Reflections
on Marriage

Edited by *William Stephens*

Florida Atlantic University

THOMAS Y. CROWELL COMPANY · NEW YORK

ESTABLISHED 1834

Reflections on Marriage

Contents

Introduction

I. The Mysteries of Love

1. From *The Many Faces of Love*   3
   HUBERT BENOIT

2. From *The Art of Courtly Love*   39
   ANDREAS CAPELLANUS

3. Romantic Love   47
   HUGO BEIGEL

4. Romantic Love   63
   ALBERT ELLIS

5. Contributions to the Psychology of Love   84
   SIGMUND FREUD

6. The Good-Bad Girl   109
   MARTHA WOLFENSTEIN and NATHAN LEITES

II. Marital Adjustment

7. Predictors of Marital Adjustment   119
   WILLIAM STEPHENS

8. Patterning in Marriage   134
   ROLAND THARP

III. *The Marriage Relationship: Clinical Views*

9. The Folklore of Marital Relations—The Great Coital Myth   175
   ALBERT ELLIS

10. Adultery: Pros and Cons   197
    ALBERT ELLIS

11. From *Games People Play*   206
    ERIC BERNE

12. Binds and Unbinds   238
    DOROTHY JONES

IV. *Marriage in the Social Matrix*

13. Day In, Day Out   251
    LEE RAINWATER, RICHARD COLEMAN
    and GERALD HANDEL

14. The Wives of Management   271
    WILLIAM H. WHYTE, JR.

15. Permissiveness and Sex Roles   292
    DAVID RIESMAN

16. On Social Regression   305
    PHILIP E. SLATER

INTRODUCTION

Marriage and the family, although it appears as a course title in college catalogues, is ill viewed as a distinct field of study. Rather it is a generalized topic, a problem area, on which separate traditions of thought and inquiry converge. It may be approached by way of sociology, psychology, anthropology or philosophy. Any one of these "fields," in fact, presents a bewildering mix of approaches, orientations, and realms of discourse, all bearing upon marital relations. All that can be done in a single book is to follow one approach, or to sample from among them. It is the latter course that we will take.

Although I hope the audience will be varied, the selection has been prepared with primarily the college undergraduate in mind: a young person in the process of discovering himself (or herself), who has experienced love, in one form or another, and who wonders about marriage. In making the selections, personal relevance to young people has been the prime value. A second criterion was variety of approach: to bring together a broad sampling of viewpoints. A third concern was to choose writings that would contribute to an expanded awareness. Bold and original thinkers and intellectual radicals are heavily represented: Benoit, Freud, Berne, Ellis, Riesman, Slater.

If one essays to seize a student where he lives, and transport him into new and unaccustomed realms of awareness, there is an attendant risk. Many a late-adolescent, no doubt, already bears a heavy burden of wondering, confusion and self-doubt; to add to this load is a dubious service. Such an overburdened reader may gain some comfort from this: what follows are, in the main, *reflections* on marriage. Little of it is "proven fact." Most is speculation, interpretation, musings, possibilities, "ideas." The sentences to follow are punctuated by the conventional period. Just as appropriately, question marks might have been used.

I

The Mysteries of Love

Hubert Benoit begins the discussion with an extraordinarily penetrating treatise on types and essences of love: possessive love, erotic love, benevolent love, falling-in-love, adoration. The next three selections treat notions of romance as they developed in Western culture. The first, by Andreas Capellanus, is a statement from the thirteenth century, when it all began. Then, Hugo Beigel recounts the history of romantic love, and draws parallels between historic conventions of love and adolescent feelings. Finally, Albert Ellis analyzes the modern ideology of romantic love, and the expectations that flow from it; he discusses the pernicious effects that romance has on sex relationships.

The last two selections, by Freud and by Wolfenstein and Leites, are on a different level; they treat unconscious motives and fantasies that drive persons in their quest for love and direct the choice of love objects. Both Freud and Wolfenstein and Leites have something to say about sexual competition. They also discuss incompatibilities that can develop between tender and sensual feelings, and subterfuges that may be undertaken to resolve the conflict.

1

From THE MANY FACES OF LOVE

HUBERT BENOIT

In Which We Distinguish Three Kinds of Love

Benevolent love—Appetitive love—Adoration
A few words on the first and second of these three

THE AUTHOR: Words are labels that simplify. They are most useful in practical life; without them, our thinking could neither give shape to ideas nor make use of them. So I have nothing to say against words; it is not their fault if they are also snares and often lead us into error.

The word "love" is one that conceals the most dangerous pitfalls. For the thing it signifies is, you will agree, one of the most important in human life. The word, the label, covers a whole psycho-physiological world of extreme complexity.

SOURCE: Hubert Benoit, *The Many Faces of Love*, trans. Philip Mairet, (New York: Pantheon Books, Inc., 1955), pp. 1–12, 45–53, 93–103. Copyright © 1955 by Pantheon Books, Inc. Reprinted by permission of Random House, Inc.

Driven by the demon of curiosity I have, like so many others, lifted this label to find out what is underneath; and with the passing years I have been made well aware that the world it denotes is illimitable, that I shall never see the whole of it. Yet I have seen enough to feel assured that it is not a formless chaos, and that from the study of love, certain principles emerge which enable one to understand, at least approximately, any individual case of love.

PRINCIPLES

It is well known that, in the name of "love," human beings humiliate and injure one another in interminable conflicts, every one of which wastes an incredible amount of energy, and yet is based upon misunderstanding. An emotional conflict is like a dialogue between the deaf, each of whom thinks he is understanding the other and is being understood, when neither is doing so. And all because they have been ensnared by the same word, which they are attaching to things that are quite different, sometimes even opposed. The word being the same, they take the things to be identical; the misery is that they are not, and neither party sees what is the matter.

One cannot study love without very quickly seeing that the word serves to denote three wholly different realms of psychology. The verb "to love" may mean "to will the good of," or it may mean "to desire" or "to adore."

THE YOUNG WOMAN: How can you say that these refer to entirely different realms? Don't we often will the good of someone we desire, and always of one whom we adore?

THE AUTHOR: We do not always will the good, even of one whom we adore. And then, the fact that these three kinds of love may be experienced at the same time by the same person does not prevent their being different. It is just because one and the same human relation may involve several different realms and simultaneously that the world of the psyche is so complicated. If the feeling between human beings were always that of good will alone, or of desire, or of adoration, the distinction between them would have been imprinted upon the human mind categorically since the earliest ages.

When we speak of "loving" without any qualification, the first meaning that comes to mind is "willing the good of . . ." The word love, in general, calls up the ideas of benevolence, alliance in the face of danger, devotedness to another person's interest, of peace in agreement. But we also say that we "love" chicken; and the murderer in the Sunday newspaper informs us that "he killed her because he loved her too much." Some ambiguity here, is there not?

THE YOUNG WOMAN: There is a perfectly clear opposition. I would call it absurd to use the same word for things so radically different. The second case—if I rightly understand your alimentary allusion—represents the urge to satisfy sexual hunger.

THE AUTHOR: Yes, but it is not only sexual. Any pleasure that I procure by means of another being, every affirmation of myself that he or she affords me, is a kind of nourishment; for my essential hunger is to find myself affirmed by the external world or, by its means, to affirm myself. Whenever I find anything that can thus nourish me, I see it as a potential satisfaction of this hunger, and I say I love it. To love, then, may mean "to want," "to be hungry for," "to wish to be nourished by"; while at other times it means "willing the good of another," that is, "wishing to nourish" that other. Here is an opposition indeed.

THE YOUNG WOMAN: How do you explain it?

THE AUTHOR: Note first of all that, if there is opposition between wishing "to nourish myself by means of the other" and "to nourish the other," the psychological opposition does not necessarily appear in action. My own nourishment is not necessarily incompatible with that of another. The bandit who rapes a girl in a ditch satisfies his sexual hunger at her expense; but a man may be attentive to the pleasure of a woman in the act of love, gratifying her desire at the same time as his own. We are not always faced with the alternatives of eating another or being eaten. There are many nourishments that can be taken in community. I may even be able to nourish myself

alone thanks to someone else, but not at their expense; when
I look at a beautiful woman, I may experience a pleasure that
is nourishing to me; this may even occur without her knowledge. All the exchanges between beings may be regarded thus,
as a giving or taking of nourishment, gross or subtle in form:
and though they are always eating one another, it is not necessarily to their mutual destruction.

THE YOUNG WOMAN: You were about to explain in what way
benevolent love and appetite love are radically distinct, but
now you show me how easily they fuse together.

THE AUTHOR: They do not fuse, they co-exist; but because of
their common co-existence we do tend to confuse them in our
minds. And they have to be distinguished. Suppose, for instance, that a young man, infatuated with desire for a young
girl, gets into her room one evening by some trickery and asks
her to give herself to him; when she refuses, he tries to take
her by force; and, enraged by her resistance, he ends by stran-
gling her. You will allow, I think, that in such a case one
could not see the slightest trace of benevolent love.

Now consider an entirely opposite case: a man is acquainted
with an unhappy woman; she is, let us say, the widow of a
friend of his; he feels no desire at all towards her, but a lively
sympathy. He goes to see her, listens to her troubles, consoles
her and offers to render, on the following day, some service of
which she is in need. This time, benevolent love is in evidence.

THE YOUNG WOMAN: Yes, but you have wisely abstained from
saying that there is not the least trace of appetitive love. For
though your man has no sexual desire for this woman, he may
nevertheless enjoy the devoted part he plays towards her, the
gratitude he receives—in short, the noble image of himself that
he sees reflected in her mind and in his own.

THE AUTHOR: Excellent, madam, you are a very apt pupil! By
anticipating what I was about to tell you, you facilitate my
task. I will explain a little later how it is that benevolent love
does not and cannot exist in a state of purity. No human deed

is done unless the doer finds in it some affirmation of himself; a completely distinterested action would be meaningless, because it would present itself as an effect without a cause. That man often deceives himself in this respect, and is so prone to believe in his "disinterestedness" is due to his weakness for seeing himself like God, a First Cause; and if we so easily manage thus to delude ourselves, it is because the interest that we have in some of our actions can be of a very subtle nature, and is liable to pass unperceived. I willingly concede, then, that we never nourish others without deriving nourishment ourselves at the same time in one way or another: but observe that it is possible to nourish ourselves *at the expense* of others, more or less to their destruction, and that the appetite for such nourishment is often called "love." So true is this, that nearly everybody seems to consider that *attachment* to another is undeniably a sign of love. Attachment, the fear of losing someone, or "possessiveness," represents only an egoistic state of need for the other person; namely, to keep him or her for one's own nourishment; yet you will notice that nearly everyone calls that "loving." Do they not say, of a husband who wastes away after his wife's death, "How he loved her!"—even if the conjugal life of the husband was spent in tyrannical exploitation of his wife, and although his ill-treatment may have helped to bring her to the grave?

THE YOUNG WOMAN: I see well enough that benevolent love ought to be distinguished from appetitive love, since there may be appetite without benevolence. But is not the distinction doubtful after all, for, as you have just said, benevolence does not exist without appetite?

THE AUTHOR: If two things are found to be sometimes in opposition, we have no right ever to confuse them with one another. Where they exist together it must be side by side, without ceasing to be distinct. One can verify this quickly enough by a little sincere self-analysis. Will you just consider the love you have for your baby? You take every care of it, in that your benevolent love is clearly apparent; you feel, how-

ever, a lively delight in being busied about it; you are proud
of its health and beauty, you dream happily about its future.
I am sure you are looking forward to the moment when you
will presently go back to it. Is this not evidently appetitive?
Do you not say, indeed, that you could "devour" your little
one with kisses? If you examine yourself sincerely, you will see
that there are two different personages corresponding to these
two kinds of love, sometimes associated and at other times
opposed. You have, for instance, read books about education;
you know that it can be harmful for a child to feel that it is
adored, and at a moment when your appetitive love prompts
you to show it some excessive tenderness your benevolent love
prevents your yielding to it.

THE YOUNG WOMAN: I have indeed been conscious of these two
kinds of loving, and found it disturbing. My love for my child
seems less genuine, somehow, when I think of the pleasure I
take in it. I wish I could love benevolently without being
appetitive at all. Is it really not possible for us to experience
a love that is purely benevolent, wholly altruistic?

THE AUTHOR: Ah! I thought you would ask me one day or another about "true love"—and that you would conceive that
love as exclusively altruistic. "True love" is not exclusively
altruistic; it lies beyond both egoism and altruism, surpassing
both at once. But that "surpassing" belongs to the timeless
realization of the human being. Let us, if you please, restrict
ourselves for the present to the study of love as it is experienced
by those we meet in our everyday life.

First Remarks Upon Adoration

The experience of "falling in love"—The lover is in
love with love—The modest rôle played by the object
of adoration—First encounter with "the plane of
images"

THE AUTHOR: The study of the third kind of love, adoration, is rendered peculiarly difficult by its combinations with the other two. It has nevertheless to be clearly distinguished from them. The difficulty is the greater because the distinction here is based less upon behaviour than upon the perception of an interior condition. Many people say absurd things about this kind of love because they have no experience of it, or one that is inadequate; we shall find that relatively few people know it—at least, not in the full development of its pure form.

THE YOUNG MAN: Is not the use of the term "adoration" questionable? Is not the verb "to adore" commonly used in respect of appetitive love? A mother declares that she "adores" her child; people say that a masochistic woman "adores" being beaten; and plenty of women and effeminate men talk about adoring film stars, mystery stories or even cocktails.

THE AUTHOR: True enough, but you will admit that is an abuse of language, an improper use of terms. The word "adore" implies an idea of "divinity," of the perception of the holy, of the infinite, of something beyond this world. And I was actually about to show you how man attains, in the love that is adoration, to some perception of "the divine." As I have said, the intermixture of the diverse modes of love complicates our analysis: I will therefore commence our study of adoration with as simple, as pure an instance as possible, of this kind of love. It is at its beginning, on the first few occasions of its manifestation, before it has become involved with anything else, that this phenomenon appears in its purest form. A man meets a woman, and is suddenly aware of a rare emotion. If he has not yet had this experience, he suddenly feels that he tastes a new quality of life, different from any that he has experienced before. He has generally, no doubt, an impression that this woman is in some way "different from the others," but this impression, which as we shall see is illusory, is neither invariably present nor really interesting. If the man is capable of perceiving intuitively what is happening to him, it is *in himself* that he will recognize something of a reality and an import far beyond the ordinary. He feels a change of his inner being, a new "state of mind," and that not only in so far as he sees the woman; his perception of everything else is altered, too. This impression intensifies as his love develops. It is as though his eyes were being subtly modified, and were revealing to him a wholly different aspect of the world. In this new aspect of things those that existed before are still present, nor can one say that anything new and different from the old appears; no, things remain what they were, but *his vision* of them has changed. To define this change of aspect is far from easy; but I will try to indicate two things about it—on the one hand, there is a heightening of colour: what was grey before becomes alive with colours; on the other hand, the world loses what I would call a "third dimension," the depth which had given it its dangerous reality; it becomes, like the décor of a theatre, something less than real, benign, smiling and reassuring. The lover feels buoyant in a world relieved of menace; his breast expands, he feels he is breathing more freely in a purer air.

Preoccupations that had obsessed him cease to worry. The lover is introduced, as it were, by what has come to pass within him, to a hitherto unknown domain to which such words as fairyland or magic would be appropriate—a domain that realizes and surpasses his previous dreams. This new world has, as I said, a dimension less than his previous world of reality; but it has a dimension more than his previous dreamland, which was one-dimensional, merely linear. The new world reconciles dream and reality in its two dimensions; does not such a lover say "I feel I am living in a dream!"

THE YOUNG MAN: Sir, you are waxing lyrical!

THE AUTHOR: It is a lyrical state I am describing. The least cultured person is capable, in this state, of writing as though inspired. I have read most moving letters, written by quite simple people when they were in love, containing passages of a literary excellence worthy of genius.

THE YOUNG MAN: I am surprised to see how small a part is played by the loved one in your psychological descriptions of the lover. One might think she had no importance for him. But is he not in fact "crazy for her"?

THE AUTHOR: That is a good objection, upon which I hope to satisfy you presently. For the moment, let it suffice to say that the lover is not "crazy *for* her," as commonly supposed; he is crazy *about* her. Upon a deeper analysis of this phenomenon, you will find that the beloved object is playing a far more modest rôle than the two lovers imagine. Before looking into the reasons for this, let us observe what is happening within the lover, transforming his attitude not towards the outer world in general, but towards the beloved person. We are supposing that the man in question is eminently capable of adoration and living through the first phases of a love of that description—that is to say, our example is one of the *purest possible* adoration. If our lover is also highly capable of introspection, he becomes aware that the *image* of the woman he loves remains continuously present to him. The image is not a continuously conscious one, because conscious attention cannot focus on two points at once, and the lover, who is still living his daily life, has to give more or less attention to it. But whenever this man returns to contemplate the beloved image after some temporary distraction from it, he has a quite peculiar impression that he had not really been absent from her, that she has remained with him all the while he was elsewhere. He has, as it were, a sort of "second sight," sometimes conscious and sometimes subconscious, which remains continuous underneath the discontinuity of ordinary perceptions. Even in reveries fully devoted to her, all the imaginary decorations of his fancy are revolving around this one beloved image, subconscious and fixed. Such a lover may become aware that his perception of the loved one—his "ideal," his image of her—fulfills a function in his inner world analogous to that of light in the world without: without light we would see nothing, yet we do not see the light itself: light shining in a void, where there is nothing to reflect it, is wholly invisible. So also the beloved woman, in so far as she becomes a part of the lover's interior world, is the source of a special revelation of the external world; but in this world the physical woman is one reality among others, and not, as a separate external object, uniquely significant. Moreover, it happens, often enough, that a lover can vividly recall the features and facial expression of any of his ordinary acquaintances, and yet cannot evoke a clear image of the beloved visage. Nor, when she is present, does his contemplation of her countenance ever exhaust the riches of his impression. For in truth it is not the reality of her face that he sees, and he does not form an impression of it that could live in his memory. He is like a man caught in the beam of a lighthouse; in that situation you have a great impression of light, but you cannot see the lighthouse as it really is.

THE YOUNG MAN: Would you say, then, that the beloved woman is everything to her lover or that really she is nothing to him?

THE AUTHOR: She is everything to him, in that she represents, in his interior world, the unseen source of an infinitely more lively vision of the world, but she is nothing to him in objective, external fact. That is, the lover, though he usually believes he loves the woman, is in reality loving the subjective state that the image of the woman enables him to experience. Remember the profound phrase of St. Augustine, *"Amabam amare."* He says "I loved loving," not "I loved women."

THE YOUNG MAN: You are sure you are not indulging a taste for paradox, when you assert that the lover does not love the woman he adores?

THE AUTHOR: Why, no; it is you who have just used a paradoxical expression. The adoration of the lover is not in truth centered upon her; but he loves "something"—what it is I will explain—by means of her; that is quite another thing. To give you a little rest from my abstractions, let us consider how, in actuality, the majority of adoring lovers behave towards the supposed objects of their love. If you happen to have a friend who is now living in that condition, and who is not unwilling to describe intimate feelings, let him confide in you at length. He will be prolix about his states of soul, and about the perfections he sees in the woman he loves, which justify those states of soul. But you will notice how very little he puts himself in the woman's place or tries to see things as she sees them—that is the least of his worries. For he is not contemplating this woman as a distinct and independent consciousness existing outside himself, he is not interested in her subjective reality. He is attentive to his own subjectivity, and to the objectivity of the woman only so far as it concerns him. To him she is not a human person but an object, precious to his own personality. Often he seems to hate the years that she lived before he came to know her, as though he denied her the right to be herself apart from him. In so far as the woman is an independent being the lover wants to do away with her, to date her rebirth from the day he met her and thenceforth allow her only to live and grow with the life and growth of the image of her in his mind.

THE YOUNG MAN: There is doubtless much truth in what you say; but then one sees so many examples of extreme solicitude in adoring lovers. They so strongly desire or fear, for the beloved, what she herself desires or fears. These, you must allow, do not confine their love to what is within themselves.

THE AUTHOR: You are right; but that is because some admixture of benevolent love with adoration is practically obligatory. This woman, who is so necessary to my inner state of adoration that she seems even to be its cause, is so deeply associated with my condition that I depend on her existence and tremble at any threat of it. An association, which I will prove to be fortuitous, between the beloved woman and the inestimable state of adoration, makes her precious to me; I have need of her—but that is appetitive love. Then, needing her existence, I clutch at whatever favours it; and that is benevolent, altruistic love. For all that, adoration is not in itself altruistic, and simply as its object, the woman is divested of personality. Actual cases are, I admit, seldom so pure that one could fairly say the woman did not count at all as a subjective personality: but such cases exist, and if there were no more than one of them, that would be concrete evidence enough to confirm what I say, and to support the abstract reasons that I will presently put forward.

THE YOUNG MAN: Before passing on to these abstract reasons, which I fear I may find hard to follow, can you enlighten me further at the level where I feel more at ease? I have a kind of intuition you may be right, but my ingrained opinions make me resistant.

THE AUTHOR: Yes, I can; but here you will not understand me unless you have yourself both loved with an intense adoration, and have yet retained, in the midst of that inebriation, a capacity for lucid reflection. Such a lover has the inward, intuitive perception of what I am about to say. In those moments when the woman he adores is before him, he tries to objectify his inner, subjective enchantment, to seize it in some tangible reality. He looks at her, he searchs her face and form with his physical eyes in an ardent effort to find out and localize the "charm" that has captivated him. Then in a flash, the spell snaps. It is as though the charm took fright and fled, vanishing in every direction from the visage it deserts. The lover realizes that this woman is of all things in the world that which he sees the least, which has the least degree of independent reality for him, and he thinks, clairvoyantly: "After all, what is she to me?" In that instant he sees that the woman, such as she is in and for herself, is nothing to him, that she merely happened to touch the switch which released an enchantment within him.

THE YOUNG MAN: I have, as it happens, had just the experience you mention. I was frightened by it. I said to myself, "Then I am not truly in love."

THE AUTHOR: Just so; we always presume to love "truly" without having learned to do so. Forget for awhile your preconceptions about "true" love; all I will say for the moment is that adoration is not to be identified with it. In adoration, so far as it is distinct from the other kinds of love, the beloved object releases the internal reaction, but is not part of it; I would compare it to the catalyzing agent in chemistry. The adoring lover has no tension towards an object perceptible to the senses, towards any temporal creature. The verb to love, in this connotation, is intransitive. The English language very rightly expresses the intransitive character of adoration as "being in love"; the beloved image accompanies the lover through the realm of love, but for the adoring lover that realm itself is all.

THE YOUNG MAN: But how can one reconcile the episodic and merely external rôle played by the real woman, with the immeasurable importance the adoring lover assigns to her?

THE AUTHOR: To answer that question I must anticipate, and call your attention to a delicate but major distinction we shall soon have to draw—the distinction between the plane of sensations and the plane of images. The woman who is loved plays an episodic part upon the plane of the sensations, inasmuch as she is a real perception, while on the plane of images her importance is immeasurable, inasmuch as she is perceived in the lover's inner world. The mental image has to be constantly present if the reaction that she catalyzes is to endure: the real woman need not be present except insofar as the image has need of her in order to be born and to be kept in being. To a lover of great imaginative power, the real woman is hardly necessary. The presence of the object is necessary in order to live the first two kinds of love, but not this kind.

Appetitive Love Reconsidered

*The plane of "images" and that of sensation—Desire
for self-affirmation, material and psychic—The desire
to be oneself—The conditions required for valid introspection—Desire to be sexually desired—Desire to
be "adored"—Ambivalent attitude of the one who is
adored.*

THE AUTHOR: Shall we now leave the question of adoration in
love, and come back to love of the two other kinds? We shall
do so better equipped to understand them. Our study of adoration, of the love which, in its pure state, is experienced wholly
on the plane of images, will have familiarized you with the
important psychological notion of the *plane of images,* as distinct from the plane of concrete reality, the *plane of sensations.*
Without this distinction, very many psychic phenomena would
remain incomprehensible to us.

THE YOUNG WOMAN: Will you be so good as to give an example.

THE AUTHOR: Suppose that your husband is unfaithful to you,
with a woman less good-looking, and for whom he has no sentiment of love. You ask yourself, "What can he see in her that is
lacking in me?" You look for the reasons of your husband's
infidelity upon the plane of sensations, but they may very well
not be there: the other woman may be no prettier than you,
nor any more clever and pleasing in sexual dalliance. Your
husband's relation with the woman differs from his relation to
you, not on the plane of sensations but on the plane of images:
he meets with her in a different psychological situation because
she is not his wife, and the sexual act with her may take on a
higher value for him; he may feel himself much more *affirmed*
by it. The act is materially the same, but not so psychically,
not upon the plane of images. That may modify the play of
the sexual function altogether.

THE YOUNG WOMAN: Yes, I see what you mean by that.

THE AUTHOR: This duality of planes, and the fact that the majority of human actions take place upon both of them at once, is what makes our psychic life so complex. You must take it into account if you want to steer your way through this complexity. The motives of appetitive love, for instance, we shall find upon both planes. In such love, a man seeks self-affirmation, by creating or by nourishing himself; he loves another person because her being nourishes his own. But this other person, the object of such a love, may nourish him in very various ways. I love my wife—among other ways in which I love her—because she takes care of my material comfort, for the *service* she renders at the practical level. But I also love her because she esteems me, is considerate for me, values my company, and so on, that is to say, I find her affirmative of me upon the subtler plane of images, the plane of totality. If I like to criticize someone else, to humiliate him, and he lets me do it, he is affirming me by allowing himself to be denied by me—all upon the subtle plane—and I may become dependent on him, attached to him, acquire the habit or appetite for the self-affirmation I procure through him. When a masochistic woman tells you, for instance, about the ill-treatment she suffers from her sadistic husband, she ends by saying, "All the same, you know, in his way he loves me"; nor is she deceived, so far as appetitive love is concerned. One of the most important kinds of appetitive love is sexual desire, and this again we find upon two levels; I may be seeking merely physical self-affirmation in the exercise, thanks to the woman, of the sexual function; but I am just as likely to be in search of a subtler affirmation of myself. I may regard the sexual act as a personal victory, and all the more so if my mistress be beautiful, much sought after, celebrated, or virtuous.

There is one kind of appetitive love that we must learn to identify without fail—one that I may have occasion to mention to you again, for it plays a very important part in human emotional relations—and that is the desire I feel for one who desires me. This may sound almost like a bad joke, a playful

labouring of the obvious. But first note how constantly we
meet with it in practice. For example—here is the mistress of
a household where, for several days, a friend of her husband
has been entertained as a guest. This friend has shown throughout his visit, both by his words and his behaviour, how much
pleasure it gave him. The situation has pleased him, the cooking, his bedroom, the company of his host and hostess, have
all equally pleased him; and he shows sincere regret when he
has to leave. The mistress of the house is delighted; she feels
enhanced in value, because what she has and what she has
done is so highly appreciated by their friend: she likes him for
this, and rejoices to see him come back for another visit. This
friend has enjoyed, on the plane of sensations, spending his
holiday in these conditions; perhaps upon the plane of images
too, if the consideration which has been shown him is one of
the causes of his enjoyment; he will like the hostess who has
procured it for him. The hostess, for her part, will have loved
this friend, on the plane of images, for having shown such
esteem and so much appreciation of what she was able to do
for him, all of which she feels as part of herself—of her image
of herself.

Take another example—you have come back several times
to these conversations: by doing so you show a kind of appetite
for what I say, and what I say to you is an expression of myself;
I feel that by your listening you are affirming me. I, in my
turn, have a desire for the affirmation you offer me, and I like
you with an appetitive liking in so far as you do affirm me. I
am hungry, as it were, for your hunger for me, and for yourself in so far as your hunger confirms an aspect of myself.

THE YOUNG WOMAN: You make me smile. One would think you
were a watchmaker deliberately taking his tiny mechanisms
apart.

THE AUTHOR: Only I don't take them apart: I simply open the
cases so that we may note with precision—but also with discretion—what is going on inside. Had we not, for the moment,
excluded all ethical considerations, this inquiry would be in-

discreet; it might throw all the wheels out of gear and seriously damage the works. Unhappily, that is what the man who tries looking into himself by himself practically always does. He forgets to leave his "moral" prejudices outside the door of his psychological laboratory, for he fancies he already has a valid ethics. This makes him from the very beginning unable to see anything clearly as it is, since he is bound to preserve his cherished illusions: and to the extent that he is baffled by his psychic mechanisms he tries to take them to pieces, rather like a child trying to find out how its doll says "mamma"—which merely makes it speechless. Introspection is dangerous, in so far as you think that the pretty mechanisms are "good" and the ugly ones "evil"—broadly, in as much as you confuse aesthetics with ethics. Just look around at your friends, and you will see that those who are great introspectives are always more or less neurotic. One can hardly venture to explore one's interior world alone, so difficult is it to do so impartially and without aesthetic prejudice. A man needs to be supported by the impartiality of someone else, and it is here that one sees the usefulness of a psychologist, of one who has gone beyond this terrible confusion between the aesthetic and the ethical.

THE YOUNG WOMAN: Will you understand me if I say that, "amused" as I may be to look at these mechanisms with you, it also makes me rather uncomfortable?

THE AUTHOR: That discomfort is very natural. The human being identifies himself with his mechanisms. Instead of seeing that a certain mechanical personage within himself loves in such-and-such a manner, he tells himself "I love after this fashion." He assumes, towards his own internal mechanisms, the *animistic* attitude assumed by the savage towards inanimate external objects. He credits them with an autonomous life, whereas they are only passing forms of his own living autonomy. He cannot feel himself to be a free temporal being, as his fictitious divinity requires him to be, without believing that his inner personages, the constituents of his "Self" are free; so he never sees them as the mechanisms that in fact they

are. The discomfort you feel at a glimpse of your mechanisms
in their reality derives from the fact that they contradict your
divine fiction, your illusion that, without having done any real
work within yourself, you exist already and are an autonomous,
perfectly free being, independent of the outer world. Yet if
this at the same time pleases you, if it is somehow agreeable,
that is because such instants of clairvoyance are working
towards your real liberation. For, though your presumption of
being already free brings a momentary appeasement whenever
you renew it, it does nothing to liberate you, and cannot really
neutralize the profound anguish inherent in a state of actual
unfreedom. Every step towards a true knowledge of oneself
tends, on the other hand, towards the neutralization of that
anguish. But would you like us to return to our watchmakers'
technique? For, I can assure you, that is how we shall have to
begin.

THE YOUNG WOMAN: Yes. So much the worse for my disquiet,
and for loss of the illusions about myself which I doubtless
cherish. I believe the prize is worth the pains, and that there is
treasure at the end of the arduous road. Our talks are gradually
awakening in me a kind of taste for the adventure, risks and
all.

THE AUTHOR: Knowledge of oneself is indeed the greatest of
human adventures, the one of which all outward adventures
are only the symbols. And you can brave the risks, since you
have a guide. But let us return to our subject.

It is in the sexual sphere that we shall discern, with the
greatest clarity and conviction, the play of this desire to be
desired by another: here too we shall best see how irrational
such an appetite is. A woman realizes that a man desires her;
she has no desire for him at all; nevertheless you will often
see her happy to meet this man and to bask in his desire for
her.

THE YOUNG WOMAN: That's not true always. For my part, if I
feel that a man wants me only sexually, this irritates me, and
I keep well out of his way.

THE AUTHOR: What irritates you is not that he wants you sexually but that he has no other desire for you *except that:* it is not that he affirms you by regarding you as sexually desirable, but that he belittles you by ignoring other aspects of yourself to which you attach higher value, aspects which the man ought to recognize, you feel, if he wants to distinguish you from other women. If you subtract the offense that this negation gives you, you will see that you feel the sexual desire of which you are the object as an affirmation of yourself. It could not be otherwise: in so far as you are coveted by the man, he is seeing something precious in you, you have a certain value in his eyes, and up to this point this is affirmative of you. Don't you know that we evaluate ourselves according to our reflections mirrored in the minds of other people? This self-valuation is a matter of relativity and comparison. The man's desire affirms you, because it goes towards you *in preference* to other women. If you saw that this man were behaving in the same way towards every woman, his desire would cease to have that meaning. The woman who is attacked in a wood by the local satyr does not feel at all affirmed, because the desire in this case does not *distinguish* her from any other woman. We feel affirmed, as a rule, only by what distinguishes us, for affirmation of a self takes place on the plane of images, of the "Ego,"—that is, within one's assumption that one is an autonomous, total being.

THE YOUNG WOMAN: I do feel that my sense of being affirmed by the man's desire for me is somewhat irrational. But then it also seems to me natural.

THE AUTHOR: But all of our spontaneously affective life is essentially irrational and at the same time essentially natural. Let us say more simply, if you like, that the emotional nature of man is not in the least rational.

THE YOUNG WOMAN: Evidently I have said something silly. I should have said that it seemed to me logical. It is logical that I should appreciate myself when I am appreciated by another, and that I should be gratified by it.

THE AUTHOR: This comes to much the same thing: the affective life is logical, but irrational, because the logic proceeds from non-rational premises. The value attributed to you by this admirer is attached to appearances which do not constitute your reality. If you were thirty years older, he would not have seen this value in you, but would you not still have been "you"? You see, then, more simply still, that when this man seems to single you out and affirm you, he is really only distinguishing and affirming the personage within himself which has a desire for you; he expects, by seducing you, to affirm an aspect of himself: you are the victim of a mere optical illusion. And what I am saying would apply just as well, evidently, to the two examples I gave you a little while ago.

THE YOUNG WOMAN: Oh, dear! How right you are! How are such delusions possible?

THE AUTHOR: We shall have to talk a little more metaphysics to deal with that question. The man who affirms himself by possessing you refills, by that means, what he felt as a kind of emptiness: he recovers, thanks to you, the sense of being a totality, a free "being," a self-sufficient, real entity. While thus re-affirming himself in time, he is really seeking self-affirmation on the plane of virtually timeless "being." But this plane of "being" transcends all those limitations which make human beings feel themselves to be distinct one from another, the distinction that is also annihilated on this plane during the act in which the man and you participate, or imagine that you do —between the man's self-affirmation and your own. Upon this plane there is no optical illusion, for the "being" affirms itself in him and in you at the same time. The optical illusion arises when this idea projects itself upon the lower plane of the affective mechanisms: *there* you are deceived if you think you are being affirmed by this man, who is dreaming of nothing but his own affirmation. I beg your pardon for a digression which you must have found obscure; but you asked me for it. Never mind if you have hardly understood me. This kind of explanation is not necessary to what immediately concerns us.

It is enough if you realize clearly that you feel the other person's affirmation of yourself and that you *like* it, you desire it, for that reason.

THE YOUNG WOMAN: I do realize it, but without the least satisfaction, for now I see myself as ridiculous.

THE AUTHOR: To the degree that you come to see your mechanisms for what they are—and they are quite harmless as soon as you cease to attach absolute importance to them—you learn to laugh at yourself; and then you feel how good it is to be humorously detached, how much it liberates you. That a woman should feel flattered because a man desires her is indeed a subject for comedy. It is as if the prey were to preen itself with pride when it saw the carnivore watching it and licking its chops. A book was published lately about women in houses of prostitution, and the author tells us that every woman has her "bad days" when no client chooses her; and that she deplores this, not only from the financial point of view: she feels humiliated by it. The observation is interesting, because in such a case every sentimental consideration is excluded, and yet one finds, even here, that to be "chosen" is to be preferred; although one is only a prey, there is this notion of preference to whatever other prey is available. Observe, moreover, that the notion of preference is not indispensable. Suppose that circumstances should expose a woman to the advances of some prisoner, long deprived of women; that he solicits her sexually, without hiding the fact that his desire is for any woman whatever, and that she consents in compassion. She may feel flattered simply to see the intensity of the appetite, the erotic ecstasy to which he is aroused with her, and the profound relief he experiences afterwards. This would not be a case of feeling preferred, but only of being *enjoyed,* of being valuable.

THE YOUNG WOMAN: What, then, are the feelings of a woman when the man loves her with adoration?

THE AUTHOR: Her feelings will usually be the same but much stronger. The man who adores her will have every kind of

desire for her, since appetitive love is mingled with his adoration. Divinizing her as he does, beholding her as a totality, he
will want her in every possible way. He will hunger for the
sight of her, to hear her, to know what she is thinking, what
she feels; to know about her past life, to meet her friends, and
to enjoy her body. And the woman feels herself affirmed accordingly. More often than not, she also contracts a lively appetitive love for him—that is, a strong attachment. By seeing
her as someone unique and incomparable he gives her, upon
the plane of images, a concentrated and most savoury nourishment, with which her insatiable Ego is delighted. Sometimes
you will see the woman deprecating adorational behaviour in
her lover; this does not mean, however, that she disdains such
exquisite nourishment, but that, owing to some previous experience, she is so much afraid of losing it that she also fears to
receive it. This is an instance of the "fear of loving," which we
will study some other time. For the moment, let us rather consider what happens within the adored woman when, as is
rather rarely the case, the adoration of which she is the object
is pure, or nearly so. Her reaction is complicated by the complex behaviour of so pure a lover. In truth, as we have seen,
he is not *attached* to the real woman; attachment arises only
from appetite, not from adoration. But this lover's love for
something intangible has to be *acted out* on the plane of concrete reality; we must return to this later in more detail, but
I think you will have already perceived the peculiarity of the
adorational situation, where the lover has to act as though he
were concerned with a real woman, although it is only his
image of her that matters to him. The lover feels and acts as
though he were devotedly attached to the real woman, and yet
only in so far as this is favourable for maintaining his ecstatic
interior condition let us not forget that it is only this interior
state which he is really attached to, which he is afraid of losing
and jealously guards. Whenever it would be prejudicial to his
condition to behave with attachment towards the real woman,
the lover both feels and behaves according to his genuine non-
attachment to her.

THE YOUNG WOMAN: In fact, the lover who adores is playing a sort of comedy. Is he aware of this?

THE AUTHOR: Hardly; practically not at all. I will return to that point; but at present we are concerned with the reactions of the adored woman. The lover suspends the comedy of attachment to the real woman whenever it threatens to hinder his adoration. For instance, the woman may behave in such a way as to excite the jealousy of her adorer; he would be expected to feel resentment against her; but every negative feeling is opposed to adoration and therefore inadmissible. So he does not do what is expected; he neither feels nor acts jealously, thereby showing his genuine detachment from the actual woman. She, for her part, feels surprised and humiliated. She is avid for the attachment of her lover which is such an affirmation of her, and feels negated when he suddenly appears to be free of the attachment of which at other times, she had such clear proofs. Moreover, her own interior attitude towards this curious lover is ambivalent; she loves him with a strongly appetitive love for the adoration he offers her, manifested in an unlimited attachment which he declares is necessary to his life; but on the other hand she nurses a strong resentment against him for the moments when he appeared to have taken back all that he gave her, thereby subjecting her to a disagreeably cold douche. This inwardly ambivalent attitude shows itself in equally ambivalent behaviour; sometimes she heaps favours upon her adorer, at others she makes him suffer as much as she can. The more the lover's adoration is *pure,* the better he can escape suffering, to which he would react with a resentment he does not want to feel; but the more he is, in consequence, unassailable, the more the woman redoubles her attacks. We will return again to the details of this interesting duel, when I will show you some of the unhappy conclusions to which it may lead.

Erotic Love

> *Sexuality on the plane of images—The quest for ex-*
> *citation, not for sexual satisfaction—Erotic images*
> *are purely mental—Their classification—External*
> *erotic images; erotic literature—Concrete erotic ob-*
> *jects—Erotic situations—The influence of sexual*
> *reality upon erotic pleasure*

THE AUTHOR: We can now begin the study of the erotic, that is,
of sexuality experienced wholly or in part upon the plane of
images. This is not a fourth kind of love: erotic love is a
mixture of the elements we already know; it consists necessarily
of adoration and of sexual desire, and may include benevolence also.

Erotic love presents itself in indefinitely varied forms, but in
all of them we find one essential characteristic; in erotic love,
a man feels that he is affirmed not by the satisfaction of the
sexual function but by *sexual excitation,* namely, the urge
towards that satisfaction, whether it follows or not. Already,
then, you can see that this is something more subtle than
sexual love in itself. In the internal genesis of the sexual act,
it is at one stage above the act; it is not a will to the sexual act
but to the desire; it is, in fact, a desire for the sexual tension.
One might say, in terms of physiology, that it is a tendency to
erection but not to ejaculation. That there is also a tendency
towards ejaculation in the end, somehow to finish and come
to rest, is no contradiction of what has just been said. That this
should be so is quite logical, for there is, as I will show you, a
certain antagonism between the image and the reality. So
long as I remain in desire for a sexual discharge that has not
yet occurred, it exists in anticipation, it is merely *in view,*
which means that it is upon the plane of images. Sexuality
lived upon the plane of images is thus a tension towards the
desire and not to the act. André Gide, in one of his books,

makes an *apologia* for this tension and recommends the reader to prefer it to the satisfaction. It is true that the desire, because it is on the subtle plane of images, is far more alluring than the satisfaction, of a savour more refined, more piercing, more exalting; but as for recommending it, that is what I call a premature ethic, and it assumes—one scarcely knows why—that a thing is "better" if it is more pleasurable.

What I have just outlined in the abstract is what we find in the concrete when we study the erotic in its simplest and purest form. Here is a man who, quietly installed in an armchair, is day-dreaming and amusing himself with merely mental erotic images: he views an erotic film in his imagination. I am speaking now, of course, of man in the sense of human being; for this might also be happening in a woman. The pleasure that our subject is feeling in the state of desire to which his images arouse him tends not to a sexual appeasement but simply to a tension.

THE YOUNG MAN: But is there not, in every tension to the exercise of a function, a kind of suffering, which the activity of the function is meant to appease?

THE AUTHOR: True. But that suffering is felt only when, for one reason or another, the subject sees that satisfaction is impossible. To be hungry as you sit down to table is quite agreeable, it is hunger with no food in prospect that is painful. Suppose that a man were inexorably deprived, by external or internal obstacles, of any sexual satisfaction whatever: he would dislike any erotic images that might occur to him, would not encourage them, and, if he could not repress them, would endure them with suffering. But now imagine a man who is sure of being able to satisfy his sex urge in one way or another if he wants to; this man will derive only gratification—at least in the beginning—from feeling the tension of desire. I said "at least in the beginning," for a moment will come, if the state of tension is prolonged, when suffering will supervene and drive the subject to satisfaction. Imagination tires, the images grow dull, one's flight in the world of images becomes heavy; it is as though the function wearied of a fruitless effort and wanted

an end of it. But this moment comes after a length of time
that varies greatly according to the subject's imaginative power.
If the subject has powers of imagination as great as those we
mentioned in connection with pure adoration, the moment
when imagination weakens may be long retarded; so long, perhaps, that there is no longer any desire for satisfaction, so
much libido having been discharged in the imaginations themselves. Thus it is quite possible that the Marquis de Sade, in
the prison where he produced his erotic writings, did not have
to resort to solitary indulgence.

THE YOUNG MAN: Is there not a grave objection, in the minds
of many people, against this holding of erotic picture-shows
within oneself?

THE AUTHOR: Indeed there is; less so than against onanism,
but of the same nature, since the erotic cinema is obviously a
kind of mental masturbation: these are what one calls "evil
thoughts"; many people banish them altogether, or at least try
to do so. But many also admit them, welcome and even cultivate them: they would not boast about it, but they feel no
objection within themselves.

Erotic images are naturally of the most varied kinds; but we
can classify them into a few categories, and this is worth doing
because we shall be meeting them again later on, embodied in
actual instances.

First of all the image may be of an erotic object that is static,
immobile. Here we encounter for the first time the typical and
powerfully symbolic image of the "female nude" which is dominant in the modern West.

But human imagination is much more like a cinema than a
magic lantern and, as a rule, the erotic images move and go
through certain motions. Their erotic action may take on innumerable forms, but we can distinguish the cases in which the
subject plays a part from those in which he does not but only
views what happens. When he participates it is not by a solitary sexual act but an action that puts the subject in relation
with an erotic object, his attention being fixed upon the gestures of this object which does this or that to him; or conversely

he may imagine that it is he who is doing something to the object. Scenes in which the subject is passive gratify his feminine component, those in which he is active gratify his virile component. But they may do both, at once or alternately. Note, moreover, that the erotic activity is not necessarily such as is properly called sexual; it may be any action whatever which, for the subject, according to the circumstances of his life, is charged with erotic significance.

When the subject himself plays no part, he sees the action performed by a single object, or often by two, sometimes more than two; his attention will frequently be fixed chiefly upon one of these personages with which he identifies himself and which is, so to speak, his part in the play. Sometimes the scene is not directly viewed by the subject, he may be listening to spoken words or reading a letter which describes the action. In that case it is verbal expression, words, which have the most erotic power: this occurs with strongly intellectual men or women for whom words have a potent reality. The pleasure is heightened by the fact of being still further detached from reality and more completely upon the plane of images.

Sometimes the erotic situation is not even visualized by the words but remains only mental. A man may, for example, imagine with keen erotic enjoyment that he is the lover of a Mrs. X, without imagining any erotic action that brings him into the picture: the mere abstract image of being this woman's lover may have an erotic value for him because he sees himself stealing the erotic image from someone else.

These generalizations are certainly inadequate but they cover, I think, the majority of erotic images. Note, before we pass on from these merely imaginary games, that they nearly always produce some excitation in the sexual organs, the significance of which you will see presently.

THE YOUNG MAN: Meanwhile I must say, sir, that I find all this decidedly unpleasant. Can you tell me just why I do so?

THE AUTHOR: Because you have been looking at all these mechanisms detachedly, from the outside. When you are identified with one of them, immersed in the sensation that it procures you, you feel it as unique, as something quite "real" in its uniqueness. But when you rise above this mechanical level and take a purely intellectual view of it, you see these mechanisms for what they are, common and of a merely relative reality: the sight gives you a glimpse of mechanic action itself, which is the cause of your deepest sufferings, and so you feel ill at ease.

THE YOUNG MAN: That must be the explanation. I feel as if I were looking on at a play of soulless marionettes.

THE AUTHOR: You have first to see where your soul is not, if you are one day to find it.

The erotic images that we have just now roughly classified, are, as we have seen, entirely fabricated by the imagination of the subject; they were not endorsed, encouraged or embellished by anything in the outer world. I began with these because it is better to proceed from the simple to the complex, when one is trying to explain the complex. And the essential, primordial basis of erotic love is the image formed in the subject's mind.

But the erotic imagination often attaches itself to some external object and makes use of it. And at an intermediate stage between the quite internal fantasy and the attachment to a real external object, we now come to the external erotic image —that is, to erotic pictures, photographs and literature. The subject makes use of the drawings, photos or writings produced by others; or he may produce such things himself to correspond more closely with his favourite fantasies.

On this point I will offer only a few observations: first, it is of interest to note that the perception of an external erotic image releases excitation in the sexual organs in a less automatic manner than does the perception of an internal image fashioned by the subject himself. To put it plainly, the man who imagines an erotic scene in detail almost necessarily has an erection, and that is why the use of the interior image prompts the subject more strongly to resort to manual excitation: you know the vulgar jibe about books one has "to read with one hand."

THE YOUNG MAN: What is the explanation of this?

THE AUTHOR: That it is the internal, cerebral image that constitutes the real stimulus, and this image is bound to be clearer when the subject is depending on himself to produce it, and nothing outside is taking on a part of the work. Eroticism is sexuality lived upon the plane of images, or at least finding there the point of departure for its play within the mind. And this is typically human; the animal cannot perceive images within itself that do not start from perceptions of the real. Try showing a photograph of a bitch to your dog. The real bitch not being present, the dog cannot fashion any internal image of it, so your photograph leaves him stone cold.

THE YOUNG MAN: Is an animal capable of imagination if given a concrete stimulus?

THE AUTHOR: Evidently it is. If I show my dog his leash he leaps for joy, because he sees within himself an image of going for a walk. But he is unable to start imagining anything from a point that is not real; he lacks the intellectual faculty of abstraction which is a specifically human attribute. Eroticism also is peculiar to man alone, of all animals that inhabit the Earth.

The external images that release our erotic feeling are often so remote from concrete reality that they vividly illustrate what I have just said. For instance, you feel suddenly aware of an erotic feeling when glancing through the headlines of a newspaper: you look for the cause of this, and then discover in a corner of the page a little advertisement in which a few badly-drawn outlines suggest, very conventionally, a nude woman: just two sinuous, symmetrical lines, and that was enough to release the erotic mechanism; or it may have been no more than a single word that caught your eye and had, for you, some erotic association. Believe me, it is always the mental image that counts. Eroticism is cerebral sexuality, that is, sexuality that starts in the brain.

Another point of interest: external images that are designed to arouse erotic excitation are almost always aesthetic. The inaesthetic aspects of the sexual function are carefully excluded.

THE YOUNG MAN: Are there not, however, drawings, photographs and obscene writings that are quite inaesthetic and yet excite some people?

THE AUTHOR: Yes, there are. But that is a peculiarity we shall have to study with what are called the "perversions." Then you will see that the taste for the obscene, which at first sight contradicts this need for the aesthetic, is, rightly interpreted, a confirmation of it. Let us leave this aside for the present, and conclude that, as a general rule, erotic pictures and literature eliminate the inaesthetic aspects of sex. The sexual organs are not depicted: the nude women have charming heads of hair but are otherwise hairless, for hair on the body is closely linked in man's mind with his animality. They are always pretty in face and figure; their breasts never sag, their flesh is never unshapely but always looks firm and healthy; and they are young. Sometimes they are entirely naked, but also frequently adorned with the last underwear that veils and precedes that condition; thus showing very well how the erotic impulse, directed towards sexuality, stops short of it in order to enjoy and prolong the excitation before ending or not ending it. The legs and thighs have a special erotic value because their outlines are directed towards, and suggest without revealing, the sexual organ; as in the French Cancan, where the frills and the stockings allure the spectator's attention to something they deny him. The aesthetic qualities of these images overcome the repugnance that man feels for certain aspects of the sexual; such images evoke a sexuality that is as "ideal" as, in his heart of hearts, man wishes that it were.

Erotic literature is very difficult to write, because the verbal image shocks more readily than the visual image. If the writer is not to disgust a portion of his readers and consequently to fail in erotic effect, he has to find euphemisms for the "breast" or "hips": he must suggest everything by periphrasis. Yet this too may irritate by keeping too far off the subject; the Marquis de Sade in his intoxication, could not desist from sometimes calling things by their names and dotting all the i's, but then the effect is merely comic.

THE YOUNG MAN: It is a fact that the word shocks more than the visual image does. But why is that?

THE AUTHOR: Imagine yourself inviting a young woman to come to your bachelor flat and look at your Japanese prints, and that she assents. She knows what such a proposal signifies and forms a pretty accurate idea of what may happen to her. All the same, she would probably not have agreed to visit you in your rooms if you had told her your intention in so many words; it is simply a question of terminology.

THE YOUNG MAN: That is well known; but after all, why is that so?

THE AUTHOR: Because to use plain language would be giving conscious recognition, in one's thought, to the reality of the animal desire. The woman does not want to give intellectual recognition to her animal desire, for it is in her thought that there is a prejudice against it. The refusal of plain language is the outward sign of an inward falsehood that the woman has to tell herself, if she is to gratify her desire without coming into collision with the prejudice that would forbid it. Evidently she knows why she is going to your bachelor flat, but she can only go there upon condition of not intellectually recognizing why she goes. If she did recognize this, there would no longer be an erotic act in view but a merely sexual one, which would not attract her.

THE YOUNG MAN: I now understand better why erotic literature has nearly always seemed to me disappointing—why it falls short of its aim. For it brings into play the intellectual function and with it one's antisexual prejudice, and the author is constantly being obliged to say too much or too little.

THE AUTHOR: That is correct. Obscene literature is on the contrary extremely easy to write, but it disgusts the majority of readers.

We come now to real erotic objects. These too, like external erotic images, derive their value from the mental image which they evoke. Note, by the way, the parallelism that exists between these three stages—the mental erotic image, the external erotic image and the real erotic object—and the three objects of love that is adoration—the internal image of the divine projected, the image of the adored woman, and the real woman.

The real erotic objects will not detain us very long, for they closely resemble the erotic images, internal and external. We find the nude woman again, in the music hall, with the same aesthetic qualities and the utmost suppression of animal attributes; she wears at least panties, or is in any case depilated, she is young, or appears to be, and is pretty. The girl in the "burlesque" shows of New York gradually undresses, slowly drawing the men's attention from the periphery of her body to the sexual centre, but stopping short of complete revelation. This is the most typically exciting exhibition of sex, in which it is most evident that what counts, in eroticism, is excitation far more than gratification. Remember Goethe, in Italy, contemplating beautiful women, naked and motionless upon a couch; it is very probable that this subtle artist did not at the time experience any localized excitation, and that he derived all his enjoyment of the situation from the cerebral image that it liberated.

Ballroom dancing is an erotic diversion; the woman is not seen in the nude, but her nudity is evoked by the contact. The eroticism of clothing is concretely manifested, as it exists upon the plane of images internal and external: clothing is erotic to the extent that it reveals the body without exhibiting any inaesthetic attributes; the partially unclothed woman is always more "erotic" than the woman entirely naked, unless the beholder can proceed to action. By association, the undergarment or any accessory of dress may be an erotic object to a fetishist; and that demonstrates clearly the erotic value of the symbolic, of things that suggest what is not clearly shown.

Eroticism on the plane of reality may be independent of any concrete object but dependent on the concrete "situation." This recalls the importance of abstraction. The beholder enjoys not only tracing his own mental images in what he is looking at, but above all the idea, or abstract mental image that he is in a position to look at; similarly, the exhibitionist enjoys the idea of being seen. A great part of the pleasure given by an erotic situation proceeds, as a rule, from its being *unwonted* from the standpoint of the accepted social conventions, a breach of the veto of prejudice, a victory over the authorities, over "moral" prohibitions. Hence marriage, considered in itself, is an anti-erotic situation; for it is a regular one, blessed by all the authorities. As Marie Dubas used to sing, "It's so nice when it isn't allowed"; it is the bachelor flat, not the domestic hearth, that is appropriate to the erotic. Eroticism is released with the abandonment of all those "good manners" which require a man and a woman to feign ignorance of those dissimilar anatomical conformations which make a particular kind of contact possible; then, all at once, their words and gestures are an admission that they too are sexual beings. It happens quite suddenly; a look may be enough to sweep away the elaborate barrier that kept the two beings separated below the chin and to bring their bodies into one powerful magnetic field. A highly imaginative person is very sensitive to this instantaneous rupture of the conventionally asexual relations; for him, the fall of the barrier opens up a whole world, closed until a moment ago: he enters into a magic realm that has been too often forbidden him.

THE YOUNG MAN: Does not the fact of coming to the sexual act itself, and to satisfaction of the desire, put a stop to the play of eroticism?

THE AUTHOR: Not necessarily. Indeed, the reverse is possible. The real object is different from the image, but may just as well exalt it, as repress or destroy it. To give you an idea of this, I will resort to a rather far-fetched comparison. An actor, before going on to the stage, may get stage fright, from an imagination of the position he is about to take up before the judgment of the public. Once he has entered upon the stage his fright will perhaps vanish, partially or completely; but another actor in the same situation will become still more frightened and feel himself partly or completely incapacitated. What has happened in these two cases? In the former, the real situation has overcome the man's image of the situation; in the latter, facing the real situation has intensified his imagination of it. It will depend upon whether the situation that is faced has been, in the subject's experience of life, an occasion of exaltation or humiliation to his Ego. If it has been one of exaltation, it will derive thereby a positive force which enables the man to dismiss the image of humiliation; but if it has been an occasion of humiliation it will have a negative force and intensify the image formed in his fright. We find analogous phenomena in the erotic life, but different, because the erotic image of the situation is always an exalting and not a depressing image. If, in my experience of life, a certain erotic experience has been favourable and has affirmed me, the image I have of it will be reinforced when I arrive at the act in reality. If, on the other hand, the real situation reminds me of an old humiliation, the image will be diminished or destroyed when I come to action.

Usually, the subject presents himself in a real erotic situation that has associations with memories of an affirming and agreeable character, and such a situation does not displace the erotic image, but supports and heightens it as the drawings or photographs did. If such a man were to analyze himself correctly in the course of the sexual experience he then undergoes, he would find out that he was living this experience on the plane of images and on the plane of sensations at the same time; which is to say that, while actually doing this or that, he sees himself doing it, and enjoys it in his mind as well as genitally. He would also observe that his most exquisite pleasure was derived from the image—I say the most exquisite, not the most intense. Moreover, if the sexual act took place upon the plane of sensations only, it would come quickly to its termination. It is on the plane of images that the genital sensations which precede the orgasm are enjoyed, and have earned the name of "voluptuousness." Their quality is due to imaginative anticipation of the orgasm. If lovers expert in the erotic art retard the orgasm as long as possible, it is because they prefer their excitation to their sexual satisfaction. And that, as we said at the beginning, is the special characteristic of eroticism, of sexuality upon the plane of images.

Often, indeed, in a strongly erotic person, sexual satisfaction may exclude for the moment all sense of the function upon the plane of sensations, but not upon the plane of images; sexual excitation persists, although the organs are pacified. *Lassata sed not satiata,* as used to be said of Messalina.

THE YOUNG MAN: May not the erotic image then be different from the situation actually experienced?

THE AUTHOR: Quite so. The human being may, during a sexual act, maintain his excitation and thereby the activity of the function by elaborating images that do not coincide with his real situation. A man may, while he lies with one woman, imagine himself lying with another, or in any other erotic situation he chooses. But the creation of such images is in general too incompatible with the real situation.

THE YOUNG MAN: You have now and again used the expression "cerebral sexuality." Why do you not use it always, in preference to "sexuality on the plane of images," which is pretty cumbersome?

THE AUTHOR: Because, when one speaks of "cerebral sexuality," it suggests, in the minds of many people, a psychological phenomenon almost devoid of connection with the genital zone; and that is quite a wrong idea. You must understand that it is the same sexuality which finds the point of origin for its activity in a genital or in a cerebral excitation. The brain and the genital organs are closely connected; according to certain schools of thought there is a genital brain that is distinct from what is properly called the brain and related to it. In a man who is capable of sexuality upon the plane of images, this will practically always be associated with sexuality on the plane of sensations; and it is on the plane of images that the sexual impulses will take their conscious origin. Note, however, that an imaginative erotic impulse normally presupposes a genital apparatus ready for action. The interaction between the two planes is intimate and lends itself to combinations of indefinite complexity: the little we have said makes no pretence of being a full examination of this question.

2

From THE ART OF COURTLY LOVE

ANDREAS CAPELLANUS

Introduction to the Treatise on Love

We must first consider what love is, whence it gets its name, what the effect of love is, between what persons love may exist, how it may be acquired, retained, increased, decreased, and ended, what are the signs that one's love is returned, and what one of the lovers ought to do if the other is unfaithful.

What Love Is

Love is a certain inborn suffering derived from the sight of and excessive meditation upon the beauty of the opposite sex, which causes each one to wish above all things the embraces of the other and by common desire to carry out all of love's precepts in the other's embrace.

That love is suffering is easy to see, for before the love becomes equally balanced on both sides there is no torment

SOURCE: Andreas Capellanus, *The Art of Courtly Love*, abr. and ed., Frederick W. Locke (New York: Frederick Ungar Publishing Co., Inc., 1957), pp. 2–6, 24, 28, 42–43. Copyright 1941 Columbia University Press.

greater, since the lover is always in fear that his love may not gain its desire and that he is wasting his efforts. He fears, too, that rumors of it may get abroad, and he fears everything that might harm it in any way, for before things are perfected a slight disturbance often spoils them. If he is a poor man, he also fears that the woman may scorn his poverty; if he is ugly, he fears that she may despise his lack of beauty or may give her love to a more handsome man; if he is rich, he fears that his parsimony in the past may stand in his way. To tell the truth, no one can number the fears of one single lover. This kind of love, then, is a suffering which is felt by only one of the persons and may be called "single love." But even after both are in love the fears that arise are just as great, for each of the lovers fears that what he has acquired with so much effort may be lost through the effort of someone else, which is certainly much worse for a man than if, having no hope, he sees that his efforts are accomplishing nothing, for it is worse to lose the things you are seeking than to be deprived of a gain you merely hope for. The lover fears, too, that he may offend his loved one in some way; indeed he fears so many things that it would be difficult to tell them.

That this suffering is inborn I shall show you clearly, because if you will look at the truth and distinguish carefully you will see that it does not arise out of any action; only from the reflection of the mind upon what it sees does this suffering come. For when a man sees some woman fit for love and shaped according to his taste, he begins at once to lust after her in his heart; then the more he thinks about her the more he burns with love, until he comes to a fuller meditation. Presently he begins to think about the fashioning of the woman and to differentiate her limbs, to think about what she does, and to pry into the secrets of her body, and he desires to put each part of it to the fullest use. Then after he has come to this complete meditation, love cannot hold the reins, but he proceeds at once to action; straightway he strives to get a helper to find an intermediary. He begins to plan how he may find favor with her, and he begins to seek a place and a time opportune for talking; he looks upon a brief hour as a very long year, because he cannot do anything fast enough to suit his eager mind. It is well known that many things happen to him in this manner. This inborn suffering comes, therefore, from seeing and meditating. Not every kind of meditation can be the cause of love, an excessive one is required; for a restrained thought does not, as a rule, return to the mind, and so love cannot arise from it.

Between What Persons Love May Exist

Now, in love you should note first of all that love cannot exist except betwen persons of opposite sexes. Between two men or two women love can find no place, for we see that two persons of the same sex are not at all fitted for giving each other the exchanges of love or for practicing the acts natural to it. Whatever nature forbids, love is ashamed to accept.

What the Effect of Love Is

Now it is the effect of love that a true lover cannot be degraded with any avarice. Love causes a rough and uncouth man to be distinguished for his handsomeness; it can endow a man even of the humblest birth with nobility of character; it blesses the proud with humility; and the man in love becomes accustomed to performing many services gracefully for everyone. O what a wonderful thing is love, which makes a man shine with so many virtues and teaches everyone, no matter who he is, so many good traits of character! There is another thing about love that we should not praise in few words: it adorns a man, so to speak, with the virtue of chastity, because he who shines with the light of one love can hardly think of embracing another woman, even a beautiful one. For when he thinks deeply of his beloved the sight of any other woman seems to his mind rough and rude.

What Persons are Fit for Love

We must now see what persons are fit to bear the arms of love. You should know that everyone of sound mind who is capable of doing the work of Venus may be wounded by one of love's arrows unless prevented by age, or blindness, or excess of passion.

An excess of passion is a bar to love, because there are men who are slaves to such passionate desire that they cannot be held in the bonds of love—men who, after they have thought long about some woman or even enjoyed her, when they see another woman straightway desire her embraces, and they forget about the services they have received from their first love and they feel no gratitude for them. Men of this kind lust after every woman they see; their love is like that of a shameless dog. They should rather, I believe, be compared to asses, for they are moved only by that low nature which shows that men are on the level of the other animals rather than by that true nature which sets us apart from all the other animals by the difference of reason.

In What Manner Love May Be Acquired, and in How Many Ways

It remains next to be seen in what ways love may be acquired.

A beautiful figure wins love with very little effort, especially when the lover who is sought is simple, for a simple lover thinks that there is nothing to look for in one's beloved besides a beautiful figure and face and a body well cared for.

But a wise woman will seek as a lover a man of praiseworthy character—not one who anoints himself all over like a woman or makes a rite of the care of the body, for it does not go with a masculine figure to adorn oneself in womanly fashion or to be devoted to the care of the body.

Likewise, if you see a woman too heavily rouged you will not be taken in by her beauty unless you have already discovered that she is good company besides, since a woman who puts all her reliance on her rouge usually doesn't have any particular gifts of character. As I said about men, so with women—I believe you should not seek for beauty so much as for excellence of character. For since all of us human beings are derived originally from the same stock and all naturally claim the same ancestor, it was not beauty or care of the body or even abundance of possessions, but excellence of character alone which first made a distinction of nobility among men and led to the difference of class.

Character alone, then, is worthy of the crown of love. Many times fluency of speech will incline to love the hearts of those who do not love, for an elaborate line of talk on the part of the lover usually sets love's arrows a-flying and creates a presumption in favor of the excellent character of the speaker. How this may be I shall try to show you as briefly as I can.

The Easy Attainment of One's Object

The readiness to grant requests is, we say, the same thing in women as overvoluptuousness in men—a thing which all agree should be a total stranger in the court of Love. For he who is so tormented by carnal passion that he cannot embrace anyone in heartfelt love, but basely lusts after every woman he sees, is not called a lover but a counterfeiter of love and a pretender, and he is lower than a shameless dog. Indeed the man who is so wanton that he cannot confine himself to the love of one woman deserves to be considered an impetuous ass. It will therefore be clear to you that you are bound to avoid an overabundance of passion and that you ought not to seek the love of a woman who you know will grant easily what you seek.

The Love of Peasants

If you should, by some chance, fall in love with a peasant woman, be careful to puff her up with lots of praise and then, when you find a convenient place, do not hesitate to take what you seek and to embrace her by force. For you can hardly soften their outward inflexibility so far that they will grant you their embraces quietly or permit you to have the solaces you desire unless first you use a little compulsion as a convenient cure for their shyness. We do not say these things, however, because we want to persuade you to love such women, but only so that, if through lack of caution you should be driven to love them, you may know, in brief compass, what to do.

In What Ways Love May Be Decreased

Now let us see in what ways love may be decreased. Too many opportunities for exchanging solaces, too many opportunities of seeing the loved one, too much chance to talk to each other all decrease love, and so does an uncultured appearance or manner of walking on the part of the lover or the sudden loss of his property. Love decreases, too, if the woman finds that her lover is foolish and indiscreet, or if he seems to go beyond reasonable bounds in his demands for love, or if she sees that he has no regard for her modesty and will not forgive her bashfulness. Love decreases, too, if the woman considers that her lover is cowardly in battle, or sees that he is unrestrained in his speech or spoiled by the vice of arrogance.

Other things which weaken love are blasphemy against God or His saints, mockery of the ceremonies of the Church, and a deliberate withholding of charity from the poor. We find that love decreases very sharply if one is unfaithful to his friend, or if he brazenly says one thing while he deceitfully conceals a different idea in his heart. Love decreases, too, if the lover piles up more wealth than is proper, or if he is too ready to go to law over trifles.

The Rules of Love

I. Marriage is no real excuse for not loving.

II. He who is not jealous cannot love.

III. No one can be bound by a double love.

IV. It is well known that love is always increasing or decreasing.

V. That which a lover takes against the will of his beloved has no relish.

VI. Boys do not love until they arrive at the age of maturity.

VII. When one lover dies, a widowhood of two years is required of the survivor.

VIII. No one should be deprived of love without the very best of reasons.

IX. No one can love unless he is impelled by the persuasion of love.

X. Love is always a stranger in the home of avarice.

XI. It is not proper to love any woman whom one should be ashamed to seek to marry.

XII. A true lover does not desire to embrace in love anyone except his beloved.

XIII. When made public love rarely endures.

XIV. The easy attainment of love makes it of little value; difficulty of attainment makes it prized.

XV. Every lover regularly turns pale in the presence of his beloved.

XVI. When a lover suddenly catches sight of his beloved his heart palpitates.

XVII. A new love puts to flight an old one.

XVIII. Good character alone makes any man worthy of love.

XIX. If love diminishes, it quickly fails and rarely revives.

XX. A man in love is always apprehensive.

XXI. Real jealousy always increases the feeling of love.

XXII. Jealousy, and therefore love, are increased when one suspects his beloved.

XXIII. He whom the thought of love vexes, eats and sleeps very little.

XXIV. Every act of a lover ends in the thought of his beloved.

XXV. A true lover considers nothing good except what he thinks will please his beloved.

XXVI. Love can deny nothing to love.

XXVII. A lover can never have enough of the solaces of his beloved.

XXVIII. A slight presumption causes a lover to suspect his beloved.

XXIX. A man who is vexed by too much passion usually does not love.

XXX. A true lover is constantly and without intermission possessed by the thought of his beloved.

XXXI. Nothing forbids one woman being loved by two men or one man by two women.

3

ROMANTIC LOVE

HUGO G. BEIGEL

The rise of the divorce rate, viewed as a threat to the marital institution, has led sociologists and psychologists to examine more closely current practices in marital selection. Owing to the emotional atmosphere surrounding this subject, however, the eagerness to provide an antidote has sometimes engendered premature conclusions. In particular has it become fashionable to point to "romantic love" as the villain in the picture. De Rougemont,[1] for instance, calls romance "a fever" and "a passing fancy" that is "the principal reason . . . for the growing number of divorces." A similar point of view is presented in several media intended for education in family and marital relations.[2]

Contrary to such verdicts, the hypothesis is here advanced that

SOURCE: Hugo Beigel, "Romantic Love," *American Sociological Review,* XIV, 3 (June 1951), 326–34. Reprinted by permission of the author and the American Sociological Association.

[1] D. de Rougemont, "The Crisis of the Modern Couple," in R. N. Anshen, *Family, Function, and Destiny,* New York: Harpers, 1949, Chap. 16.

[2] H. Bowman, "This Charming Couple," 16mm. motion picture, New York: McGraw-Hill, 1950.

(1) courtly love and its derivative, romantic love, are not identical with puppy love,[3] but are expressions of a socio-psychological process that aims at the reconciliation of basic human needs with frustrating social conditions;

(2) in this function romantic love has not only not harmed the relationship of the sexes but has enhanced the status of women and softened the impact on the marital union of factors that endanger the ideological basis of this and related institutions without providing substitute values.

Three phases of formalized love are discernible in Western culture. The first encompasses the origin of courtly love in the twelfth century, the second its revival at the turn of the nineteenth century, and the third its present state and significance for marital selection.

The first phase is called courtly love, *l'amoor de lonh* (distant love), or *minne,* and many literary documents, poems, and epics depict its form and the feelings involved. The history and practices of courtly love have been described by Folsom,[4] Gleichen-Russwurm,[5] Vedel[6] and others. We can thus confine ourselves to summarize merely the points essential to the present discussion.

Courtly love was the conventionalization of a new ideal that arose in the feudal class and institutionalized certain aspects of the male-female relationship *outside marriage.* In conformity with the Christian concept of and contempt for sex, the presupposition for *minne* was chastity. Being the spiritualization and the sublimation of carnal desire, such love was deemed to be impossible between husband and wife. By application of the religious concept of abstract love to the "mistress," the married woman of the ruling class, who had lost her economic

---

[3] E. W. Burgess and H. J. Locke, *The Family,* New York: American Book Co., 1950.

[4] J. K. Folsom, *Family and Democratic Society,* New York: Wiley, 1943.

[5] A. von Gleichen-Russwurm, *Kultur und Sittengeschichte aller Zeiten und Voelker,* Zurich: Gutenberg Verlag, 1920.

[6] V. Vedel, *Mittelalterliche Kulturideale, Natur und Geisteswelt,* Leipzig, 1916.

function, was endowed with higher and more general values: gentleness and refinement. Unselfish service to the noble lady became a duty of the knight, explicitly sworn to in the oath the young nobleman had to take at the dubbing ceremony.[7] Part of this service was ritualized; by means of such formalization the aggressiveness of unfulfilled cravings was channeled into codes and causes. In this manner sexual covetousness was deflected and the marital rights of husbands were—theoretically at least—safeguarded. This was obviously an important provision in an age in which social rules prevented free choice of a mate for marriage with the result that basic human needs were left unsatisfied.

Courtly love—in retrospect called romantic love—consequently was not a whimsical play. In spite of the surface appearance of its aesthetic formulation, it sprang from vital needs, from a deeply felt desire for the ennoblement of human relations, and from culture-bred frustrations. It made *māze* (moderation) a masculine virtue.

The fact that it is in the first place the sexual drive that was frustrated in this love relationship suggests an analogy with adolescent love. We can assume that certain features in the development of an adolescent brought up in an earlier phase of our culture coincide with tendencies observable nowadays. Those produced by the physiological maturation of the organism, for instance, are universal, and medieval literature gives some evidence of the emotions involved in self-discovery and the experience of change at this age.[8]

While the sexual drive rises to its greatest intensity during adolescence, it is denied satisfaction. Abstinence and celibacy being among the highest religious ideals and sexual immorality being threatened with hellfire, conflicts are created that lead to feelings of guilt, depreciation of the ego, and a heightening of

[7] "Monumenta Germaniae" (leges II, 363) in F. Sturtevant, *Vom guten Ton im Wandel der Jahrhunderte,* Berlin: Bong, 1917.

[8] Chretiens de Troyes, *Percival* (Conte del graal); Wolfram von Eschenbach, *Parzival;* Hartmann von Aue, *Der arme Heinrich;* Wirnt von Gravenberg, *Vigalois.*

the ego ideal. The phantasy is quickened and the suppression of the intensified desires results in a high emotionality which seeks for vicarious outlets.[9] While sexual relations cannot be established before marriage, there is sufficient erotic stimulation from talk, from visual stimuli, and an occasional trespassing with females outside one's class to feed the hope for more. Unless hope is realized or relinquished, the adolescent strains his resources to impress any members of the opposite sex and one female in particular whose behavior allows anticipation of possible acceptance. The means are display of masculine skill and prowess which, under the influence of religious teachings, the group code, and the masculine ideal, are subordinated to socially acknowledged causes or such feats as can be interpreted as good causes. The striving to prove one's independence and manliness finds expression in the search for adventures. The female, being at the same time the weaker competitor, the object to be obtained, and the substitute for the mother, grows to be the ideal audience and the representative for the super-ego; this has the effect that softer virtues often take precedence over coarser forms of behavior. While, in general, the adolescent does not aim at permanent possession of the female, any sign of approval by her is interpreted as acceptance and props up the wavering self-esteem. For this service she is idealized; even the refusal of sexual gratification is taken as an indication of greater self-control and moral strength. Such greatness, on the other hand, reflects favorably on the quality of the one accepted, who tries to live up to moral perfection and thus to the beloved's assumed higher standard. Vows of self-improvement alternate with feelings of unworthiness and moments of expansive self-feeling.

The adolescent's showing-off attitude has its counterpart in the medieval knight's search for adventures and in the tournaments he fought for his mistress. Love tests are frequent. Certain feats like those of Ulrich von Lichtenstein, who sent his

---

[9] K. C. Garrison, *The Psychology of Adolescence,* New York: Prentice-Hall, 1950; A. H. Arlitt, *Adolescent Psychology,* New York: American Book Co., 1933.

little finger to his mistress and drank the water in which she had washed, or of Peire Vidal, who had himself sewn into a bear's hide and hunted,[10] have their parallels in the adolescent's obsessional yearning to impress the chosen female by valiance, self-sacrifice, and self-punishment. As do adolescent relations, courtly love provided partial satisfactions of the sexual desire. The lover having become a *drutz*[11] had the right to accompany his lady to her bedchamber, to undress her to the skin, and to put her to bed. Sometimes he was even allowed to sleep with her if he promised to content himself with a kiss. The love symbols are similar; the adolescent feels the one-ness with the beloved by wearing a lock of her hair or a ribbon near his heart as the knight felt it when he tied her veil around his armor; and as the mistress wore her gallant's blood-stained shirt so may a girl today wear her boy's pin, blazer, or baseball hat.

Such and many more similarities provoke the conclusion that courtly love represents the aesthetization of adolescent feelings which, though recognized as precious, are rarely experienced in adulthood with the same ardor. Under the influence of the cherished tales of oriental love refinement, the pyre of adolescent emotions was artificially kept burning, producing that subtler form of male-female relations that exploited the elations and depressions of enforced chastity for the ennoblement of the mind and gave the newly consolidated ruling class moral distinction over the crude indulgence of the masses.

The cultural significance of this concept lies in the fact that the idealization of the female initiated her social elevation and that it introduced voluntary fidelity, restraint, and the magnanimous gentleness of the male consciously into the relation between the sexes, qualities that were not considered essential or even possible in a marriage based on the semi-patriarchal concept of the Middle Ages. As the idea spread, it influenced

---

[10] H. Jantzen, ed., *Dichtungen aus mittelhochdeutscher Fruehzeit; Goeschen*, 137, Leipzig, 1910.

[11] Gleichen-Russwurm, *op. cit.* The lover who has reached the fourth and highest state in the ritual of courtly love and is accepted.

greatly the emotional development of the group as a whole. This penetration became evident when romantic love, the bourgeois adaptation of courtly love, was propagated by the Romanticists.

Presupposing the knowledge of the historic and socio-economic roots of the Romantic movement,[12, 13] we limit ourselves again to an outline of those trends that have direct bearing on our subject.

In formulating the idea of romantic love, the Romanticists merely propounded a concept that had become a socio-psychological necessity. Starting in the fourteenth century, the dissolution of the broader family had progressed to the point where its economic, religious, and political functions were gone. With increasing urbanization the impact of social isolation made itself felt upon the individual. As a result of industrialization and mercantilization the father's authority had decreased and the children remained longer under the more emotionally-oriented care of the mother, a fact that, together with the child's loss of economic function, effected a gradual change in personality, especially in the male personality. Reformation, revolutions, and wars had shaken the foundations of beliefs and traditions. Being the first to feel the pinch of the technological development on the treasured ideology of individualism, the Romanticists rebelled against the progressing de-humanization, the all-devouring materialism and rationalism, and sought escape from these dangers in the wonders of the emotions. In the basic feelings of humanity they hoped to find security and a substitute for the eliminated cultural values.

Under the increasing discomfort in a changing civilization, the aristocratic class had found a way to alleviate the defects of a family-prescribed monogamous marriage by dividing duty and satisfaction; the woman reserved her loyalty for her husband and her love for her gallant. Continuing on the tracks

12 R. M. Meyer, *Die Literatur des 19. und 20. Jahrhunderts,* Berlin: Bondi, 1921.

13 L. Walzel, *Romantik; Natur und Geisteswelt,* Leipzig, 1915, Vols. 232, 233.

laid by the concept of courtly love, the nobles of the seventeenth and eighteenth centuries in Austria, Spain, France, the Netherlands, etc. still adhered to the tenet that love and marriage were irreconcilable. Yet, love had dropped its cloak of sublimation. The medieval concept had drawn a line between the spiritual and the animalicsexual, between love and marriage. The court society of the Baroque[14] and the Rococo periods, by rewarding the gallant's deeds and duels with carnal favors, actually integrated sex and love—though only outside marriage. The adaptation noticeable in the ascending bourgeois class followed the same line—integration of sex and love —with the important difference that their economic struggle, their tradition of thrift, their religious ideas, (which, reformed to further their purposes, gave them moral support in their ultimate contest with the group in power[15]) did not permit them to accept illicit relationships as a solution of the problem. Yet, they had not remained unaffected by the ideology of earthly love. The refined concept had filtered down from the castles to the cities. Marriage, to be sure, was still arranged on a family basis with an eye on business, and the status of the wife was by no means enviable. But the verbiage of courtly love had entered the relation of the sexes. However, it was addressed not to the married woman, but, for the first time, to the marriageable maiden. Of course, this was hardly possible before the betrothal since, as an anonymous writer, Ursula Margareta, wrote in her diary published posthumously in 1805,[16] "the association with the opposite sex was not yet invented then (about 1760) . . . and we were shielded from them as from chicken pox." But during the months between engagement and marriage the bethrothed was expected to "court" the girl and to display his emotional fervor in conversation, gifts, and poetry.

[14] M. Carrière, "Barocque," in Gleichen-Russwurm, *op. cit.*, vol. 11.

[15] R. H. Tawney, *Religion and the Rise of Capitalism*, Penguin Books, Harmondsworth, England, 1938.

[16] "Alte und neue Zeit; Taschenbuch zum geselligen Vergnuegen, 1805," reprinted in Sturtevant, *op. cit.*

Preceded by the English novelist Samuel Richardson (1689–1761), who is credited with having said first that love is needed for marriage, the men of letters of those days pointed out both the immorality of the aristocratic solution and the sterility of the bourgeois pattern. Visualizing love as an antidote to the insecurity produced by social and technological changes, they propagated its legitimization and thus its perpetuation in marriage. The model for the bond between the sexes was the complex of feelings so graciously depicted in medieval romances, and its realization was henceforth called romance or romantic love.

We thus encounter a third stage in the development of love relations. The first admitted certain formalized features of adolescent feelings into the adult relationship to bridge the dichotomy between sublimated sex desires and the prevailing sex-hostile ideology; the second justified with love adulterous sex relations to ease the burden of an unreformed monogamy; the third aimed at the integration of love and marriage. It was promulgated by the first spokesmen of the bourgeois culture, who pleaded for the right of the young people to make their own choice for marriage on the basis of their feelings. No longer was there to be a cleavage between the spirituality of love and the marital sex relation, but the latter was to be sanctified by the former. This combination raised—though only ideologically at first—the woman of the middle class to the status which heretofore only the aristocratic lady had achieved in relation to the man.

Like courtly love, the concept of the Romanticists leaned noticeably on adolescent experiences. Though less ritualized than *minne,* romantic love acknowledged the value of certain pre-adult emotions. It established a hierarchy of characteristics that marked predestined affection. Foremost among them was emotional instead of rational evaluation, an attitude that contrasts clearly with the adult behavior normally aspired to, but is typical of adolescence, in which the rational powers do not operate at their optimum. Economic and status considerations were belittled. The female was idealized because of her ('nat-

ural') kindness, her intuition, and her nearness to nature. The
male conceived of himself as a restless, striving, and erring
deviate, spoiled by civilization, who, inspired by the female's
love, might find the way back to his better self. This tendency
corresponds to the adolescent's moments of magnified feelings
of inferiority in the face of the female's greater poise and
virtue and the elation when he is accepted nevertheless. While
in the romantic concept the adventures of the mind were valued over fighting and fencing, conflict, self-recognition, sensitivity and the preservation of one's "true" and original self
were elevated to moral qualities. The analogy to the adolescent's defensive attitude toward practical adult goals is evident.

The romantic love relationship itself was pervaded by melancholy and *Weltschmerz* (world-woe), another trend that is
generally encountered in adolescence when the young person,
having severed his emotional ties with his protective elders and
craving new attachments, finds himself abandoned and, in
comparison with the still child-like ego ideal, inadequate.
From the same experience, on the other hand, results the claim
to uniqueness and originality. Owing to his maturing mental
powers, his broadening experience and knowledge, the adolescent frequently senses suddenly some of the discrepancies
between reality and the moral teachings of his group, especially
those which are antagonistic to the fulfillment of his desires.
In this whirl of contradictions, wishes, rebellious emotions, and
thoughts he feels like a castaway or like a revolutionary, chosen
for the fight against either the traditions or the temptations,
like a hero or like a sinner, full of defiance or full of resolu-
tions to prove himself better than anyone else. Simultaneously
proud and afraid of his discoveries, he seeks reassurance, someone to confide to, a companion who confirms the value of his
ideas and thus of his personality.

Unable to turn to his parents, who in a quickly changing
world are no longer considered revered guides but old-fashioned
antagonists, he can find assurance only with a friend who
seems to be shaken by similar convulsions and consequently
"understands." After a period of homosexual friendships, the

social conventions, the ideal of masculinity, and the sex drive usually direct the choice toward heterosexual relations, the same relations whose secrecy, mood of conspiracy, exuberations and depressions were the raw material for romantic love which, minimizing the sexual aspect, introduced friendship between the sexes.

By the end of the nineteenth century love had won its battle along the whole line in the upper sections of the middle class. It has since been regarded as the most important prerequisite to marriage. The American concept that considers individual happiness the chief purpose of marriage is based entirely on this ideology.

This fact must, however, not be confused with the allegations that the combination of romance and marriage is a specific American feature[17] or that marriage in this country is influenced to a unique degree by romantic love.[18] Doubtful as such assertions are in the absence of quantitative studies, they tend to create the impression that the majority of marriages are based on romantic love and that there is a deplorable causative relation between this circumstance and the record the United States holds regarding divorce. Actually, while estimates as to the frequency of love as a motive for marriage vary, marital counselors are agreed that love is more often presented as a reason for an intended marriage than feelings and circumstances warrant.

There arises, however, a second question. Is this love identical with the formalized concept of romantic love?

Certainly, the all-pervading melancholy is relatively rare among young adults; the mood of lovers, though still vacillating between joy and depression, is, on the whole, less sentimentally sad and, owing to their greater independence and the diminishing outside interference, is based more often on anticipation of marital joys, cooperation, "having fun together," and pursuit of common interests. As contact between the sexes

---

17 Burgess, *op. cit.*

18 F. E. Merril, *Courtship and Marriage*, New York: Sloane Associates, 1949.

is freer, partial sexual outlets are frequently provided. And while such activities may still be followed by feelings of guilt, these seem to be greatly attenuated by a presumed necessity caused by a socially cultivated sexual competition. Sex competition, on the other hand, particularly potent among girls, tends to blur the line between the excitations of love and those of an aggressive ambition. As a result of the prevailing dating convention and its concomitant early initiation of the sexes on a social basis, the over-idealization of the female (the keynote in both courtly and romantic love) is curbed. The love conventions of the twelfth and the nineteenth centuries were grants made by the man to the female; love in our day and in this country, conversely, has become a demand of the female, who is in the privileged position to extend or withhold sexual favors. Her own desire probably being lessened by culturally necessitated repressions, she frequently uses such favors to reward or stimulate emotional expressions without regard to her own sex drive. Thus it appears that the modern love concept is not identical with romantic love, but is a derivative, modified in concord with the conditions of our age and based more on ego demands than on ideal demands.

But whatever form it takes, love is rarely the only consideration upon which marriage is contracted. Rather, it is one selective factor operating within the controls imposed upon the mates by our culture. These controls involve age, race, religion, ethnic origin, and class,[19] and the thus defined field is furthermore narrowed by regional proximity.

Under these circumstances, to blame love for the failures of marital unions in general is therefore unjustified, especially since a great number of marriages are contracted for reasons other than mutual love. In any case, however, the divorce rate cannot be taken as the sole indication of failure. In blaming its rise on the inadequacy of love as a selective agent, the judges omit several considerations, such as whether marriages con-

[19] A. B. Hollingshead, "Cultural Factors in the Selection of Marriage Mates," *American Sociological Review*, 15 (Oct. 1950), 619–627.

tracted for economic or similar reasons do not work out worse and whether every failing marriage ends in divorce. Overlooked also is the fact that divorce is now more generally available than before. What marital life in the leading group looked like before the admission of either love or divorce can be gathered from any studies of the Baroque and Rococo periods. To give but one example: in 1716, Lady Montague[20] wrote that in Vienna every woman of social standing had two men, her husband and her lover. Everyone knew of it and it was a serious offense to invite a lady to a party without asking both of her men.

Matters were similar for men in the higher social classes of all civilized countries with the exception of Spain where, in the seventeenth century, a man was said to have three women, his wife for representative purposes, his *manceba* (lady friend) for sexual, and his mistress for aesthetic conversations.[21] Thus, it was obviously not the combination of love and marriage that destroyed marital relations in Western culture.

Rather, the integration of love with marriage is an attempt at adjustment in the light of social concepts that outgrew the inadequate monogamous institution. Undoubtedly, love is not the panacea as which it is sometimes presented. But it is less often the affectionate feeling that hampers the evaluation of the future mate's personality than it is the disregard of personality factors when the determination to get married results in confusing thwarted ambition or feelings of inferiority with love.

As with every institutionalized emotion, a certain amount of pretense is, of course, to be expected. Since love is considered the noblest motive for marriage, many people will profess love even though they have married for different reasons, family pressure, for instance, or material security or betterment of status.

20 Carrière, *op. cit.*
21 Sturtevant, *op. cit.*

But pretense need not be so evident. Sexual cravings are easily mistaken for love. As a matter of fact, love has attained an exceptional state with regard to sex. It has become the condition that allows the woman to lift the severe sex taboo imposed on her; the implicit supposition is that she may enter a sex relationship only when she is motivated by affectionate feelings. While this requirement is officially waived only when she marries, it frequently serves as an extenuating circumstance when she enters an illicit relationship. She certainly is judged differently when she succumbs to the latter for pecuniary considerations. As a result, the male uses the language and gestures of love to obtain temporarily desired sexual favors, and the female frequently interprets his "line" as love to avoid losing his attention.

Equally dangerous is self-deception. Especially in early marriages it happens often that undiluted adolescent feelings—such as the relief felt when the need to assert one's power and personality or one's independence, or the desire to escape depressing home restrictions is satisfied—are experienced as love and allowed to determine the selection of the mate. This tendency is greatly augmented since the motion picture industry, innumerable magazines and hack-written novels have undertaken to carry a cheap counterfeit of romantic love to the masses. The heroines of these products do not know of any attraction to a man except overwhelming, unconquerable, unerotic, and absolutely unselfish love that strikes at first sight, breaks down all bars of class or education, unfailingly cures all moral defects and inevitably solves all possible problems when it is transposed into marriage. Identifying herself with these stereotypes the young female movie-goer recognizes similarities between these and her own problems, and longing for the promised elations she views any approaching male under the aspect of marriage—the happy ending of the industrio-cultural literary products without any consideration of personality or moral values. Not being able to find the expected miracles in her mild likings, she tries to approximate her models by inflating her meager feelings. By autosuggestion and imitation she can usually convince herself of the unfathomable depth of her affection to anyone who speaks of love.

There is no doubt that such pressure cooker recipes for happiness do not presage well for marriage. But such immature ideas cannot be blamed on love itself, nor can they minimize the function love has actually attained in selection for marriage. For with the collective aspect of marriage, family coherence, and the economic function of wife and offspring gone, there are no other positive agents left for mate selection except economic factors, sex, and personality assets.

The first, though important, does not guarantee satisfaction in the marital union. As a matter of fact, the intolerableness of the economic dependence of the female on the male has added impetus to the acceptance of the love concept. In our time, social and economic near-equality has given women sufficient independence to allow most of them a choice. They need not—at least not to the same extent as in former times—accept their husband's will and whim as their lot. With the social control weakened in this respect, only affection or consideration of the children can bind a woman to her husband.

Sex as a selective agent is ineffectual in our culture since the premarital testing of sexual compatibility is interdicted. Instead, the attraction produced by psycho-sexual emotions is taken as an indication of mutual suitability. It does not, of course, fulfill this expectation, but feelings of love, of which this attraction is a part, are the closest substitute for tests. Even so, for the female whose training still compels her to repress all sex-tinged desires, it is, next to the psychotherapist, only love that helps her to overcome her inhibitions.

Similarly is it true that emotions provide no objective measurement for the future mate's personality. What love does, however, is to satisfy man's most urgent psychological needs, those produced by social isolation, by lack of any conceptual hold on the world in which he lives, and by lack of work satisfaction. Exposed to the high tensions of the modern work day and an unceasing brutal competition, man seeks relief in emotional satisfactions. Of these, few are available outside love. Reduced through technological progress to a negligible nut in an incomprehensible machine, confused by tumbling and contradictory moral values, he can regain the feeling of self-importance only in love. Only here can he find shelter from an inimical world, and, like the medieval knight take off his armor without fear. Only here can he be himself and expect to be accepted in all his imperfection and with all his unfulfilled secret yearnings.

Thus love—and only in connection with it marriage—has become the state from which compensation for all emotional frustrations is expected. True, such high expectations are likely to make the marital union precarious. It is doubtful, however, whether the imperfect remedy can be blamed for the illness. For, the emancipation of the female, her demand for mutuality of sex satisfactions, and the higher educational level of the middle classes have equally contributed to the brittleness of the marital institution. Yet, who would think of doing away with them even if he could?

Nor is it sensible to argue that marriage is irreconcilable with romance because sexual fulfillment and the intimacies of everyday life break down the idealization resulting from the sublimation of the sexual desire. Of course, the burning craving cannot last. But while it is true that the aura of divinity is not habit-resistant, it is also a fact that in a sexually gratifying relationship that has been built on love, that is, on understanding and mutual assistance in emotional conflicts, on moral support and common interests, on mutual confirmation and emotional security—unavailable anywhere else—the chance of creating an atmosphere of loyalty and friendship, tolerance and confidence are greater than in any other.

To summarize: courtly love, romantic love, and their modern derivative should be considered 'cultural phenomena evolved from basic human feelings that have gradually developed forms useful as replacements for discarded or decaying cultural concepts. Love aims at and assists in the adjustment to frustrating experiences. To measure its effect on marriage it must be judged in its true form and not in poor falsifications. Seen in proper perspective, it has not only done no harm as a prerequisite to marriage, but it has mitigated the impact that a too-fast-moving and unorganized conversion to new socio-economic constellations has had upon our whole culture and it has saved monogamous marriage from complete disorganization.

It is not impossible that with the progressing de-individualization inherent in our industrial orientation, sexual reproduction will some day be entirely divorced from individual personality preferences and based on a scientific biological-eugenic basis. So long, however, as human society has not taken this ultimate step, love provides one of the few positive factors in mate selection, allowing relief and emotional gratification in the enormous stress of civilization. It is not free of shortcomings; the solution, however, for the alleviation of ills concomitant to any cultural innovation and its integration with an old unreformed institution cannot be to dissuade young people from love, but only to aid them in the discrimination of those qualities in themselves and the prospective mate which must balance each other to ensure the satisfaction of emotional, sexual, and personality needs and, in so doing, the greater durability of their union.

4

ROMANTIC LOVE

ALBERT ELLIS

*"We raise our daughters in convents," said Anatole
France, "then marry them off to pirates." There is
just about that degree of actual education for the
lives they actually will lead, in the way Americans
raise their children, particularly in their attitudes
toward sex. What we teach is an unreality, and the
failure to recognize reality is one of the first roots
of neurosis and psychosis.*

The pattern of courtship in American and in practically all of
Western civilized society is, as we have just seen, that of the
Sex Tease. In following this pattern, the modern woman,
whether she consciously knows it or not, is forcibly striving to
do two major things: First, to make herself appear infinitely
sexually desirable—but finally approachable only in legal marriage. Second, to use sex as bait and therefore to set it up as
something special. If she gives in too easily to sex pleasure,
she loses her favorite man-conquering weapon. Hence she must
retain sexuality on a special plane, and dole it out only under
unusual conditions.

SOURCE: Albert Ellis, *American Sexual Tragedy* (New York: Lyle Stuart,
Inc., 1962), pp. 97–121 with deletions. Reprinted by permission of the
author and publisher.

The idealized aspect of this philosophy of let-us-women-stick-together-and-only-employ-sex-for-special-baiting-purposes is what we usually call romantic love. For at the very core of modern romance is a tight rope tautly stretched between, and uneasily dividing as well as soldering, gratified and ungratified, over- and under-evaluated sexuality. Where non-romantic types of love prevail—as they do in numerous primitive, peasant, and Eastern cultures—sex is either enjoyed for its own sake or is hedged in by practical (socio-economic, status-giving, marital, or other) restrictions. Where romance is the rule, sex is virtually never enjoyed for itself. It is invariably hemmed in by idealistic, non-practical love restrictions. Romanticisim, hand in hand with the sex tease game of American courtship, often plays up the verbal and plays down the active expression of human sexuality.

To understand modern romantic love, we should first know a little about its origins and history. Although the history of love may be traced to the beginnings of mankind, romantic love seems to have been born in Western Europe during the Middle Ages. It is, as Finck has pointed out, "A modern sentiment, less than a thousand years old."[1]

The so-called Dark Ages which preceded the twelfth century was an epoch of acute socio-economic, religious, philosophic, and esthetic rigidity. The individual of the day was born into a world which, to the largest possible extent, predetermined his work, his thoughts, and even his emotions. Against this church-bound and custom-ridden condition of living, romanticism was something of a reflexive, and certainly a healthy, rebellion.

Like most rebellious movements, however, romantic love at first tended to take to extremes its floutings of the established social order. Thus, where the amorous ideal has emphasized sexual fidelity, *courtoisie* love frequently glorified adultery. Where eighth century love was based on patriarchal traditions, tenth century troubadours extolled woman-centered, female-worshipping *amour*. Where the priests preached divine love, the courtiers deified human love. Where Christianized conjugality was truly coffined, cabined, and confined, romantic love emphasized freedom of choice—and of parting. As Denis de Rougement has observed: "The cultivation of passionate love began in Europe as a reaction to Christianity (and in particular to its doctrine of marriage) by people whose spirit, whether naturally or by inheritance, was still pagan."[2]

Just as an insurgent political group will often, both prior and subsequent to its victory, take over many of the trappings of the vested interests it is undermining, romantic love borrowed from the Christianized version of love that preceded it. It preempted many of the mystical, irrational, evangelical aspects of early Christianity. Fighting the restrictions imposed by a mighty religion, it eventually became almost a religion in its own right.

It should be noted that man achieves so-called free will almost in direct inverse ratio to his becoming a socialized human being. The mere fact that one has, and early in one's life is raised by, duly conditioned and biased parents reduces one's possible free will to meagre amount; the fact that one, additionally, is raised among hundreds of other human beings, and among humans who have a long history and an intrenched culture, further reduces one's potential free will to near-zero proportions. Romanticism, therefore, by very virtue of its being a philosophy with quite well-defined rules of the game of living, eventually leads to virtually as much restriction and human determination as does medieval or other non-romantic philosophies. To be human is to be, in one degree or another, predetermined in one's thoughts, feelings, actions. One merely has a choice of what *kind* of determination one will live by. And even that choice is largely chimerical: since, as it for example happened, early Christianity and its heir-apparent, medievalism, actually determined most of the trappings of the romantic revolt that followed. Small wonder was it, then, that soon after its inception romantic love blanketed itself in religiosity and traditionalism.

Again, although romantic love was in part a reaction against the sexual repressiveness of early Christianity, it quickly took on so many characteristics of the Christianized love that it was trying to replace that, in its own right, it became antisexual. As Emil Lucka observed: "As time went on the barrier erected between true spiritual love and insidious sensuality became more and more clearly defined; the former pervaded the erotic emotion of the whole period. Parallel with chaste love, sensuality continued to exist as something contemptible, unworthy of a noble mind." The cycle, curiously enough, was then complete: romantic love, which originated as a revolt against Christian antisexuality, soon was conquered by its victim: so that, at least in some of its extreme manifestations, it became itself a bulwark against pagan sensuality.

Three notable facts, however, kept the antisexual elements of medieval romantic love within the bounds of practicality and sanity. In the first place, it was not, when it first originated, a mass phenomenon. The troubadours and their ladies followed the romantic patterns, to be sure. But the peasants, footsoldiers, common tradesmen and artisans, and other members of the community tended to remain scrupulously orthodox. In the second place, while the troubadours and lords maintained romantic attachments to the ladies of the day, these were invariably adulterous, and not marital, attachments. Marriages, at this time, were socio-economically arranged, and had little or nothing to do with love either in their courtship or post-courtship stages. In the third place, although the troubadours and courtiers could fall romantically in love with their ladies, they also could, and invariably did, find plenty of girls from the peasant and other classes with whom they could roll in the hay. They could therefore well afford to use love as a special ritual for the unattainable lady while they used sex as a pleasant pastime and an essential ingredient of their relations with women of the lower classes.

Medieval romanticism was in several ways an exceptionally class-limited form of love; and it hardly interfered with sex activity, which the courtier could always have, practically for the asking, with a wife, prostitute, or girl of the lower classes for whom he had very frank sex desire and, usually, no romantic love whatever. Under such conditions, the courtier could easily build love into a mystical, religious, antisexual emotion —while he was gaily, and quite unromantically, fulfilling his sexual needs at the same time.

Up until the twentieth century, vestiges of this medieval pattern of romantic love have persisted. Although the nineteenth century male was supposed to show some degree of romantic love for his wife, several non-romantic aspects of sex and marriage also were so widespread in the 1800's as to be virtually socially sanctioned. Males of the upper class in Europe and America frequently had their regular mistresses; while lower class males often frequented brothels. Marriages, particularly among the gentry, were often arranged by parents, or at least had to be entered into with parental permission; and in a country like the United States, where the frontier still existed and where women tended to bear several children and to work just as hard as their husbands, there was relatively little opportunity for romantic love in marriage, even when some measure of it existed in courtship.

Only in our own day, for the first time in history, has romantic love become ubiquitous. Whereas our forefathers expected only relatively few gentlemen and gentlewomen to love romantically, we expect every male and female to do so. There are several reasons why romantic attitudes have become so democratized today. For one thing, romantic love is facilitated by small families, by weakened religiosity, by the freedom of women, and by social mobility, all of which are considerably more prevalent today than they were a century or more ago. For another thing, modern living arrangements and technological inventions (such as kitchenettes, automobiles, and birth control appliances) make it easy for households to be moved and for families to break up, and this in turn favors romantic concepts of love. Our present concepts of individual freedom, democracy, and personal adventurousness also encourage romanticism. Finally, we have literally taken up the cudgels for romantic love and actually preach its precepts in our schools, fiction, drama, movies, and television performances. "Romantic love is to a large extent a convention developed by society,"[3] and in our own society we have deliberately adopted this convention and promulgated it with a vengeance.

All love is not, of course, romantic love. Love itself consists of any kind of more or less intense emotional attraction to or involvement with another. It includes many different types and degrees of affection, such as conjugal love, parental love, familial love, religious love, love of humanity, love of animals, love of things, self-love, sexual love, obsessive-compulsive love, etc. Although *romantic* has become, in our day, virtually a synonym for *loving,* romantic love is actually a special type of love, and has several distinguishing features.

A summary description of the characteristics of romantic love—or more accurately of the romantic lover—will help clarify. The romantic lover is unrealistic: he over-evaluates and fictionalizes his beloved. He is verbal and esthetic about his love. As Tolstoy remarked of the lovers of his day, "Many people's love would be instantly annihilated if they could not speak of it in French."[4] He is aggressively individualistic: he insists, utterly, on his own romantic love choice, and on all but absolute lack of restraint in that choice. This aspect of romantic love was taken so seriously by the famous Comtesse de Champagne's twelfth century Court of Love that it held, in one of its decisions, that "love cannot extend its rights over two married persons. For indeed lovers grant each other all, mutually and freely, without being constrained by any motive of necessity, whereas husband and wife are holden, by their duty, to submit their wills to each other and to refuse each other nothing."[5]

The romantic lover, furthermore, frequently is in love with love rather than with his beloved; and he may well repeat, with Elizabeth Barrett Browning, "If thou must love me, let it be for naught except for love's sake only." He is monopolistic, in that he normally devotes himself to one paramount love object. As Folsom has noted, "Romantic love is intensely mo-

nogamous *at any one time.* Yet, essentially, its loyalty is to *love*
rather than to a person."⁶

The romantic lover is demanding: he wishes to be loved, in
his turn, by his beloved; to be loved madly, completely, mono-
polistically; and for himself, rather than for his position and
accomplishments. He is perfectionistic: he strives for not merely
a fine, good, lasting, happy relationship with his beloved, but
for the finest, greatest, most lasting, most ecstatic amour.

The romantic lover is, as we previously noted, antisexual.
He acknowledges the value of sexuality only when it is linked
to love. He is sentimental and tends to overact and overstate
the greatness of his love. He is passionate and intense: he is
supposed to love madly and to be violently in love, rather than
affectionately loving.

The romantic lover is changeable, and frequently goes from
one violent passion to another. He is jealous, often intensely
so, of his beloved. He tends to emphasize physical attractiveness above all else. Finally, in today's world, the romantic lover
invariably stresses marrying only for love, and is likely to believe that one should never remain married when love dies.
For him, too, the death of love from his marriage tends to
become sufficient license for every sort of adultery. In the high
name of romantic love, he is free to pursue his true passion
at any cost.

The romantic lover believes, in sum, two basic propositions
which Ernest W. Burgess lists as follows: "1. That the highest
personal happiness comes from marriage based upon romantic
love. 2. That love and marriage are essentially personal and
private and are, perhaps, even more than other aspects of life,
to be controlled by the individual himself."⁷

This, in general, is what the romantic lover is; or, in other
words, these may be said to be the *facts* of romantic love. Even
more interesting, however, are some of the current American
beliefs and attitudes—or folklore—concerning love. For several main tenets about romantic amour are constantly being
drilled into the eyes and ears of the American public; and,
apparently, some measure of belief in these tenets ultimately

comes to be held by this public. Our mass media are full of assertions, implicit and explicit, about the nature of romantic love, some of which we shall now document.*

1. Romantic love is a feeling that takes you unawares, at first sight or a reasonable facsimile thereof, and quickly cooks your goose.
2. When once you really and truly fall in love, your emotion is deathless, and not even complete rejection by your beloved will serve to make you fall out of love again.
3. Romantic love is more than welcome at any age, and oldsters, as well as youngsters, should hasten to let themselves fall in love.
4. Romatic love, when it is reciprocated and fulfilled, leads to unalloyed, ecstatic happiness.
5. When romantic love is unrequited, or when one's lover deserts, it is the most painful, agonizing feeling possible.
6. Romantic love is a completely irrational, illogical feeling that makes lovers do the maddest things.
7. Romantic love is worth making any sacrifice for, and the greater the sacrifice the greater, presumably, the love.
8. True love is utterly monogamous, and once you fall in love—honest and truly—you can never love another—even though your beloved is worthless, unloving, or already married.
9. Romantic love is an all-important emotion, without which life is dull, pitiful, and meaningless.
10. Love has the power of life and death over men and women and can make them do, or not do, almost anything.
11. Love transforms sexuality and makes it truly good. Sex without love is nasty and worthless.
12. A true lover gives in completely to his beloved, and becomes entirely subservient to her wishes and whims.

The impression could easily be given, from the material thus far presented in this chapter, that romanticism monopolizes

---

* Dr. Ellis cites excerpts from magazine stories, novels, journal articles, biographies, films and songs, that play upon these themes. These have been omitted here.—Ed.

our contemporary philosophies of love and marriage. This is not entirely true: since dissident, non-romantic voices are also heard from time to time. A *Modern Bride* writer, for example, tells us that "we are hampered by ideas of love that represent a combination of infantile and adolescent patterns, instead of those appropriate to a grown-up." In a tale in *Gay Love Stories* the heroine says: "I—don't want romance or glamour—I want —genuine affection, tenderness . . . " In an article in the magazine, *Wake,* we are informed that mature love is selfless and does not demand super-romantic requitement. An *American Sociological Review* article by William L. Kolb points out that our society puts considerable pressure on young people not to marry just for love, but for more logical, socio-economic reasons. Even some of our popular jokes contain unromantic implications, as this one from *Joke Parade:* "A young woman wrote in her diary, after the loss of her husband, 'My sorrow is more than I can bear.' Several months later, leafing through the diary she came to the entry, paused, and then added the word 'alone.' "

Despite these criticisms of romantic love, and for all the jokes current about it, the fact remains that our mass media overwhelmingly favor the belief that romantic amour is incredibly delightful, delicious, and delectable and that a life not rooted in romantic affection is detestable, deleterious, and damnably dull. While not even a dozen non-romantic or anti-romantic views were found in the course of surveying literally hundreds of mass media outlets, several hundred distinctly romantic attitudes were uncovered.

The ubiquity of ultra-romantic philosophies in our mass media, particularly when combined with the unromantic and often harsh realities of modern life, leads to serious (conscious and unconscious) conflicts and disturbances on the part of virtually all the members of our society. Some of the reasons for these conflicts and disturbances are as follows:

1. Romanticism is, almost by definition, passionately untrammeled and unrestricted. But our courtship customs, as we

indicated in the previous chapter, are normally hemmed in by many practical and nonromantic considerations. Consequently, the swain who is romantically enamored of his girlfriend must almost necessarily encounter parental objections, financial difficulties, sexual tabus, and other limitations. It may therefore be predicted that, quite aside from his girlfriends' reacting negatively to him, most of his romantic attachments will never get the chance to bud or will be cruelly nipped before they have consequentially flowered. Although the sex tease of courtship which is prevalent in our society nicely dovetails with romanticism's antisexuality, our other courtship restrictions are mainly antithetical to romance: they, to some extent, encourage romantic dreams—but savagely combat the fulfillment of these dreams.

2. The kind of romantic love which is enthusiastically espoused by our mass media is based on many assumptions which, ordinarily, are not sustained by the realities of either living or loving. Thus, it is assumed that romantic love does not change; but, on the contrary, it most often does. It is assumed that romantic love survives the lover's aging processes and the beloved's loss of youth and beauty; but, most frequently, it does not. It is assumed that it is easy to tell "true love" from "infatuation"; which, of course, it isn't. It is assumed that romantic love brings nothing but ecstatic joy; when, actually, it often brings worry, responsibility, loss of independence, and all kinds of anguish. It is assumed that having steady sex relations with one's beloved will make one romantically love her more; when, in point of fact, it frequently makes one love her less. It is assumed that if a pair of romantic lovers have children, their offspring will help increase their mutual ardor; when, in numerous instances, children seriously sabotage romantic ardor. Similarly, numerous other assumptions about romantic love are made in our popular publications and productions which, in reality, are distinctly false. Consequently, the utter, terrible disillusionment of many or most romantic lovers becomes eventually assured.

3. Romanticism, again almost by definition, implies a considerable degree of fiction, of facing away from instead of toward reality. The romantic lover exaggerates, overestimates, sees his beloved as she really is not. But life, particularly in our technologically influenced world, is hardly fictional; and adjustment to life, as we psychologists have been stressing for many years, means full acceptance of reality. Neurosis, in the last analysis, invariably includes a considerable degree of failure to recognize reality. If, then, romantic love also includes a failure to recognize reality, we should expect it importantly to overlap with neurosis at several points. This means that we, on the one hand, are trying to raise our children to be realistic and, on the other hand, to be non-realistic—that is, romantic. Not only, then, are we directly raising them to be at least semi-neurotic, but we are heading them for a virtually irreconcilable conflict between their romantic and non-romantic aspirations: which conflict, in its turn, is only likely to intensify their neurosis.

4. Many romantic ideals, such as those concerned with purity, dedication, holy affection, and the deification of physical beauty, supply us with perfectionistic goals which will inevitably be unachievable by most of us, and will lead to grim disappointment and disillusionment. The result, particularly where sexuality is at issue, is likely to be neurotic and psychotic feelings of dirtiness, failure, guilt, inadequacy, profanation of what is considered to be holy, and so on. Human happiness, as has long been known, is a ratio between what people expect and what they get from life. When their expectations are ultra-romantic, and hence unrealistic, failure to achieve their level of aspiration must inevitably ensue: with consequent unhappiness and a tendency toward emotional disturbance.

5. Romantic love, in our culture, is supposed to lead to engagement and marriage; but its tenets, actually, are largely opposed to the type of marriage which exists among us. Normal marriage has numerous socio-economic aspects which are antithetical to the maintenance of romantic

(though not necessarily other types of) love. Thus, married couples must be concerned about purchases, repairs, sickness, insurance, child care, entertainment, business success, in-laws, relatives, friends, education, cooking, cleaning, shopping, mending, sleeping facilities, and hundreds of other practical aspects of modern living which are utterly nonromantic and which tend to restrict emotional outpourings of a romantic nature.

Romanticism, moreover, puts a premium on intense amative *feelings:* which are notoriously changeable and fleeting. Romantic courtship usually follows a highly erratic pattern, and includes considerable affectional promiscuity. Romantic marriage, quite logically, tends to follow this same pattern and to result in numerous separations and divorces—at which our society hardly looks with equanimity.

Marriage usually becomes a relatively calm, steady relationship that is not too demanding emotionally: since few married couples have available a great reserve of sustained, intense emotional energy. But romanticism, as Gross has pointed out, demands "constant and unequivocal demonstrations of affection."[8] An individual who is raised to crave romantic love is rarely content with anything but the sustained emotional intensity which is thoroughly non-indigenous to everyday marital domesticity. Hence the almost inevitable dissatisfaction of the arch romanticist who marries.

Romantic love, again, is largely based on the sexual teasing and blocking of modern courtship. Its very intensity, to a large extent, grows out of the generous promises combined with the niggardly actualities of sex fulfillment which exist during the courtship stages. When, after marriage, the sex blockings of the courtship days are necessarily removed, the intensity of romantic love which partly stemmed from these blockings may easily fade; and the result is a relatively (romantically) loveless marriage—which, by the very premises of romanticism, is considered to be worthless and must be broken up.

Romantic love, because it is an idealized, perfectionist emotion, particularly thrives on intermittent rather than steady association between two lovers. During courtship, fellows and girls see each other for relatively few hours per week, when they are well-rested, well-fed, and well-accoutered for having a good time. On such a basis, they are at their best and their handsomest or loveliest, and can reasonably well live up to perfectionist ideals. Marriage, however, invariably means domesticity: meaning, a constant, more or less monotonous, living together on an hour after hour, year after year basis. This type of domesticity, probably, is as well designed to sabotage romantic love as is any other mode of social living. Indeed, if romantic lovers wanted, with perfect logic, to induce their passions to endure for a maximum period of time, they might well ban, under almost any circumstances, marital domesticity. But, in our society, they do just the opposite: they, as it were, condemn themselves to living under the same roof, for perhaps forty or fifty years, with their beloveds. The result, in terms of their own romantic ideals, is almost invariably frightful.

6. Romantic love, in our culture, is essentially opposed to the other modes of love which we also, in one way or another, espouse. It is particularly opposed to conjugal or familial love which our religious institutions and (increasingly) our schools are continually upholding. Moreover, most of our married women, once they see that their early romantic love for their husbands does not last, tend to raise their sons and daughters, and particularly perhaps the former, in a Momistic, family-tied manner that brooks little romantic opposition. Mother-centered sons are not encouraged to fall madly in love with the girl next door; and many of them, in point of fact, are raised so that they cannot possibly romantically love anyone. When, because of the pressurizing and pulling influences of their culture (particularly, the novels, films, and television shows of this culture), they do become romantically attached to a woman, they are almost automatically propelled right into the center of a bitter struggle for their

souls between their mother and their wife. Since romanticism, with its unrealistic idealizations and demands, can
afford no such struggle, it usually gets the worst of the
conflict, and the consequent wrestle with reality is often
agonizing.

7. Of the several possible logical culminations of romantic love
that theoretically may, and presumably should, occur, virtually none are consciously permitted to occur; so that its
usual end is desultory, unplanned, and heartbreaking. Some
of the possible logical culminations of romantic love are
these:

(a) Romantic love may, under some circumstances, be
sustained by severely limiting the period of its expression.
Thus, Somerset Maugham has the heroine of his play, *The
Constant Wife,* declare that she is going off to stay with her
lover only for a period of six weeks "Because I'm putting a
limit to our love it may achieve the perfection of something
that is beautiful and transitory."[9]

(b) Romantic love may flower indefinitely if lovers consciously become varietists and change their individual partners while continuing their romantic patterns of attachment.

(c) Romantic lovers may, quite logically, engage in plural
love affairs and thus, by having two or more romantic partners simultaneously, avoid much of the monotony and
domesticity which normally dooms romanticism.

(d) Romantic lovers may keep their love alive by consciously renouncing its fruition. Thus, Ibsen has his lovers
in *Love's Comedy* break with each other just as they are
about to marry, with the heroine ecstatically removing her
engagement ring, casting it into the fjord, and exclaiming
to her lover: "Now for this earthly life I have forgone thee,
—But for the life eternal I have won thee!"[10] George Moore,
in his *Memoirs of My Dead Life,* Andre Gide in *Strait is the
Gate,* Walter Van Tilburg Clark in *The City of Trembling
Leaves,* and Ben Hecht in *Erik Dorn* solve the problem of
longevity of romantic love in precisely the way Ibsen solved

it in *Love's Comedy*.[11] Theophile Gautier, in *Mlle. de Maupin,* gives one of the best summaries of this renunciation philosophy by having his heroine write a farewell letter to her lover in this wise: "You believe, perhaps, that I do not love you because I am leaving you. Later, you will recognize the truth of the contrary. Had I valued you less, I should have remained, and would have poured out to you the insipid beverage to the dregs. Your love would soon have died of weariness; after a time you would have quite forgotten me, and, as you read over my name on the list of your conquests, would have asked yourself: 'Now, who the deuce was she?' I have at least the satisfaction of thinking that you will remember me sooner than another. Your unsated desire will again spread its wings to fly to me; I shall ever be to you something desirable to which your fancy will love to return, and I hope that in the arms of the mistresses you may have, you will sometimes think of the unrivalled night you spent with me."[12]

(e) Romantic love, most logically perhaps, may be ended in the most drastic of all human acts: death. As Emil Lucka has pointed out: "One thing is certain: the great love cannot find its consummation on earth . . . The love-death is the last and inevitable conclusion of reciprocal love which knows no value but itself, and is resolved to face eternity, so that no alien influence shall reach it."[13] Denis de Rougemont concurs: "The mystic lovers in the Romance are compelled to pursue the *intensification* of passion, not its fortunate appeasement. The keener their passion, the more it can detach them from created things, the more readily do they feel that they are on the way to attaining the death in *endura* which they desire."[14]

Of these logical, or romantically selfconsistent, ways of bringing romantic love to a climax, none are consciously espoused by any number of lovers in our culture: for the good reason that the general marital philosophy of our society is quite opposed to such acts as lovers limiting the period of their love, becoming varietists, engaging in plural affairs, consciously renouncing their loves, or arranging a suicide pact with their beloveds. Instead, we espouse what might be called the most illogical climax to romantic courtship and love: consummation. For sexual and marital consummation indubitably, in the vast majority of instances, maims, bloodies, and finally kills romanticism until it is deader than—well, yesterday's romance. Noting this, the famous troubadour Peiral maintained that "I cannot believe that a true lover can continue to love after he has received the last favor."[15]

The pernicious and widespread effects of our romantic ideologies may perhaps be illustrated by considering the first ten patients I have seen this week. Patient No. 1, a 23 year old girl, keeps contending that she does not want to marry; actually, she has highly romantic ideals of marriage that aggravate her general feelings of inadequacy, so that she deems herself unworthy of ever acquiring the ideal type of partner she would like to marry; hence her stated lack of desire for the marital state. Patient No. 2, a 28 year old male, is living with a girl for whom he has considerable affection, but whom he will not consider marrying because, in some respects, she does not live up to his ideal of a tall, slim, beautiful, unearthly creature. Patient No. 3 has left his wife because, among other things, she has never lived up to his notion of romantic love during their twenty years of married life. Patient No. 4 has turned to homosexuality because, after twelve years of marriage, he still feels guilty about engaging in various non-coital sex activities with his wife (who is quite willing to engage in these activities) while he does not feel guilty, or as guilty, about engaging in these same activities with other males. Patient No. 5 feels that his wife does not love him because she is too close to her mother. Patient No. 6 cannot live comfortably with her husband, who she admits is a fine person and a good companion, because she is madly infatuated with another man who she says is quite inferior to him. Patient No. 7 has no special problems in relation to romantic love. Patient No. 8 cannot put his heart into sex relations with his wife, with whom he says he wants to keep living, because he feels that their marriage got off on the wrong foot when they married for practical, utterly non-romantic reasons. Patient No. 9 keeps falling intensely in love with males of whom she is absolutely afraid, because of fears that they may reject her, even to show any indication of her feeling, and with whom she normally parts long before any chance for real intimacy arises between them. Patient No. 10, while saying that she would marry almost any normal male who loved her and wanted to marry her, actually goes with literally scores of boyfriends every year, most of whom she soon rejects because they do not live up to her impossibly romantic, perfectionist notions.

So it goes with most of my patients, particularly my female patients: although romantic aspirations and ideals are not necessarily their main source of difficulty and disturbance, romanticism is definitely one of the chief reasons for their being considerably more unhappy and maladjusted than they would be had they more realistic goals of love and marriage. Similarly, I am sure, if we had adequate statistics on the place of romanticism in the causation of modern neurosis, we would find literally millions of instances where romantic ideologies have caused or abetted emotional disturbance.

Psychologists, psychiatrists, social workers, and marriage counselors rarely, alas, keep the kind of statistics which would be most helpful in gauging just how much maladjustment results from the inculcation in our populace of super-romantic ideals. Many case histories and clinical observations, however, have been published in regard to this point. Alfred Adler, for example, shows how a person who invents a "romantic, ideal, or unattainable love . . . can thus luxuriate in [his] feelings without the necessity of approaching a partner in reality."[16] Karen Horney demonstrates how romantic, over-evaluated love may be made "a screen for satisfying wishes that have nothing to do with it . . . made an illusion by our expecting much more of it than it can possibly fulfil."[17] John Levy points out how an individual's romantically expecting too much from marriage inevitably leads to a "universal feeling of disillusionment about marriage."[18] W. Beran Wolfe contends that "romanticism is the sexual life of the adolescent. When practiced by mature men and women it reaps a narrow horizon, a high degree of subjectivity, a desire to be pampered, to be treated like a prince or a princess."[19] Sandor Ferenczi notes that a full appreciation of reality is lacking in persons who remain fixated at the romantic stage of love.[20] Freud stresses the fact that extreme romanticism may lead to masochistic submissiveness to the love partner and to actual sexual perversion.[21] Lorine Pruette discusses a number of the childish marital attitudes to which romantic ideologies may lead.[22] Theodor Reik and Edmund Bergler show how unrealistic love attitudes, sparked by literary productions, result in many sorts of neurotic phenomena.[23]

Sociologists and anthropologists, on the basis of their studies, have also consistently demonstrated the pernicious effects of ultraromantic attitudes. Ray E. Baber has pointed out that "the fact that so frequently the response satisfactions in the early years of marriage do not come up to expectation is due to social misguidance. The literature of love has brought into being a cult of romance that dominates the thinking of both old and young, though not in exactly the same way. It is a wishful cult, ignoring the basic realities of life and building its castles in the clouds of fancy, where none but knights and ladies, princes and princesses exist."[24] J. B. Lichtenberger has noted that "we have here, in the perversion of the concept of the marriage of true affection and in the over-emphasis upon the romantic element, one of the obvious causes of the increases of divorces . . . Romantic love as the exclusive basis of marriage is hopelessly inadequate. Even connubial love can flourish only in a congenial atmosphere and often is killed by antagonisms which arise from other sources."[25] Sumner and Keller contended that it is romantic influences "which bring men and women up to matrimony with false and impossible notions and prepare them for speedy disillusionment, misery, divorce, a new attempt to reach the impossible, and so on."[26] Similar realistic observations on the effects of romanticisms have been made by many other outstanding sociological thinkers, including Folsom,[27] Green, Gross, Groves and Groves, Landis, MacIver, Mowrer, and Schmiedeler.[28] This is not to gainsay romanticism's many valuable aspects: the democracy of choice, the freedom from restraint, the aspirations to high-level individualism, the frank avowal of hedonism, the glorious potentialities for human ecstasy, and the indubitable other benefits that it valiantly espouses. The conclusion is factually and clinically inevitable, however, that romantic love, in its present form, is a very mixed blessing. Unless it evolves (as, fortunately, it may) in a somewhat saner direction, and unless it becomes a more mature and more realistic path to marriage, serious trouble will continue to result.

References

1. HENRY T. FINCK, *Romantic Love and Personal Beauty*. New York: Macmillan, 1887, p. 1.

2. DENIS DE ROUGEMONT, *Love in the Western World*. New York: Harcourt, Brace, 1940, p. 70.

3. ARTHUR GARFIELD HAYS, in V. F. CALVERTON and SAMUEL D. SCHMALHAUSEN, *Sex in Civilization*. New York: Macaulay, 1929, p. 219.

4. LEO TOLSTOY, in FREDERICK W. MORTON, *Love in Epigram;* Chicago: McClurg, 1899.

5. COMTESSE DE CHAMPAGNE, in DE STENDHAL, *On Love*. New York: Liveright, 1947.

6. JOSEPH K. FOLSOM, *The Family*. New York: Harpers, 1935, p. 74.

7. ERNEST W. BURGESS, "Sociologist Aspects of Sex Life of the Unmarried Adult," in Ira S. Wile, *Sex Life of the Unmarried Adult*. New York: Vanguard, 1934, pp. 153–154.

8. LLEWELLYN GROSS, "A Belief Pattern Scale for Measuring Attitudes Toward Romanticism." *American Sociological Review*, 1944, 9, 463–472.

9. SOMERSET MAUGHAM, *The Constant Wife*. New York: Doubleday, 1932.

10. HENRIK IBSEN, *Love's Comedy*. New York: Willey Book, 1911, pp. 470–71.

11. GEORGE MOORE, *Memoirs of My Dead Life*. London: Heineman, 1921, p. 72.

ANDRE GIDE, *Strait is the Gate*. New York: Knopf, 1936, pp. 187–89.

WALTER VAN TILBURG CLARK, *The City of Trembling Leaves*. New York: Random House, 1945, p. 395.

BEN HECHT, *Erik Dorn*. New York: Modern Library, 1930, p. 130.

12. THEOPHILE GAUTIER, *Mlle. de Maupin*. New York: Three Pay Sales Co., 1900, p. 223.

13. EMIL LUCKA, *Eros*. New York: Putnam, 1915.

14. DENIS DE ROUGEMONT, *op. cit.*, pp. 123–24.

15. PEIRAL THE TROUBADOUR, quoted in Emil Lucka, *op. cit.*, p. 129.

16. ALFRED ADLER, *What Life Should Mean to You*. Boston: Little, Brown, 1931, pp. 275–76.

17. KAREN HORNEY, *The Neurotic Personality of Our Time*. New York: Norton, 1937, p. 387.

18. JOHN LEVY and RUTH MUNROE, *The Happy Family*. New York: Knopf, 1938, p. 66.

19. W. BERAN WOLFE, *How to Be Happy Though Human*. New York: Farrar and Rinehart, 1931, p. 261.

20. SANDOR FERENCZI, *Further Contributions to the Theory and Technique of Psychoanalysis*. New York: Basic Books, 1952.

21. SIGMUND FREUD, *Group Psychology and the Analysis of the Ego*. London: International Psychoanalytic Press, 1922.

22. LORINE PRUETTE, *The Parent and the Happy Child*. New York: Holt, 1932, p. 9.

23. THEODOR REIK, *A Psychologist Looks at Love*. New York: Rinehart, 1945, p. 67.

EDMUND BERGLER, "Further Contributions to the Psychoanalysis of Writers," *Psychoanalytic Review*, 1948, 35, 33–50.

24. RAY E. BABER, *Marriage and the Family*. New York: McGraw-Hill, 1939, p. 203.

25. J. B. LICHTENBERGER, *Divorce*. New York: Whittlesey House, 1931, p. 345.

26. WILLIAM GRAHAM SUMNER and ALBERT G. KELLER, *The Science of Society*. New Haven: Yale Univ. Press, 1927, p. 2049.

27. JOSEPH K. FOLSOM, *The Family and Democratic Society*. New York: Harpers, 1950.

28. ARNOLD W. GREEN, "Social Values and Psychotherapy," *Journal of Personality*, 1946, 14, 19–228.

LLEWELLYN GROSS, *op. cit.*, p. 469.

ERNEST GROVES and GLADYS GROVES, "The Case for Monogamy." In W. F. BIGELOW, *The Good Housekeeping Marriage Book*. New York: Prentice-Hall, 1938, p. 157.

PAUL H. LANDIS, "Control of the Romantic Impulse Through Education," *School and Society*, 1936, 213.

R. M. MACIVER, *Society*. New York: Long and Smith, 1932, p. 145.

ERNEST R. MOWRER, *Family Disorganization*. Chicago: Univ. Chicago Press, 1927, p. 162.

EDGAR SCHMIEDELER, *An Introductory Study of the Family*. New York: Century, 1930, p. 169.

5

CONTRIBUTIONS TO THE PSYCHOLOGY OF LOVE

SIGMUND FREUD

A Special Type of Choice of Object Made by Men (1910)

Up till now we have left it to the creative writer to depict for us the 'necessary conditions for loving' which govern people's choice of an object, and the way in which they bring the demands of their imagination into harmony with reality. The writer can indeed draw on certain qualities which fit him to carry out such a task: above all, on a sensitivity that enables him to perceive the hidden impulses in the minds of other people, and the courage to let his own unconscious speak. But there is one circumstance which lessens the evidential value of what he has to say. Writers are under the necessity to produce intellectual and aesthetic pleasure, as well as certain emotional effects. For this reason they cannot reproduce the stuff

SOURCE: *The Standard Edition of the Complete Psychological Works of Sigmund Freud*, trans. and ed., James Strachey (London: The Hogarth Press Ltd., 1957), Vol. XI, pp. 165–190. Reprinted by permission of Sigmund Freud Copyrights Ltd., James Strachey, and the Hogarth Press Ltd.; and from the *Collected Papers of Sigmund Freud* (New York: Basic Books, Inc., 1959), Vol. IV, pp. 192–216.

of reality unchanged, but must isolate portions of it, remove disturbing associations, tone down the whole and fill in what is missing. These are the privileges of what is known as 'poetic licence'. Moreover they can show only slight interest in the origin and development of the mental states which they portray in their completed form. In consequence it becomes inevitable that science should concern herself with the same materials whose treatment by artists has given enjoyment to mankind for thousands of years, though her touch must be clumsier and the yield of pleasure less. These observations will, it may be hoped, serve to justify us in extending a strictly scientific treatment to the field of human love. Science is, after all, the most complete renunciation of the pleasure principle of which our mental activity is capable.

In the course of psycho-analytic treatment there are ample opportunities for collecting impressions of the way in which neurotics behave in love; while at the same time we can recall having observed or heard of similar behaviour in people of average health or even in those with outstanding qualities. When the material happens to be favourable and thus leads to an accumulation of such impressions, distinct types emerge more clearly. I will begin here with a description of one such type of object-choice—which occurs in men—since it is characterized by a number of 'necessary conditions for loving' whose combination is unintelligible, and indeed bewildering, and since it admits of a simple explanation on psycho-analytic lines.

1. The first of these preconditions for loving can be described as positively specific: wherever it is found, the presence of the other characteristics of this type may be looked for. It may be termed the precondition that there should be 'an injured third party'; it stipulates that the person in question shall never choose as his love-object a woman who is disengaged—that is, an unmarried girl or an unattached married woman—but only one to whom another man can

claim right of possession as her husband, fiancé or friend. In some cases this precondition proves so cogent that a woman can be ignored, or even rejected, so long as she does not belong to any man, but becomes the object of passionate feelings immediately she comes into one of these relationships with another man.

2. The second precondition is perhaps a less constant one, but it is no less striking. It has to be found in conjunction with the first for the type to be realized, whereas the first precondition seems very often to occur independently as well. This second precondition is to the effect that a woman who is chaste and whose reputation is irreproachable never exercises an attraction that might raise her to the status of a love-object, but only a woman who is in some way or other of bad repute sexually, whose fidelity and reliability are open to some doubt. This latter characteristic may vary within substantial limits, from the faint breath of scandal attaching to a married woman who is not averse to a flirtation up to the openly promiscuous way of life of a *cocotte* or of an adept in the art of love; but the men who belong to our type will not be satisfied without something of the kind. This second necessary condition may be termed, rather crudely, 'love for a prostitute'.

While the first precondition provides an opportunity for gratifying impulses of rivalry and hostility directed at the man from whom the loved woman is wrested, the second one, that of the woman's being like a prostitute, is connected with the experiencing of *jealousy,* which appears to be a necessity for lovers of this type. It is only when they are able to be jealous that their passion reaches its height and the woman acquires her full value, and they never fail to seize on an occasion that allows them to experience these most powerful emotions. What is strange is that it is not the lawful possessor of the loved one who becomes the target of this jealousy, but strangers, making their appearance for the first time, in relation to whom the loved one can be brought under suspicion. In glaring instances the lover shows no wish for exclusive possession of the woman and seems to be perfectly comfortable in the triangular situation. One of my patients, who had been made to suffer terribly by his lady's escapades, had no objection to her getting married, and did all he could to bring it about; in the years that followed he never showed a trace of jealousy towards her husband. Another typical patient had, it is true, been very jealous of the husband in his first love affair, and had forced the lady to stop having marital relations; but in his numerous subsequent affairs he behaved like the other members of this type and no longer regarded the lawful husband as an interference.

So much for the conditions required in the love-object. The following points describe the lover's behaviour towards the object he has chosen.

3. In normal love the woman's value is measured by her sexual integrity, and is reduced by any approach to the characteristic of being like a prostitute.[1] Hence the fact that women with this characteristic are considered by men of our type to be *love-objects of the highest value* seems to be a striking departure from the normal. Their love-relationships with these women are carried on with the highest expenditure of mental energy, to the exclusion of all other interests; they are felt as the only people whom it is possible to love, and demand for fidelity which the lover makes upon himself is repeated again and again, however often it may be broken in reality. These features of the love-relationships which I am here describing show their *compulsive* nature very clearly, though that is something which is found up to a certain degree whenever anyone falls in love. But the fidelity and intensity that mark the attachment must not lead one to expect that a single love-relationship of this kind will

[1] The German *'Dirne'*, here and in several other passages in this paper, is not well rendered by 'prostitute', which in English lays too much stress on the monetary side of the relation. 'Harlot' would give the sense better, if the word had not to-day acquired an antiquated and even Biblical colouring.

make up the whole erotic life of the person in question or occur only once in it. On the contrary, passionate attachments of this sort are repeated with the same peculiarities—each an exact replica of the others—again and again in the lives of men of this type; in fact, owing to external events such as changes of residence and environment, the love-objects may replace one another so frequently that a *long series of them is formed.*

4. What is most startling of all to the observer in lovers of this type is the urge they show to '*rescue*' the woman they love. The man is convinced that she is in need of him, that without him she would lose all moral control and rapidly sink to a lamentable level. He rescues her, therefore, by not giving her up. In some individual cases the idea of having to rescue her can be justified by reference to her sexual unreliability and the dangers of her social position: but it is no less conspicuous where there is no such basis in reality. One man of the type I am describing, who knew how to win his ladies by clever methods of seduction and subtle arguments, spared no efforts in the subsequent course of these affairs to keep the woman he was for the time being in love with on the path of 'virtue' by presenting her with tracts of his own composition.

If we survey the different features of the picture presented here—the conditions imposed on the man that his loved one should not be unattached and should be like a prostitute, the high value he sets on her, his need for feeling jealousy, his fidelity, which is nevertheless compatible with being broken down into a long series of instances, and the urge to rescue the woman—it will seem scarcely probable that they should all be derived from a single source. Yet psycho-analytic exploration into the life-histories of men of this type has no difficulty in showing that there is such a single source. The object-choice which is so strangely conditioned, and this very singular way of behaving in love, have the same psychical origin as we find in the loves of normal people. They are derived from the infantile fixation of tender feelings on the mother, and represent one of the consequences of that fixation. In normal love only a few characteristics survive which reveal unmistakably the maternal prototype of the object-choice, as, for instance, the preference shown by young men for maturer women; the detachment of libido from the mother has been effected relatively swiftly. In our type, on the other hand, the libido has remained attached to the mother for so long, even after the onset of puberty, that the maternal characteristics remain stamped on the love-objects that are chosen later, and all these turn into easily recognizable mother-surrogates. The comparison with the way in which the skull of a newly born child is shaped[2] springs to mind at this point: after a protracted labour it always takes the form of a cast of the narrow part of the mother's pelvis.

We have now to show the plausibility of our assertion that the characteristic features of our type—its conditions for loving and its behaviour in love—do in fact arise from the psychical constellation connected with the mother. This would seem to be easiest where the first precondition is concerned—the condition that the woman should not be unattached, or that there should be an injured third party. It is at once clear that for the child who is growing up in the family circle the fact of the mother belonging to the father becomes an inseparable part of the mother's essence, and that the injured third party is none other than the father himself. The trait of overvaluing the loved one, and regarding her as unique and irreplaceable, can be seen to fall just as naturally into the context of the child's experience, for no one possesses more than one mother, and the relation to her is based on an event that is not open to any doubt and cannot be repeated.

If we are to understand the love-objects chosen by our type as being above all mother-surrogates, then the formation of a series of them, which seems so flatly to contradict the condition of being faithful to one, can now also be understood. We

2 In the editions before 1924 this read 'deformed'.

have learnt from psycho-analysis in other examples that the notion of something irreplaceable, when it is active in the unconscious, frequently appears as broken up into an endless series: endless for the reason that every surrogate nevertheless fails to provide the desired satisfaction. This is the explanation of the insatiable urge to ask questions shown by children at a certain age: they have one single question to ask, but it never crosses their lips.[3] It explains, too, the garrulity of some people affected by neurosis; they are under the pressure of a secret which is burning to be disclosed but which, despite all temptation, they never reveal.

On the other hand the second precondition for loving—the condition that the object chosen should be like a prostitute—seems energetically to oppose a derivation from the mother-complex. The adult's conscious thought likes to regard his mother as a person of unimpeachable moral purity; and there are few ideas which he finds so offensive when they come from others, or feels as so tormenting when they spring from his own mind, as one which calls this aspect of his mother in question. This very relation of the sharpest contrast between 'mother' and 'prostitute' will however encourage us to enquire into the history of the development of these two complexes and the unconscious relation between them, since we long ago discovered that what, in the conscious, is found split into a pair of opposites often occurs in the unconscious as a unity.[4] Investigation then leads us back to the time in a boy's life at which he first gains a more or less complete knowledge of the sexual relations between adults, somewhere about the years of prepuberty. Brutal pieces of information, which are undisguisedly intended to arouse contempt and rebelliousness, now acquaint him with the secret of sexual life and destroy the authority of adults, which appears incompatible with the

[3] This point is also made by Freud in his essay on Leonardo da Vinci (1910*c*), above, p. 78.

[4] This fact had already been hinted at in Freud's *Interpretation of Dreams* (1900*a*), *Standard Ed.*, **4**, 318, and explicitly mentioned in Chapter VI of his book on jokes (1905*c*). See also above, p. 155 ff.

revelation of their sexual activities. The aspect of these disclosures which affects the newly initiated child most strongly is the way in which they apply to his own parents. This application is often flatly rejected by him, in some such words as these: '*Your* parents and other people may do something like that with one another, but *my* parents can't possibly do it.'[5]

As an almost invariable corollary to this sexual enlightenment, the boy at the same time gains a knowledge of the existence of certain women who practise sexual intercourse as a means of livelihood, and who are for this reason held in general contempt. The boy himself is necessarily far from feeling this contempt: as soon as he learns that he too can be initiated by these unfortunates into sexual life, which till then he accepted as being reserved exclusively for 'grown-ups', he regards them only with a mixture of longing and horror. When after this he can no longer maintain the doubt which makes his parents an exception to the universal and odious norms of sexual activity, he tells himself with cynical logic that the difference between his mother and a whore is not after all so very great, since basically they do the same thing. The enlightening information he has received has in fact awakened the memory-traces of the impressions and wishes of his early infancy, and these have led to a reactivation in him of certain mental impulses. He begins to desire his mother herself in the sense with which he has recently become acquainted, and to hate his father anew as a rival who stands in the way of this wish; he comes, as we say, under the dominance of the Oedipus complex.[6] He does not forgive his mother for having granted the favour of sexual intercourse not to himself but to his father, and he regards it as an act of unfaithfulness. If these impulses do not quickly pass, there is no outlet for them other than to

[5] Cf. the last paragraph of Freud's paper on the sexual theories of children (1908c).

[6] This appears to be Freud's first published use of the actual term. The concept had, of course, long been familiar to him (cf. *Standard Ed.*, 4, 263n.), and he had already spoken of the 'nuclear complex', e.g. in the paper referred to in the last footnote and in his 'Five Lectures', 1910a, above, p. 47.

run their course in phantasies which have as their subject his mother's sexual activities under the most diverse circumstances; and the consequent tension leads particularly readily to his finding relief in masturbation. As a result of the constant combined operation of the two driving forces, desire and thirst for revenge, phantasies of his mother's unfaithfulness are by far the most preferred; the lover with whom she commits her act of infidelity almost always exhibits the features of the boy's own ego, or more accurately, of his own idealized personality, grown up and so raised to a level with his father. What I have elsewhere[7] described as the 'family romance' comprises the manifold ramifications of this imaginative activity and the way in which they are interwoven with various egoistic interests of this period of life.

Now that we have gained an insight into this piece of mental development we can no longer regard it as contradictory and incomprehensible that the precondition of the loved one's being like a prostitute should derive directly from the mother-complex. The type of male love which we have described bears the traces of this evolution and is simple to understand as a fixation on the phantasies formed by the boy in puberty—phantasies which have later after all found a way out into real life. There is no difficulty in assuming that the masturbation assiduously practised in the years of puberty has played its part in the fixation of the phantasies.

To these phantasies which have succeeded in dominating the man's love in real life, the urge to *rescue* the loved one seems to bear merely a loose and superficial relation, and one that is fully accounted for by conscious reasons. By her propensity to be fickle and unfaithful the loved one brings herself into dangerous situations, and thus it is understandable that the lover should be at pains to protect her from these dangers by watching over her virtue and counteracting her bad inclinations. However, the study of people's screen-memories, phantasies and nocturnal dreams shows that we have here a par-

[7] In a discussion included in Rank's *The Myth of the Birth of the Hero* (1909) Freud (1909c).

ticularly felicitous 'rationalization' of an unconscious motive, a process which may be compared to a successful secondary revision of a dream. In actual fact the 'rescue-*motif*' has a meaning and history of its own, and is an independent derivative of the mother-complex, or more accurately, of the parental complex. When a child hears that he *owes his life* to his parents, or that his mother *gave him life,* his feelings of tenderness unite with impulses which strive at power and independence, and they generate the wish to return this gift to the parents and to repay them with one of equal value. It is as though the boy's defiance were to make him say: 'I want nothing from my father; I will give him back all I have cost him.' He then forms the phantasy of *rescuing his father from danger and saving his life;* in this way he puts his account square with him. This phantasy is commonly enough displaced on to the emperor, king or some other great man; after being thus distorted it becomes admissible to consciousness, and may even be made use of by creative writers. In its application to a boy's father it is the defiant meaning in the idea of rescuing which is by far the most important; where his mother is concerned it is usually its tender meaning. The mother gave the child life, and it is not easy to find a substitute of equal value for this unique gift. With a slight change of meaning, such as is easily effected in the unconscious and is comparable to the way in which in consciousness concepts shade into one another, rescuing his mother takes on the significance of giving her a child or making a child for her—needless to say, one like himself. This is not too remote from the original sense of rescuing, and the change in meaning is not an arbitrary one. His mother gave him a life—his own life—and in exchange he gives her another life, that of a child which has the greatest resemblance to himself. The son shows his gratitude by wishing to have by his mother a son who is like himself: in other words, in the rescue-phantasy he is completely identifying himself with his father. All his instincts, those of tenderness, gratitude, lustfulness, defiance and independence, find satisfaction in the single wish *to be his own father.* Even the element of danger has not been lost in the change of meaning; for the act of birth itself is the danger from which he was saved by his mother's efforts. Birth is both the first of all dangers to life and the prototype of all the later ones that cause us to feel anxiety, and the experience of birth has probably left behind in us the expression of affect which we call anxiety. Macduff of the Scottish legend, who was not born of his mother but ripped from her womb, was for that reason unacquainted with anxiety.[8]

Artemidorus, the dream-interpreter of antiquity, was certainly right in maintaining that the meaning of a dream depends on who the dreamer happens to be.[9] Under the laws governing the expression of unconscious thoughts, the meaning of rescuing may vary, depending on whether the author of the phantasy is a man or a woman. It can equally mean (in a man) making a child, i.e. causing it to be born, or (in a woman) giving birth oneself to a child. These various meanings of rescuing in dreams and phantasies can be recognized particularly clearly when they are found in connection with water. A man rescuing a woman from the water in a dream means that he makes her a mother, which in the light of the preceding discussion amounts to making her his own mother. A woman rescuing someone else (a child) from the water acknowledges

---

[8] *Macbeth*, V, 7. This is Freud's first extended allusion to the relation between birth and anxiety. He had already referred to the question in a footnote added in the previous year (1909) to Chapter VI (E) of *The Interpretation of Dreams* (1900a), *Standard Ed.*, **5**, 400–1, and had mentioned it in a discussion at the Vienna Psycho-Analytical Society on November 17, 1909 (Jones, 1955, 494). He dealt with it again at some length near the beginning of Lecture XXV of the *Introductory Lectures* (1916–17). But his longest discussion of it will, of course, be found in *Inhibitions, Symptoms and Anxiety* (1926d), especially in Chapters II, VIII and XI, A (b), where his former opinions are largely revised. At the beginning of his psychological studies Freud had connected the symptoms of anxiety not with the experience of birth, but with the accompaniments of copulation. Cf. the penultimate paragraph of Section III of his first paper on anxiety neurosis (1895b) and a passage near the end of the probably even earlier Draft E in the Fliess correspondence (Freud, 1950a).

[9] Cf. a passage in Chapter II of *The Interpretation of Dreams* (1900a), *Standard Ed.*, **4**, 98, and a footnote to it added in 1914.

herself in this way as the mother who bore him, like Pharoah's daughter in the legend of Moses (Rank, 1909). At times there is also a tender meaning contained in rescue-phantasies directed towards the father. In such cases they aim at expressing the subject's wish to have his father as a son—that is, to have a son who is like his father.[10]

It is on account of all these connections between the rescue-*motif* and the parental complex that the urge to rescue the loved one forms an important feature of the type of loving which I have been discussing.

I do not feel that it is necessary for me to justify my method of work on this subject; as in my presentation of anal erotism [Freud (1908*b*)], so here too I have in the first place aimed at singling out from the observational material extreme and sharply defined types. In both cases we find a far greater number of individuals in whom only a few features of the type can be recognized, or only features which are not distinctly marked, and it is obvious that a proper appreciation of these types will not be possible until the whole context to which they belong has been explored.[11]

---

[10] Dreams of rescuing are mentioned in a paragraph added in 1911 to Chapter VI (E) of *The Interpretation of Dreams, Standard Ed.*, **5**, 403. A woman's rescue dream is analysed in Freud's paper on 'Dreams and Telepathy' (1922*a*), *Standard Ed.*, **18**, 212 ff.

[11] In a paper (1920*a*) written many years after the present one, Freud demonstrated the occurrence of precisely the same type of object-choice in a homosexual girl, *Standard Ed.*, **18**, 160 f.

On the Universal Tendency to Debasement in the Sphere of Love (1912)

I

If the practising psycho-analyst asks himself on account of what disorder people most often come to him for help, he is bound to reply—disregarding the many forms of anxiety—that it is psychical impotence. This singular disturbance affects men of strongly libidinous[1] natures, and manifests itself in a refusal by the executive organs of sexuality to carry out the sexual act, although before and after they may show themselves to be intact and capable of performing the act, and although a strong psychical inclination to carry it out is present. The first clue to understanding his condition is obtained by the sufferer himself on making the discovery that a failure of this kind only arises when the attempt is made with certain individuals; whereas with others there is never any question of such a failure. He now becomes aware that it is some feature of the sexual object which gives rise to the inhibition of his male potency, and sometimes he reports that he has a feeling of an obstacle inside him, the sensation of a counter-will which successfully interferes with his conscious intention. However, he is unable to guess what this internal obstacle is and what feature of the sexual object brings it into operation. If he has had repeated experience of a failure of this kind, he is likely, by the familiar process of 'erroneous connection',[2] to decide that the recollection of the first occasion evoked the disturbing anxiety-idea and so caused the failure to be repeated each time;

---

[1] *'Libidinös.'* Here 'libidinous', as contrasted with the technical 'libidinal'.

[2] This seems to be an allusion to the slightly differently termed 'false connection' already described in *Studies on Hysteria* (1895d), *Standard Ed.*, 2, 67n.

while he derives the first occasion itself from some 'accidental' impression.

Psycho-analytic studies of psychical impotence have already been carried out and published by several writers.[3] Every analyst can confirm the explanations provided by them from his own clinical experience. It is in fact a question of the inhibitory influence of certain psychical complexes which are withdrawn from the subject's knowledge. An incestuous fixation on mother or sister, which has never been surmounted, plays a prominent part in this pathogenic material and is its most universal content. In addition there is the influence to be considered of accidental distressing impressions connected with infantile sexual activity, and also those factors which in a general way reduce the libido that is to be directed on to the female sexual object.[4]

When striking cases of psychical impotence are exhaustively investigated by means of psycho-analysis, the following information is obtained about the psychosexual processes at work in them. Here again—as very probably in all neurotic disturbances—the foundation of the disorder is provided by an inhibition in the developmental history of the libido before it assumes the form which we take to be its normal termination. Two currents whose union is necessary to ensure a completely normal attitude in love have, in the cases we are considering, failed to combine. These two may be distinguished as the *affectionate* and the *sensual* current.

The affectionate current is the older of the two. It springs from the earliest years of childhood; it is formed on the basis of the interests of the self-preservative instinct and is directed to the members of the family and those who look after the child. From the very beginning it carries along with it contributions from the sexual instincts—components of erotic interest—which can already be seen more or less clearly even

---

[3] Steiner (1907), Stekel (1908), Ferenczi (1908). Freud had written a preface to Stekel's book (Freud, 1908*f*) and wrote one later to a book of Steiner's on the same subject (Freud, 1913*e*).

[4] Stekel (1908, 191 ff.).

in childhood and in any event are uncovered in neurotics by psycho-analysis later on. It corresponds to *the child's primary object-choice.* We learn in this way that the sexual instincts find their first objects by attaching themselves to the valuations made by the ego-instincts, precisely in the way in which the first sexual satisfactions are experienced in attachment to the bodily functions necessary for the preservation of life.[5] The 'affection' shown by the child's parents and those who look after him, which seldom fails to betray its erotic nature ('the child is an erotic play-thing'), does a very great deal to raise the contributions made by erotism to the cathexes of his ego-instincts, and to increase them to an amount which is bound to play a part in his later development, especially when certain other circumstances lend their support.

These affectionate fixations of the child persist throughout childhood, and continually carry along with them erotism, which is consequently diverted from its sexual aims. Then at the age of puberty they are joined by the powerful 'sensual' current which no longer mistakes its aims. It never fails, apparently, to follow the earlier paths and to cathect the objects of the primary infantile choice with quotas of libido that are now far stronger. Here, however, it runs up against the obstacles that have been erected in the meantime by the barrier against incest; consequently it will make efforts to pass on from these objects which are unsuitable in reality, and find a way as soon as possible to other, extraneous objects with which a real sexual life may be carried on. These new objects will still be chosen on the model (imago) of the infantile ones, but in the course of time they will attract to themselves the affection that was tied to the earlier ones. A man shall leave his father and his mother—according to the biblical command[6]— and shall cleave unto his wife; affection and sensuality are then united. The greatest intensity of sensual passion will bring with it the highest psychical valuation of the object—this

[5] The 'attachment' (or 'anaclitic') type of object-choice was discussed more fully in Freud's later paper on narcissism (1914c).
[6] *Genesis ii,* 24.

being the normal overvaluation of the sexual object on the part of a man.

Two factors will decide whether this advance in the developmental path of the libido is to fail. First, there is the amount of *frustration in reality* which opposes the new object-choice and reduces its value for the person concerned. There is after all no point in embarking upon an object-choice if no choice is to be allowed at all or if there is no prospect of being able to choose anything suitable. Secondly, there is the amount of *attraction* which the infantile objects that have to be relinquished are able to exercise, and which is in proportion to the erotic cathexis attaching to them in childhood. If these two factors are sufficiently strong, the general mechanism by which the neuroses are formed comes into operation. The libido turns away from reality, is taken over by imaginative activity (the process of introversion), strengthens the images of the first sexual objects and becomes fixated to them. The obstacle raised against incest, however, compels the libido that has turned to these objects to remain in the unconscious. The masturbatory activity carried out by the sensual current, which is now part of the unconscious, makes its own contribution in strengthening this fixation. Nothing is altered in this state of affairs if the advance which has miscarried in reality is now completed in phantasy, and if in the phantasy-situations that lead to masturbatory satisfaction the original sexual objects are replaced by different ones. As a result of this substitution the phantasies become admissible to consciousness, but no progress is made in the allocation of the libido in reality. In this way it can happen that the whole of a young man's sensuality becomes tied to incestuous objects in the unconscious,[7] or to put it another way, becomes fixated to unconscious incestuous phantasies. The result is then total impotence, which is perhaps further ensured by the simultaneous onset of an actual weakening of the organs that perform the sexual act.

Less severe conditions are required to bring about the state

[7] In the editions before 1924 the word used here is the very unusual '*Unbewusstsein*', 'unconsciousness'.

known specifically as psychical impotence. Here the fate of the sensual current must not be that its whole charge has to conceal itself behind the affectionate current; it must have remained sufficiently strong or uninhibited to secure a partial outlet into reality. The sexual activity of such people shows the clearest signs, however, that it has not the whole psychical driving force of the instinct behind it. It is capricious, easily disturbed, often not properly carried out, and not accompanied by much pleasure. But above all it is forced to avoid the affectionate current. A restriction has thus been placed on object-choice. The sensual current that has remained active seeks only objects which do not recall the incestuous figures forbidden to it; if someone makes an impression that might lead to a high psychical estimation of her, this impression does not find an issue in any sensual excitation but in affection which has no erotic effect. The whole sphere of love in such people remains divided in the two directions personified in art as sacred and profane (or animal) love. Where they love they do not desire and where they desire they cannot love. They seek objects which they do not need to love, in order to keep their sensuality away from the objects they love; and, in accordance with the laws of 'complexive sensitiveness'[8] and of the return of the repressed, the strange failure shown in psychical impotence makes its appearance whenever an object which has been chosen with the aim of avoiding incest recalls the prohibited object through some feature, often an inconspicuous one.

The main protective measure against such a disturbance which men have recourse to in this split in their love consists in a psychical *debasement* of the sexual object, the overvaluation that normally attaches to the sexual object being reserved for the incestuous object and its representatives. As soon as the condition of debasement is fulfilled, sensuality can be freely expressed, and important sexual capacities and a high degree

[8] This term is borrowed from Jung's word-association experiments (Jung, 1906), and is also used by Freud in the 'Rat Man' case history (1909d), *Standard Ed.*, **10**, 210.

of pleasure can develop. There is a further factor which contributes to this result. People in whom there has not been a proper confluence of the affectionate and the sensual currents do not usually show much refinement in their modes of behaviour in love; they have retained perverse sexual aims whose nonfulfilment is felt as a serious loss of pleasure, and whose fulfilment on the other hand seems possible only with a debased and despised sexual object.

We can now understand the motives behind the boy's phantasies mentioned in the first of these 'Contributions' (above, p. 91), which degrade the mother to the level of a prostitute. They are efforts to bridge the gulf between the two currents in love, at any rate in phantasy, and by debasing the mother to acquire her as an object of sensuality.

2

In the preceding section we have approached the study of psychical impotence from a medico-psychological angle of which the title of this paper gives no indication. It will however become clear that this introduction was required by us to provide an approach to our proper subject.

We have reduced psychical impotence to the failure of the affectionate and the sensual currents in love to combine, and this developmental inhibition has in turn been explained as being due to the influences of strong childhood fixations and of later frustration in reality through the intervention of the barrier against incest. There is one principal objection to the theory we advance; it does too much. It explains why certain people suffer from psychical impotence, but it leaves us with the apparent mystery of how others have been able to escape this disorder. Since we must recognize that all the relevant factors known to us—the strong childhood fixation, the incest-barrier and the frustration in the years of development after puberty—are to be found in practically all civilized human beings, we should be justified in expecting psychical impotence to be a universal affliction under civilization and not a disorder confined to some individuals.

It would be easy to escape from this conclusion by pointing to the quantitative factor in the causation of illness—to the greater or lesser extent of the contribution made by the various elements which determine whether a recognizable illness results or not. But although I accept this answer as correct, it is not my intention to make it a reason for rejecting the conclusion itself. On the contrary, I shall put forward the view that psychical impotence is much more widespread than is supposed, and that a certain amount of this behaviour does in fact characterize the love of civilized man.

If the concept of psychical impotence is broadened and is not restricted to failure to perform the act of coitus in circumstances where a desire to obtain pleasure is present and the genital apparatus is intact, we may in the first place add all those men who are described as psychanaesthetic: men who never fail in the act but who carry it out without getting any particular pleasure from it—a state of affairs that is more common than one would think. Psycho-analytic examination of such cases discloses the same actiological factors as we found in psychical impotence in the narrower sense, without at first arriving at any explanation of the difference between their symptoms. An easily justifiable analogy takes one from these anaesthetic men to the immense number of frigid women; and there is no better way to describe or understand their behaviour in love than by comparing it with the more conspicuous disorder of psychical impotence in men.[9]

If however we turn our attention not to an extension of the concept of psychical impotence, but to the gradations in its symptomatology, we cannot escape the conclusion that the behaviour in love of men in the civilized world to-day bears the stamp altogether of psychical impotence. There are only

---

[9] I am at the same time very willing to admit that frigidity in women is a complex subject which can also be approached from another angle. The question is examined at length in 'The Taboo of Virginity' (1918*a*), p. 201 ff. below.

a very few educated people in whom the two currents of affection and sensuality have become properly fused; the man almost always feels his respect for the woman acting as a restriction on his sexual activity, and only develops full potency when he is with a debased sexual object; and this in its turn is partly caused by the entrance of perverse components into his sexual aims, which he does not venture to satisfy with a woman he respects. He is assured of complete sexual pleasure only when he can devote himself unreservedly to obtaining satisfaction, which with his well-brought-up wife, for instance, he does not dare to do. This is the source of his need for a debased sexual object, a woman who is ethically inferior, to whom he need attribute no aesthetic scruples, who does not know him in his other social relations and cannot judge him in them. It is to such a woman that he prefers to devote his sexual potency, even when the whole of his affection belongs to a woman of a higher kind. It is possible, too, that the tendency so often observed in men of the highest classes of society to choose a woman of a lower class as a permanent mistress or even as a wife is nothing but a consequence of their need for a debased sexual object, to whom, psychologically, the possibility of complete satisfaction is linked.

I do not hesitate to make the two factors at work in psychical impotence in the strict sense—the factors of intense incestuous fixation in childhood and the frustration by reality in adolescence—responsible, too, for this extremely common characteristic of the love of civilized men. It sounds not only disagreeable but also paradoxical, yet it must nevertheless be said that anyone who is to be really free and happy in love must have surmounted his respect for women and have come to terms with the idea of incest with his mother or sister. Anyone who subjects himself to a serious self-examination on the subject of this requirement will be sure to find that he regards the sexual act basically as something degrading, which defiles and pollutes not only the body. The origin of this low opinion, which he will certainly not willingly acknowledge, must be looked for in the period of his youth in which the sensual current in him was already strongly developed but its satisfaction with an object outside the family was almost as completely prohibited as it was with an incestuous one.

In our civilized world women are under the influence of a similar after-effect of their upbringing, and, in addition, of their reaction to men's behaviour. It is naturally just as unfavourable for a woman if a man approaches her without his full potency as it is if his initial overvaluation of her when he is in love gives place to undervaluation after he has possessed her. In the case of women there is little sign of a need to debase their sexual object. This is no doubt connected with the absence in them as a rule of anything similar to the sexual overvaluation found in men. But their long holding back from sexuality and the lingering of their sensuality in phantasy has another important consequence for them. They are subsequently often unable to undo the connection between sensual activity and the prohibition, and prove to be psychically impotent, that is, frigid, when such activity is at last allowed them. This is the origin of the endeavour made by many women to keep even legitimate relations secret for a while; and of the capacity of other women for normal sensation as soon as the condition of prohibition is re-established by a secret love affair: unfaithful to their husband, they are able to keep a second order of faith with their lover.

The condition of forbiddenness in the erotic life of women is, I think, comparable to the need on the part of men to debase their sexual object. Both are consequences of the long period of delay, which is demanded by education for cultural reasons, between sexual maturity and sexual activity. Both aim at abolishing the psychical impotence that results from the failure of affectionate and sensual impulses to coalesce. That the effect of the same causes should be so different in men and in women may perhaps be traced to another difference in the behaviour of the two sexes. Civilized women do not usually transgress the prohibition on sexual activity in the period during which they have to wait, and thus they acquire the intimate connection between prohibition and sexuality. Men usually break through this prohibition if they can satisfy the condition of debasing the object, and so they carry on this condition into their love in later life.

In view of the strenuous efforts being made in the civilized world to-day to reform sexual life, it will not be superfluous to give a reminder that psycho-analytic research is as remote from tendentiousness as any other kind of research. It has no other end in view than to throw light on things by tracing what is manifest back to what is hidden. It is quite satisfied if reforms make use of its findings to replace what is injurious by something more advantageous; but it cannot predict whether other institutions may not result in other, and perhaps graver, sacrifices.

3

The fact that the curb put upon love by civilization involves a universal tendency to debase sexual objects will perhaps lead us to turn our attention from the object to the instincts themselves. The damage caused by the initial frustration of sexual pleasure is seen in the fact that the freedom later given to that pleasure in marriage does not bring full satisfaction. But at the same time, if sexual freedom is unrestricted from the outset the result is no better. It can easily be shown that the psychical value of erotic needs is reduced as soon as their satisfaction becomes easy. An obstacle is required in order to heighten libido; and where natural resistances to satisfaction have not been sufficient men have at all times erected conventional ones so as to be able to enjoy love. This is true both of individuals and of nations. In times in which there were no difficulties standing in the way of sexual satisfaction, such as perhaps during the decline of the ancient civilizations, love became worthless and life empty, and strong reaction-formations were required to restore indispensable affective values. In this connection it may be claimed that the ascetic current in Christianity created psychical values for love which pagan antiquity was never able to confer on it. This current assumed its greatest importance with the ascetic monks, whose lives were almost entirely occupied with the struggle against libidinal temptation.

One's first inclination is no doubt to trace back the difficulties revealed here to universal characteristics of our organic instincts. It is no doubt also true in general that the psychical importance of an instinct rises in proportion to its frustration. Suppose a number of totally different human beings were all equally exposed to hunger. As their imperative need for food mounted, all the individual differences would disappear and in their place one would see the uniform manifestations of the one unappeased instinct. But is it also true that with the satisfaction of an instinct its psychical value always falls just as sharply? Consider, for example, the relation of a drinker to wine. Is it not true that wine always provides the drinker with the same toxic satisfaction, which in poetry has so often been compared to erotic satisfaction—a comparison acceptable from the scientific point of view as well? Has one ever heard of the drinker being obliged constantly to change his drink because he soon grows tired of keeping to the same one? On the contrary, habit constantly tightens the bond between a man and the kind of wine he drinks. Does one ever hear of a drinker who needs to go to a country where wine is dearer or drinking is prohibited, so that by introducing obstacles he can reinforce the dwindling satisfaction that he obtains? Not at all. If we listen to what our great alcoholics, such as Böcklin,[10] say about their relation to wine, it sounds like the most perfect harmony, a model of a happy marriage. Why is the relation of the lover to his sexual object so very different?

It is my belief that, however strange it may sound, we must reckon with the possibility that something in the nature of the sexual instinct itself is unfavourable to the realization of complete satisfaction. If we consider the long and difficult developmental history of the instinct, two factors immediately spring to mind which might be made responsible for this difficulty.

10 Floerke (1902, 16).

Firstly, as a result of the diphasic onset of object-choice, and the interposition of the barrier against incest, the final object of the sexual instinct is never any longer the original object but only a surrogate for it. Psycho-analysis has shown us that when the original object of a wishful impulse has been lost as a result of repression, it is frequently represented by an endless series of substitutive objects none of which, however, brings full satisfaction. This may explain the inconstancy in object-choice, the 'craving for stimulation'[11] which is so often a feature of the love of adults.

Secondly, we know that the sexual instinct is originally divided into a great number of components—or rather, it develops out of them—some of which cannot be taken up into the instinct in its later form, but have at an earlier stage to be suppressed or put to other uses. These are above all the coprophilic instinctual components, which have proved incompatible with our aesthetic standards of culture, probably since, as a result of our adopting an erect gait, we raised our organ of smell from the ground.[12] The same is true of a large portion of the sadistic urges which are a part of erotic life. But all such developmental processes affect only the upper layers of the complex structure. The fundamental processes which produce erotic excitation remain unaltered. The excremental is all too intimately and inseparably bound up with the sexual; the position of the genitals—*inter urinas et faeces*—remains the decisive and unchangeable factor. One might say here, varying a well-known saying of the great Napoleon: 'Anatomy is destiny.' The genitals themselves have not taken part in the development of the human body in the direction of beauty: they have remained animal, and thus love, too, has remained in essence just as animal as it ever was. The instincts of love are hard to educate; education of them achieves now too much, now too little. What civilization aims at making out of them

---

[11] *'Reizhunger.'* This term seems to have been introduced by Hoche and Bloch. See Freud's *Three Essays* (1905d), *Standard Ed.*, 7, 151n.

[12] Cf. two long footnotes to Chapter VI of *Civilization and its Discontents* (1930a).

seems unattainable except at the price of a sensible loss of pleasure; the persistence of the impulses that could not be made use of can be detected in sexual activity in the form of non-satisfaction.

Thus we may perhaps be forced to become reconciled to the idea that it is quite impossible to adjust the claims of the sexual instinct to the demands of civilization; that in consequence of its cultural development renunciation and suffering, as well as the danger of extinction in the remotest future, cannot be avoided by the human race. This gloomy prognosis rests, it is true, on the single conjecture that the non-satisfaction that goes with civilization is the necessary consequence of certain peculiarities which the sexual instinct has assumed under the pressure of culture. The very incapacity of the sexual instinct to yield complete satisfaction as soon as it submits to the first demands of civilization becomes the source, however, of the noblest cultural achievements which are brought into being by ever more extensive sublimation of its instinctual components. For what motive would men have for putting sexual instinctual forces to other uses if, by any distribution of those forces, they could obtain fully satisfying pleasures? They would never abandon that pleasure and they would never make any further progress. It seems, therefore, that the irreconcilable difference between the demands of the two instincts— the sexual and the egoistic—has made men capable of even higher achievements, though subject, it is true, to a constant danger, to which, in the form of neurosis, the weaker are succumbing to-day.

It is not the aim of science either to frighten or to console. But I myself am quite ready to admit that such far-reaching conclusions as those I have drawn should be built on a broader foundation, and that perhaps developments in other directions may enable mankind to correct the results of the developments I have here been considering in isolation.

6

THE GOOD-BAD GIRL

MARTHA WOLFENSTEIN AND

NATHAN LEITES

The difficulty of choosing between a good and a bad girl is one
of the major problems of love-life in western culture. The
problem is to fuse two feelings which men have found it hard
to have in relation to the same woman. On the one hand, there
are sexual impulses, which a man may feel to be bad, and
which he may find it hard to associate with a woman whom he
considers admirable. The image, and the actuality, of the
"bad" woman arises to satisfy sexual impulses which men feel
to be degrading. On the other hand, there are affectionate impulses evoked by women who resemble the man's mother or
sister, "good" women. A good girl is the sort that a man should
marry, but she has the disadvantage of not being sexually
stimulating.

There are various possible solutions to this conflict. The
attempt may be made to satisfy one of these impulses at the

SOURCE: Martha Wolfenstein and Nathan Leites, *Movies: A Psychological
Study* (New York: The Free Press, 1950), pp. 25–28; 30–33. Reprinted by
permission of the publisher. Copyright 1950 by The Free Press, A Corporation.

expense of the other, to satisfy them both but in different directions, or to combine the two impulses in a single relationship. Exclusive devotion to a good woman constituted the stock image of Victorian marriage. Oppressed by the sway of the Angel in the House, rebels might go to the opposite extreme of seeking only prostitutes. In the supposedly frequent pattern of various continental European cultures, a man might keep both a wife and a mistress. Satisfaction was thus sought for both sexual and affectionate feelings, but it was not supposed that one woman could satisfy both. Another presumably frequent arrangement has been for a young man to have relations with bad women up to marriage, after which there is a substantial shift of attachment towards the good woman. In the reverse possibility the established husband and father of a family breaks away, or is diverted by a wicked seductress.

Efforts to combine the two components produce a variety of real or imagined feminine types. The image of the bad woman may be transformed so that she becomes the object of more ideal feelings. The prostitute may be redeemed by love, as in the case of Camille. Her prostitution may be compensated for by a saintly character, as in the case of Sonia, in Dostoyevsky's *Crime and Punishment,* who walked the streets only to save her family from starvation. Her involvement in low life may seem irrelevant to the essential nature of the beautiful woman who passes through it detached and unaffected. Or the attempt may be made to glorify the bad woman, to see her as a priestess of a pleasure unspoiled by scruples (Swinburne's Dolores). Proceeding in the other direction, an effort may be made to infuse the image of the good woman with some qualities of her opposite. The good woman may appear for a time to be bad, so that she acquires an exciting aura which is not entirely dissipated when her goodness becomes established. Or the good woman may become transformed—the business-like career girl takes off her glasses. The dull wife may learn a lesson from a lover and return to her husband more pleasurable.

The man may see the beloved woman in different ways. He may mistakenly form an idealized picture of a bad woman, and suffer disillusionment. The good girl may appear to him as bad, and the eventual revelation may be in her favor. The woman also may present herself in various ways. The bad woman may conceal her badness; the good woman may pretend to be bad, or make no effort to conceal what, misleadingly, looks bad. A variety of dramatic possibilities results from combinations of the different feminine types, the ways they present themselves, and the sequence of impressions that the man gets. While Camille was being transformed by love, she deceived her lover into believing that she was still bad. His image of her declined at the same time that her character became ennobled.

Current American films have produced the image of the good-bad girl. She is a good girl who appears to be bad. She does not conceal her apparent badness, and uncertainty about her character may persist through the greater part of the film. The hero suspects that she is bad, but finally discovers this was a mistaken impression. Thus he has a girl who has attracted him by an appearance of wickedness, and whom in the end he can take home and introduce to Mother.

Usually the good-bad girl appears to be promiscuous, or to be involved with a bad man. Occasionally she appears guilty of theft or murder. The title character in *Gilda* (after whom a Bikini bomb was named) appears quite promiscuous through the greater part of the film; in the end she turns out to be a faithful and devoted woman who has never loved anyone but the hero. Gilda and the hero had been lovers before the action of the film begins and had separated because of his jealousy. When they meet again the hero has become the right-hand man of a big gambler and international schemer; Gilda has become the gambler's wife. The hero is tortured not only by seeing Gilda as his boss's wife, but also by her strenuous flirtations with other men. Eventually the boss disappears and is considered dead. Gilda has tried to persuade the hero of her continued love for him and he now agrees to marry her. But he does not believe in her. To punish her for her apparent infidelities to the boss and to himself, he holds her a virtual prisoner. His strong-arm men follow her wherever she goes and forcibly dissuade her admirers. One night Gilda appears at the swank night-club adjoining the gambling casino which the hero now runs. She sings and dances seductively and begins stripping off her clothes (she doesn't get much farther than her long black gloves) while men from the audience rush forward to assist her. The hero, who enters just in time to get a glimpse of the climax of the performance, sends his men to carry her out.

While episodes of this sort present the image of the beautiful promiscuous woman, they are interspersed with occasions when Gilda pleads with the hero to believe that she has never loved anyone but him. In the end it turns out that what the hero saw was a deceptive appearance, and what Gilda told him was quite true. An understanding police official, who interests himself in their affairs, persuades the hero of this. All the carryings-on of Gilda with other men have been motivated by her love for the hero, whom she wished to hold by making him jealous. Once this has been explained to the hero by an impartial observer, everything is cleared up.

The hero's distress when he believed in Gilda's promiscuity did not impel him to look for a more quiet domestic type. In the end he finds that he can eat his cake and have it. He gets the girl with the aura of innumerable men in her life, and the guarantee that she is a good girl and belongs to him alone.

In *Till the End of Time*, the hero has several occasions for suspecting the heroine of promiscuousness, but each time this is successfully explained away. While the image of Gilda seemed intensely bad till the final explanation, the image of this heroine fluctuates back and forth between apparent lapses and virtuous explanations. The figure of the beloved woman who continually allays doubts about her fidelity with plausible explanations is familiar. Only in other versions this woman was deceiving her man. His suspicions were well founded, and her explanations were false. In the case of the good-bad girl this is reversed. What the man sees turns out to be illusory; what the woman tells him is true. Deceptive circumstances have been substituted for the deceiving woman. And the denouement in which the trusting man realizes that his beloved is false has been replaced by the happy outcome in which the suspicious hero learns that the seemingly bad girl is really good.

In *The Big Sleep,* the heroine appears involved with a shady night-club owner, who turns out to be a gangster and murderer. The hero, a private detective, who has been hired by the heroine's father, finds the girl trying to block his investigations. Her efforts seem related to her connection with the night-club owner. The hero appears unexpectedly at the night-club and finds the heroine there singing with the band and apparently very much in her element. Later she wins a lot of money at roulette. The night-club owner seems reluctant to let her leave when she is so much ahead. Under pressure from the hero she leaves, but is immediately held up by the night-club owner's thugs. The hero is convinced that this is all an act put on to conceal from him some guilty partnership between the girl and the night-club owner, to fool him into thinking that their relations are unfriendly. After more confusion of this sort, it finally comes out that it is not the night-club owner whom the heroine is trying to shield, but her unfortunate sister who has committed a murder. Since the night-club owner knows about this killing he is able to blackmail the heroine. It was to pay the blackmail that she had to come to the night-club so often.

In *The Strange Love of Martha Ivers,* the combination of badness, seeming badness, and goodness in the heroine is quite complicated. The girl has just come out of jail, to which she had been sent for stealing a fur coat. She explains to the hero that the coat was given to her by a boy-friend who later disappeared. Thus she did not steal the coat, but wasn't she rather friendly with the thief? In another episode she is forced by the wicked district attorney, who is still pursuing her for the crime she didn't commit, to play a rather mean trick on the hero. She gets the hero to go with her to a café where, by pre-arrangement, a man appears who claims to be her husband

and demands that the hero come outside and fight. The hero is then forced into a waiting automobile in which several thugs beat him up. The heroine later has a chance to explain the whole thing to the hero; she really has no husband, and so on. In this series of bad appearances and explanatory denials, one or two bad things remain that are not explained. However, since the girl repeatedly turns out to be so much better than she seemed, there is probably the feeling that with a few more explanations, for which the film perhaps didn't have time, she could be shown to be completely good.

The good-bad girl has supplanted the vamp of earlier American films. The vamp created the illusion of exclusive passionate attachment to the hero, but was in the end found out to be untrue. The hero at first believed in her, later became disillusioned. The picture was the reverse of that of the good-bad girl, whose apparent badness rouses the hero's suspicions but is later explained away. In a Greta Garbo film of the 20's, *Flesh and the Devil*, the hero fell in love with a seductive woman who responded passionately to the advances she provoked. He was forced to go away and, during his absence, she married his best friend. On the hero's return a bitter quarrel arose between the two men. They were about to shoot each other in a duel, but, suddenly remembering their old friendship, fell into each other's arms. The wicked woman was, by an appropriate accident, drowned. The dangerousness of the vamp was associated with the man's intolerance for sharing her with other men. Her seductive appearance and readiness for love carried a strong suggestion that there had been and might be other men in her life. But while the hero loved her, he excluded this possibility from his thoughts. When the proof of her infidelity was established, he renounced her. The good-bad girl is associated with a greater tolerance for sharing the woman, although this sharing remains subject to limitations. The hero believes that the woman he loves is involved with other men. While this disturbs him, it does not drive him away. In effect, the woman's attraction is enhanced by her association with other men. All that is needed to eliminate unpleasantness is the assurance that these relations were not serious (only apparent).

The good-bad girl is perhaps a melodramatic reflection of the American popular girl, whose attractiveness is directly proportional to the number of men she goes out with. The American attitude is in contrast to that of cultures where attractive women are secluded, where men feel that the attractiveness of a beautiful woman for other men is a liability. The man who guards the beautiful woman whom he loves from the eyes of others believes that if they only look at her they will start making plans to go to bed with her. American courtship patterns are based on a series of breaks between looking and going to bed. It is possible to look and go no further, to kiss and go no further, to pet and go no further. The attractiveness of the popular girl derives from her association with many men, combined with the assurance that she has not gone too far with them. In the case of her movie counterpart, the good-bad girl, the hero's doubts express uneasy fantasies about the possibly more serious involvement of the girl with these other men. The films express the man's uncertainty about whether the girl has only gone so far and no further, and the difficulty of holding in check his own fantasies about her relations with other men. The happy outcome reassures us that the system works. The girl's relations with other men were only apparent (did not go too far sexually). Her attractiveness for other men then ceases to arouse anxiety and becomes positive. Where the vamp evoked a complete sexual response, and so could not be shared without intense jealousy, the good-bad girl is sexy in a different sense. Her attractiveness is not in her inducement to passion, but in her (harmless) association with other men.

In comedies it may be manifest that the girl's associations with other men are harmless. She may, to the knowledge of the audience, construct a pretense of such relations in order to interest the man she wants. The desired man may see through the pretense, and nevertheless he favorably influenced by the appearance of the girl with other men. In *Every Girl*

Should Be Married, the hero is mostly aware that the heroine has contrived the semblance of a relationship with a rich playboy in order to make herself attractive to him. Eventually she draws a third man into her scheme, a hillbilly radio comedian who poses as her old sweetheart from back home. Although the hero also recognizes the comedian, he is moved to oust these pseudo-rivals and claim the girl. Her desperate efforts to make herself appear to be associated with other men achieve the desired result. (The hero's positive reaction despite his awareness of what goes on behind the scenes appears related to a larger trend. There seems to be a fairly widespread American tendency not to devalue an effect though one sees how it is achieved—whether it is the technique of a movie trick shot, or the beautiful complexion derived from assiduous application of a certain soap.)

Another film reflection of the popular girl with her many escorts is a frequent dance pattern in musicals where a girl dancer appears with a chorus of men. Her relation to them is stylized and superficial as she dances with each in rapid succession, not favoring one more than another. The male chorus alternate their attentions to the girl with routines in which they dance together in amicable accord. This parallels a frequent comedy theme of playful woman-sharing which has no negative effect on the friendly relations between the men. The girl's potentiality for bestowing true love on one man alone may be expressed by her singing, while she dances with several dozen men, a song whose sentiment is that of exclusive love: "You do something to me that nobody else can do" (*Night and Day*). Thus in her dance the girl gratifies the wish of the man who will eventually win her to see her associated with other men, while in her song she satisfies his demand for assurance that she is not emotionally involved in these other relations.

II

Marital Adjustment

This section is devoted to empirical studies. It is comprised of two review articles, both of which summarize conclusions drawn from measurement-based research.

The second article, by Roland Tharp, is by far the more ambitious and the more profound. It focuses on two general problems: (1) What are the determinants of mate choice? What leads one person to marry a particular other person rather than someone else? (2) What determines whether a marriage will succeed or fail, be relatively happy or unhappy, be harmonious or filled with conflict? In other words, Tharp marshals the data in a search for causes, a quest for understanding. He also has things to say about research strategies and methodology, and about alternative interpretations of data. Since he is speaking to his colleagues, fellow researchers and social scientists, at times the discourse gets "technical"—unavoidably so. The Tharp article was chosen, in part, for what it has to say, and, in part, as a representative of one of the major traditions of inquiry into marital relations—the scientific.

The first article, "Predictors of Marital Adjustment," attempts much less and makes lighter demands on the reader. Empirical studies have turned up an array of social-background variables that correlate with indices of marital adjustment. These permit a variety of statements about what types of marriages are likely to succeed and what types are likely to fail. They also enable some qualified predictions as to the chances of particular future marriages. We turn now to this first article.

7

PREDICTORS OF MARITAL
ADJUSTMENT

WILLIAM STEPHENS

A life insurance company, in issuing policies and setting premium rates, is guided by actuarial tables. Given a few facts about a prospective customer, the company "knows the odds" that this person will live a specified number of years. If he is twenty years old, the chances that he will still be alive thirty years from now are fairly good. If he is forty-five, the chances are less good. Other factors, aside from age, enter into the calculus of life expectancy. Women, as a group, live longer than do men. Healthy persons live longer than do diabetics and cardiac patients. Accountants live longer than do steeplejacks.

Life expectancy, then, can be predicted. For a particular individual, the prediction may fall wide of the mark. But for large groups of people, the actuarial tables do well enough to enable the insurance companies to stay in business. Even for the single individual, the predictors have something significant

This selection is published here for the first time.

to say. They give a probabilistic—if not a certain—knowledge of the future. They tell you the odds.

Using the actuarial model, one can also say something about the life expectancy of marriages. One cannot predict with certainty about a particular marriage. Neither can we quote precise odds. However, we do have evidence that certain types of people are more apt to make successful marriages, are less prone to divorce, than are other types. The marital adjustment studies point to numerous signs. If, for a certain prospective marriage, the signs are generally good, that marriage stands an excellent chance for success. If the signs are generally negative, the future of that marriage looks bleak.

Suppose that you are a girl, and a boy has just proposed to you. Suppose further that in the interval between the proposal and your "yes" or "no" you could be as coldly rational as the insurance company executive. In this unlikely event, the marital adjustment studies have something to say to you:

1. If you are very young you should wait a few years before getting married. As people grow older, their chances of making a successful marriage increase.

2. If you have known him for a long time—and still want to marry him—your chances of success are better than if the period of acquaintanceship, prior to marriage, is short.

3. If your beloved is divorced, the chances are fair that he will get divorced again—from you.

4. If you and he are religious, this is a good sign. If you are both of the same faith, this also augurs well.

5. The more education you (and he) have had, the better your chances for a good marriage.

6. If your parents are happily married, this is a good sign. The odds improve if your fiance's parents are also happily married.

These are just a few of the predictors. There are many more, and they will be discussed presently.

The Studies

The bibliography at the end of the article lists studies that have documented various social-background correlates of marital adjustment. These studies were done over the past forty years. With two exceptions, they were conducted in this country. Aside from a few studies of divorce, based on court records, all derive from interviews and questionnaires—survey data. In any given study, various traits of a person or a married couple—age at marriage, religion, brothers and sisters, residence, education, and so on—are correlated with an index of marital adjustment. Indices of marital adjustment (marital happiness, success of the marriage, or what have you) are of three types. (1) A few studies use ratings. A couple is rated, by the researcher or by an acquaintance, as to whether their marriage is successful (i.e., adjusted, "good") or unsuccessful (maladjusted, "bad"). (2) Many a study uses divorce. Some marriages within the sample have ended in divorce; others have not. The assumption is that, on the whole, the non-divorced marriages have been more successful than the others that did end in divorce. Allowance is made for a certain percentage of "errors"; in particular, miserable but stable marriages that go on and on. (3) The third type of marital adjustment index is questionnaire-based. A sample of couples is given a standard list of questions to answer. The questions ask, in one form or another, and in relation to various aspects and areas of married life: "How are you getting along?" A couple answers the questionnaire; the answers are scored, using a standard scoring key and scaling convention; and thereby the couple is assigned a score on degree of marital adjustment.

All these indices are admittedly crude, tainted with an unknown amount of measurement error. They do, I think, permit certain conclusions which are likewise crude: cautious statements as to the presence and direction of associations;

statements that permit a large margin for error. If, for example, we find that people who marry young have a higher divorce rate than do other people who marry when they are older, this gives us some basis for concluding that age at marriage has something to do with subsequent marital adjustment. If this same correlation turns up in eleven separate studies (as is the case), done in different places at different times, using a variety of marital adjustment indices, our conclusion would seem even better-grounded. It may be that age at marriage, in itself, is not a determinant of marital adjustment. Still, it would seem to be a trustworthy actuarial sign: if you marry young, your chances of success are somewhat diminished since, in the past, early-marrying people have been more prone to divorce, and have scored relatively badly on marital adjustment tests.

Actually, the persuasiveness of the evidence varies somewhat, from one predictor to the next. For some, like age at marriage, findings from all studies agree.[1] For level of education, on the other hand: most study findings return a positive correlation with marital adjustment; but a few do not. Along with agreement between studies, the danger of systematic bias must be taken into account. Some of these correlations might, conceivably, have nothing to do with marital adjustment. Take, for example, the finding that divorce predicts divorce; a divorced man, if he remarries, is more likely (than a previously unmarried person) to get divorced. Perhaps divorced men really are poor risks. Or perhaps they are merely people who are better able to break out of a marriage, once it has gone sour. In other words, readiness to seek divorce might be the controlling variable here; not ability to make a good marriage.

In general, I think, the greatest danger of systematic bias lies with the studies that use questionnaire-based marital adjustment indices. These are, of course, subject to distortion: lying, positive thinking, viewing-with-rose-colored-glasses on the part of questionnaire respondents. Some respondents are, no doubt,

[1] Agree, that is, as to the *direction* of the association. Agreement as to the strength of the association or the shape of the curve is, of course, too much to ask.

more candid than are others. For some predictors, individual differences in respondent-honesty could produce positive correlations with the quetionnaire-based marital adjustment test scores. Take the finding that persons who report their parents were happily married tend to report that they too are happily married. Exaggeration, in a positive direction, by a certain fraction of the sample could have produced this correlation. This sort of danger is alleviated, to some degree, by two characteristics of the data. (1) For some of the predictors, such as age at marriage and place of residence, it is hard to imagine how untruthful questionnaire responses could produce this sort of systematic bias. (2) For a given predictor, evidence typically comes from many studies; some of these employ the marital adjustment tests, but others use divorce as the index of marital adjustment. Information on divorce does not come from questionnaires; hence it cannot be influenced by respondent-lying. If the same effect holds up across both types of studies, confidence in the data increases.

We are now ready to review seventeen predictors. I have grouped them into three classes—A, B, and C—on the basis of an admittedly arbitrary judgment as to the persuasiveness of the supporting evidence. In the Class A predictors I have the highest confidence. For the Class B predictors, evidence seems a bit less persuasive. With the Class C predictors I am still impressed, but still less confident. The judgment is based on the two criteria that were just discussed: extent of agreement between studies, and a guess as to the danger of systematic bias.

Class-A Predictors

1. AGE AT MARRIAGE. Eleven studies here, and they all agree. Five find early marriages more prone to divorce. The other six find early-marrying persons scoring relatively low on marital adjustment tests. (Burgess and Cottrell 1939; Bernard 1934; Burchinal 1960; Christensen and Meissner 1953;

Hart and Shields 1926; King 1952; Locke 1951; Landis and Landis 1958; Monahan 1953; Rountree 1964; Terman 1938.) What is an "early" marriage? What is too young? Perhaps about eighteen for girls, and twenty for men. However, the general trend across the studies is: up to the late twenties at least, the older you are, the better your chances.

2. LENGTH OF ACQUAINTANCESHIP. The longer you've known him, the longer you have gone together, the longer the engagement: the better your chances. Six studies, all agreeing. (Burgess and Cottrell 1939; King 1952; Locke 1951; Locke and Karlsson 1952; Popenoe and Neptune 1938; Terman 1938.) How long is long enough? Date him for at least a year; but the longer the better.

3. PREMARITAL PREGNANCY. Don't let it happen to you. (Christensen and Meissner 1953; Geismar and La Sorte 1963; Rountree 1964.)

4. RELIGIOSITY. An atheist is a relatively poor risk. Eight studies suggest this; there is one dissenter. (Kirkpatrick 1937.) The index of religiosity is, generally, frequency of church attendance; also used in Sunday school attendance, formally belonging to a church, and stating (or not stating) a religious preference on the marriage license application. (Burgess and Cottrell 1939; Burchinal 1955; Chesser 1957; King 1952; Landis 1946, 1949; Locke 1951; Schroeder 1938.) Also, marriages performed by a minister, priest, or rabbi stand a better chance than those joined by a Justice of the Peace. (Burgess and Cottrell 1939; Christensen and Meissner 1953; Schroeder 1938.)

5. SIMILARITY OF FAITH. Mixed-faith marriages: Catholic-Protestant, Catholic-Jew, Protestant-Jew; these show higher divorce rates than do same-faith marriages. Nine studies, all agreeing. (Chancellor and Monahan 1955; Gordon 1964; Kirkpatrick 1937; Landis 1949; Vernon 1960; Vincent 1959; Monahan and Chancellor 1955; Monahan and Kephart 1954; Weeks 1943.)

6. SOCIAL CLASS. It is best not to be poor. Fourteen studies return a positive correlation between social class (signified by

income or by husband's occupation) and a marital adjustment index. (Burgess and Cottrell 1939; Census 1953; Christensen and Meissner 1953; Goode 1956; Hamilton 1929; Kephart 1955; King 1952; Land 1932; Locke 1951; Monahan 1955; Roth and Peck 1951; Schroeder 1938; Weeks 1943; Williamson 1952.) Two studies find no relationship. (Bernard 1934; Terman 1938.) The one nationwide study, done by the Census Bureau, returns an impressive correlation between income and divorce rate. On the subject of occupations: two old studies find that travelling men, whose occupations take them away from home a good deal, are also poor risks. (Burgess and Cottrell 1939; Land 1932.) Beware of travelling salesmen, railroad men, transcontinental truck drivers.

What of social class differences: a rich girl marries a poor man, or vice versa? Two studies indicate that this, also, may be a negative predictor. (Kirkpatrick 1937; Roth and Peck 1951.)

Class-B Predictors

7. LEVEL OF EDUCATION. If we merely view the studies that use marital adjustment tests or ratings, there is no relationship to speak of. Three of these return a positive correlation between years of schooling and marital adjustment. (Burgess and Cottrell 1939; Landis 1946; Terman 1938.) One shows a weak negative correlation. (Hamilton 1926.) Three show no relationship at all. (Bernard 1934; Kirkpatrick 1937; Geismar and La Sorte 1963.) The eight studies that use divorce, however, all agree: the more years of schooling, the lower the divorce rate. (Census 1953; HEW 1957; Glick 1957; Glick and Carpenter 1958; Locke 1951; Monahan 1961; Schroeder 1938; Terman and Oden 1947.) A number of them are based on nation-wide probability samples. It looks as if there is something here.

8. PREVIOUS DIVORCE. Past divorce is a predictor of future divorce, upon remarriage. Five studies agree. (Census 1949;

Christensen and Meissner 1953; Monahan 1952, 1953, 1958.)
There is one dissenter. (Locke 1951.) Two more studies use
something other than divorce to indicate marital adjustment: Geismar and La Sorte (a marital adjustment rating),
and Locke and Klaussner (a marital adjustment test). Both
find that previously divorced *grooms* represent a poor risk;
but this is *not* true for previously divorced *brides*.

9. DIVORCED PARENTS. Children of divorced parents tend to
score low on marital adjustment tests. (Burgess and Cottrell
1939; Hamilton 1926.) They are more apt to get divorced
or separated. (Landis 1955; Schroeder 1938.) Geismar and
La Sorte, using marital adjustment ratings, found that
divorced parents represented a negative predictor for
grooms (again), but not for brides.

In six more studies, *happiness of parents' marriage* (as
judged by the respondent) correlates positively with scores
on marital adjustment tests. (Burgess and Cottrell 1939;
Hamilton 1929; Locke and Karlsson 1952; Popenoe and
Wicks 1937; Terman 1938; Terman and Buttenwiser
1935.) There is one dissenting study. (Locke 1951.)

There is an impressive mass of data here. Agreement is
high. But systematic bias may be a real factor.

10. WHERE THEY WILL LIVE. Live in the country or in a small
town; don't live in the city. (Census 1958; Burgess and
Cottrell 1939; Carter and Plateris 1963; Christensen and
Meissner 1953.)

11. PARENTS' APPROVAL. Get it first. Four studies all agreeing.
Either the old folks really know something, or parental
objections generate a self-fulfilling prophecy effect. (Burgess and Wallin 1953; King 1952; Locke 1951; Locke and
Karlsson 1951.)

12. SOCIABILITY. People who report they (and/or the spouse)
are joiners, have "lots of friends," are "popular": these
persons tend to score high on the marital adjustment tests.
(Burgess and Cottrell 1939; Burgess and Wallin 1953; King
1952; Locke 1951; Locke and Karlsson 1952; Terman and
Oden 1947.)

Class-C Predictors

13. DIFFERENCES IN AGE. If the groom is much older—or much younger—than the bride: this looks as if it may be a negative predictor. Five studies find this negatively correlated with marital adjustment; two studies report no association. (Christensen and Meissner 1953; Burgess and Cottrell 1939; Geismar and La Sorte 1963; King 1952; Kirkpatrick 1937; Locke 1951; Terman 1938.) What is "much older?" Perhaps five years or more. It is hard to say, given the low degree of concensus among studies.

14. BROTHERS AND SISTERS. Being an only child, without brothers or sisters: this looks as if it may be a negative predictor. Two studies assert that it is. (Burgess and Cottrell 1939; Terman 1938.) A third study disagrees. (Kirkpatrick 1937.) A fourth returns mixed results (Hall 1965.)

15. RELATIONSHIP WITH PARENTS. In two old studies, persons who report they had a lot of conflict with their parents tend to have low marital adjustment scores. (Terman 1938; Burgess and Cottrell 1939.)

16. THE RELATIONSHIP BEFORE MARRIAGE. This seems to be one indicator of how the couple will get along after they are married. If the engagement relationship is tempestuous and strife-torn, chances are the marriage will be too. (Burgess and Wallin 1944; Locke 1951; Geismar and La Sorte 1963.)

17. MENTAL HEALTH. In three studies, an index of mental health correlates positively with an index of marital adjustment. (Burchinal 1957; Eshleman 1965; Robbins and O'Neal 1958.)

Clifford Kirkpatrick (1963) has made an even more extensive literature review. He cites still more predictors. Generally, these are the type that I would place in "Class C" or below; the supporting evidence, in my view, is not impressive. Here are some examples, all positive predictors: the wife is pretty; they are in good health; they are similar in personality and values and have common interests.

Discussion

The picture that emerges is: a great many variables correlate with marital adjustment indices; and, as is typical of survey data, the correlations generally are rather weak. It is impossible to firmly establish the relative importance of all these variables: which are really important, which do not particularly matter. I would guess that no single predictor counts for very much; but that all the predictors, taken together, definitely count for something. The seventeen predictors, given above, could be used as a checklist. Thus, for a contemplated marriage: if the signs are unfavorable on only two of the predictors, this is very good, because it means that the signs are favorable with respect to the other fifteen. If, on the other hand, the prospective marriage rates bad on ten of the predictors, this is reason to pause.

Needless to say, this long list of variables still leaves much unaccounted for. No doubt the most crucial events, the interpersonal mechanisms on which marriages actually succeed and fail, are hardly touched by the survey data. We have, in a sense, been examining surface phenomena; the data, as they have been used here, contribute little to any deeper understanding of causal mechanisms. If one is willing to interpret further and to speculate, it is possible to employ questionnaire data in a quest for understanding. This is what Roland Tharp does in the next article.

One more general conclusion: the data seem to say that conventional people and conventional marriages stand the best chance. Girls: marry a Rotarian who is active in his church, who gets on well with his parents, who has never been divorced, who is about your age, whom you have known for years. Don't get pregnant first. Don't marry without your parents' blessings. Don't marry until you are out of school. Marry your own kind, *vis à vis* religion and social class position. And stay out of big cities.

Conceivably, all these precepts are spurious. The entire conventionality effect might be one huge, ramified case of systematic bias. Perhaps it merely happens that conventional people are less willing to seek divorce, and less able to face the truth about their marriages when they take marital adjustment tests. Perhaps, but I think not.

References

JESSIE BERNARD, "Factors in the Distribution of Success in Marriage," *American Journal of Sociology*, XL (1934), 49–60.

LEE G. BURCHINAL, "Research on Young Marriage: Implications for Family Life Education," *The Family Life Coordinator*, IX (1960), 6–24.

BUREAU OF THE CENSUS SERIES P-20, NO. 23, March 4, 1949. "Marital Status, Number of Times Married, and Duration of Present Marital Status: April, 1948."

U.S. Census of Population: 1950. Vol. IV, Special Reports, Part 5, Chapter 5, 1953.

———, *Current Population Reports,* Series 20, No. 87, November 14, 1958.

ERNEST W. BURGESS and LEONARD S. COTTRELL, *Predicting Success or Failure in Marriage* (New York: Prentice-Hall, Inc., 1939).

ERNERT W. BURGESS and HARVEY J. LOCKE, *The Family* (New York: American Book Co., 1945).

ERNEST W. BURGESS and PAUL WALLIN, "Marriage Adjustment and Engagement Adjustment," *American Journal of Sociology*, XLIX (1944), 324–30.

————, *Engagement and Marriage* (Philadelphia: Lippincott, 1953).

HUGH CARTER and ALEXANDER PLATERIS, "Trends in Divorce and Family Disruption," *HEW Indicators*, September 1963.

LORING CHANCELLOR and THOMAS MONAHAN, "Religious Preference and Inter-religious Mixtures in Marriages and Divorces in Iowa," *American Journal of Sociology*, LXI (1955), 233–39.

HAROLD T. CHRISTENSEN and HANNA H. MEISSNER, "Studies in Child Spacing: III-Premarital Pregnancy as a Factor in Divorce," *American Sociological Review*, XVIII (1953), 641–44.

EUSTACE CHESSER, *The Sexual, Marital, and Family Relationships of the English Woman* (New York: Roy, 1957).

RAYMOND J. CORSINI, "Understanding and Similarity in Marriage," *Journal of Abnormal and Social Psychology*, LII (1956), 327–32.

————, "Multiple Predictors of Marital Happiness," *Marriage and Family Living*, XVIII (1956), 240–42.

LEONARD W. FERGUSON, "Correlates of Marital Happiness," *Journal of Psychology*, VI (1938), 285–94.

LUDWIG L. GEISMAR and MICHAEL A. LA SORTE, "Factors Associated with Family Disorganization," *Marriage and Family Living* (1963), 479–81.

PAUL C. GLICK, *American Families* (New York: Wiley, 1957).

PAUL C. GLICK and HUGH CARPENTER, "Marriage Patterns and Educational Level," *American Sociological Review*, XXIII (1958), 294–300.

WILLIAM J. GOODE, *After Divorce* (Glencoe, Ill.: Free Press, 1956).

ALBERT I. GORDON, *Intermarriage* (Boston: Beacon Press, 1964).

EVERETT HALL, "Ordinal Position and Success in Engagement and Marriage," *Journal of Individual Psychology*, XXI (1965), 154–58.

GILBERT V. HAMILTON, *A Research in Marriage* (New York: A. & C. Boni, 1929).

HORNELL HART and WILMER SHIELDS, "Happiness in Relation to Age at Marriage," *Journal of Social Hygiene,* XII (1926), 403–8.

JEROLD S. HEISS, "Interfaith Marriage and Marital Outcome," *Marriage and Family Living,* XXIII (1961), 228–33.

WILLIAM K. KEPHART, "Occupational Level and Marital Disruption," *American Sociological Review,* XX (1955), 456–65.

CHARLES E. KING, "A Research Technique of Marital Adjustment Applied to a Southern Urban Minority Population Group," *Factors Making For Success or Failure in Marriage Among 466 Negro Couples in a Southern City* (Ph.D. thesis, University of Chicago, 1951).

——, "The Burgess-Cottrell Method of Measuring Marital Adjustment Applied to a Non-white Southern Urban Population," *Marriage and Family Living,* XIV (1952), 280–85.

CLIFFORD KIRKPATRICK, "Factors in Marital Adjustment," *American Journal of Sociology,* XLIII (1937), 270–83.

——, *The Family: As a Process and Institution* (New York: Ronald, 1963).

CLIFFORD KIRKPATRICK and JOHN COTTON, "Physical Attractiveness, Age, and Marital Adjustment," *American Sociological Review,* XVI (1951), 81–86.

JUDSON T. LANDIS, "Marriages of Mixed and Non-mixed Religious Faith," *American Sociological Review,* XIV (1949), 401–7.

——, "The Pattern of Divorce in Three Generations," *Social Forces,* XXXIV (1955), 213–16.

——, "Social Correlates of Divorce or Nondivorce among the Unhappy Married, *Marriage and Family Living* (1963), 178–83.

JUDSON T. LANDIS and MARY G. LANDIS, *Building a Successful Marriage* (New York: Prentice-Hall, 1958).

RICHARD O. LANG, "A Study of the Degree of Happiness or Unhappiness in Marriage," Quoted in Burgess and Cottrell, *Predicting Success or Failure in Marriage.* (Master's Thesis, University of Chicago, 1932).

HARVEY J. LOCKE, "Predicting Marital Adjustment by Comparing a Divorced and a Happily Married Group," *American Sociological Review*, XII (1947), 187–91.

——, *Predicting Adjustment in Marriage* (New York: Holt, 1951).

HARVEY J. LOCKE and GEORG KARLSSON, "Marital Adjustment and Prediction in Sweden and the United States," *American Sociological Review*, XVII (1952), 10–17.

HARVEY J. LOCKE and WILLIAM J. KLAUSNER, "Marital Adjustment of Divorced Persons in Subsequent Marriages," *Sociology and Social Research*, XXX (1948), 97–101.

HARVEY J. LOCKE and MURIEL MACKEPRANG, "Marital Adjustment and the Employed Wife," *American Journal of Sociology*, LIV (1949), 536–38.

THOMAS P. MONAHAN, "How Stable are Remarriages?", *American Journal of Sociology*, LVIII (1952), 280–88.

——, "Does Age at Marriage Matter in Divorce?", *Social Forces*, XXXII (1953), 81–87.

——, "Divorce by Occupation Level," *Marriage and Family Living*, XVII (1955), 322–24.

——, "The Changing Nature and Instability of Remarriages," *Eugenics Quarterly*, V (1958), 73–85.

——, "Educational Achievement and Family Stability," *Journal of Psychology*, LV (1961), 253–63.

THOMAS P. MONAHAN and LOREN E. CHANCELLOR, "Statistical Aspects of Marriage and Divorce by Religious Denomination in Iowa," *Eugenics Quarterly*, II (1955), 162–73.

THOMAS P. MONAHAN and WILLIAM KEPHART, "Divorce and Desertion by Religious and Mixed Religious Groups," *American Journal of Sociology*, LIX (1954), 454–65.

PAUL POPENOE and D. W. NEPTUNE, "Acquaintance and Betrothal," *Social Forces*, XVI (1938), 552–55.

PAUL POPENOE and DONNA WICKS, "Marital Happiness in Two Generations," *Mental Hygiene*, XXI (1937), 218–23.

LEE N. ROBINS and PATRICIA O'NEAL, "Marital History of Former Problem Children," *Social Problems,* V (1958), 347–58.

JULIUS ROTH and ROBERT F. PECK, "Social Class and Social Mobility Factors Related to Marital Adjustment," *American Sociological Review,* XVI (1951), 478–86.

GRISELDA ROUNTREE, "Some Aspects of Marriage Breakdown in Britain During the Last Thirty Years," *Population Studies,* XVIII (1964), 147–63.

CLARENCE W. SCHROEDER, "Divorce in a City of 100,000 Population" (Ph.D. Thesis, University of Chicago, 1938, Private Edition; distributed by Bradley Polytechnic Institute Library, Peoria, Ill., 1939).

LEWIS M. TERMAN, et al., *Psychological Factors in Marital Happiness* (New York: McGraw-Hill, 1938).

LEWIS M. TERMAN and PAUL BUTTENWISER, "Personality Factors in Marital Incompatibility," *Journal of Social Psychology,* VI (1935), 143–71.

LEWIS M. TERMAN and MELITA H. ODEN, *The Gifted Child Grows Up: Twenty-five Years' Follow-up of a Superior Group* (Stanford, Calif.: Stanford University Press, 1947).

U. S. DEPARTMENT OF HEALTH, EDUCATION and WELFARE, *Vital Statistics—Special Reports,* Vol. 45, No. 12 (September 9, 1957).

GLENN M. VERNON, "Interfaith Marriages," *Religious Education,* LV (1960), 261–64.

CLARK E. VINCENT, "Interfaith Marriages: Problem or Symptom?", in Jane C. Zahn (ed.), *Religion and the Face of America* (University Extension, University of California, 1959).

PAUL WALLIN, "Religiosity, Sexual Gratification, and Marital Satisfaction," *American Sociological Review,* XXII (1957), 300–5.

H. ASHLEY WEEKS, "Differential Divorce Rates by Occupation," *Social Forces,* XXI (1943), 334–37.

ROBERT C. WILLIAMSON, "Economic Factors in Marital Adjustment," *Marriage and Family Living,* XIV (1952), 298–300.

8

PSYCHOLOGICAL PATTERNING IN MARRIAGE

ROLAND G. THARP[1]

After 70 years of research, the broad outlines of a systematic social science approach to marriage may be discerned. Both psychology and sociology have made extensive explorations. Before us now is the task of integration, which should map the work of both disciplines into appropriate relations with one another. Like early cartographers, we shall err; but a solid ground of data exists, and can be distinguished from unknown seas.

Marriage research began in the 1890s with Pearson's comparisons of the anthropometric characteristics of spouses. From that time until. our own, the organizing issue in all mating research has remained the same, namely, the degree of simi-

SOURCE: Roland G. Tharp, "Psychological Patterning in Marriage," *Psychological Bulletin*, LX, 2 (March 1963), 97–117. Reprinted by permission of the author and publisher.

[1] The major portion of this report was written at the University of Michigan and supported by a United States Public Health Service fellowship.

The author wishes to express his gratitude to E. Lowell Kelly for his direction and encouragement.

larity between husbands and wives. That is, do "likes marry likes" (homogamy), or do "unlikes" marry (heterogamy)? Sociology has produced convincing evidence for homogamy of several cultural variables. Hollingshead (1950) has provided both an excellent bibliography and a definitive piece of research demonstrating homogamy with respect to race, age, religion, ethnic origin, and social class. More recently, residential propinquity has been added to sociological variables influencing mate selection; Katz and Hill (1958) provide a bibliography, a review, and an integration. These factors, then, largely define that pool of opposite-sex individuals which one is most likely to meet and know; it may be called the "field of eligibles" (Winch, 1952).

Yet it is obvious that the individual psychology must be accountable to some degree for the "field of acquaintances" from which the mate must ultimately be selected. Psychological factors must affect the limits of the field, and most certainly selection from within those limits. It is perhaps such considerations that have led sociologists to extend their investigations to *psychological* factors affecting mate selection and marriage outcome.

Such investigations began in the 1920s. The pioneering work of Burgess and Cottrell, King, Locke, Terman, Kirkpatrick, and others has been presented and summarized in Burgess and Wallin's important book, *Engagement and Marriage* (1953), which also reports the results of their own study of 1,000 engaged and 666 married couples.

In all these early studies, homogamy—not heterogamy—is the trend, though relationships are of a low order among psychological variables—much lower than for the investigated cultural characteristics and social traits. For example, Burgess and Wallin reported that of the 42 items of the Thurstone Neurotic Inventory, 14 showed a greater than chance expectation for homogamy of engaged couples. None were heterogamous. The significant relationships ranged (in ratio of obtained to expected similarity) from 1.17 on "do you day-dream frequently?" to 1.04 on "when you were in school did you hesitate to volunteer in a class recitation?" Comparable results are reported for items on the Bernreuter Personality Inventory and the Strong Interest Test by Terman (1938). Homogamy, then, obtains in *assortative mating.*

Marital success was at that time (and remains) the second outcome variable of interest to researchers. Generalizing from the studies of Terman (1938), Terman and Oden (1947), and Burgess and Wallin (1953, p. 529), the latter authors present the following lists of characteristics as the most decisive in differentiating happy from unhappy marriages:

HAPPILY MARRIED	UNHAPPILY MARRIED
Emotionally stable	Emotionally unstable
Considerate of others	Critical of others
Yielding	Dominating
Companionable	Isolated
Self-confident	Lacking self-confidence
Emotionally dependent	Emotionally self-sufficient

Employing the Thurstone items (obtained before marriage) weighted for maximum discrimination, Burgess and Wallin report correlations with marital success scores of .25 for men and .18 for women. Bernreuter responses, after marriage, provide success correlations of .38 and .42 for the sexes, respectively, according to Terman. The Burgess and Wallin results were substantially replicated more than 20 years later on a grossly different sample by Burchinal, Hawkes, and Gardner (1957). That individuals' neurotic traits are predictive of marital disharmony can be accepted as a demonstrated fact.

The generalization "homogamy-with-respect-to-personality-traits" is drawn by all the classic investigators. It should be remembered, however, that most traits investigated are neurotic in character. That neurotics unite in marriage with neurotics is an observation common in psychoanalytic literature. In the light of our present knowledge of the relationships between culture and personality, homogamy of the degree reported with respect to social interests and general personality traits could likely be accounted for on the basis of the common modal personalities of individuals in common cultural groups; particularly when it is known that these cultural similarities establish the marital field of eligibles. The effect of degrees of homogamy or heterogamy on marital success has not been assessed, beyond the fact that individuals possessing those traits listed in the right-hand column above are more likely to be unhappily married, and are likely to be married homogamously, and are thereby doubly damned.

The main body of this review, then, is concerned with studies having the above-summarized information as background. More recent research can conveniently be divided into four somewhat overlapping areas: interpersonal perception, identification, complementary needs, and role theory.

Interpersonal Perception

Perception of the self and of others has lately been a central construct in influential theories and research of personality and personality change (Rogers & Dymond, 1954). Although the classic studies discussed above have used self-ratings and ratings-by-others as techniques in marriage research, Kelly (1941) was the first to consider perception of personality as an operative force in its own right: "the actual relative position of the husband and wife on a personality trait continuum are not as important in determining compatibility as the belief of the husband and wife regarding their relative positions on these scales" (p. 193). The instrument used to investigate this proposition was Kelly's 36-item Personality Rating Scale, administered for self-perception and perception of spouse to 76 couples. His results may be summarized as follows: subjects rate themselves less favorably than they rate their spouses, and less favorably than they are rated *by* their spouses. The Burgess-Terman-Miles Compatibility Index was also administered to each subject, yielding the following information: high compatibility is associated with more favorable self-ratings, but accompanied by spouse ratings which are yet more favorable. These findings hold true for both husband and wife. Kelly concludes that an individual's personal satisfaction in marriage is related both to self-regard and to the judgment of the self's inferiority or superiority vis-a-vis the spouse.

Preston, Peltz, Mudd, and Froscher (1952) extended this type of investigation to the consideration of the relationship between person-perception and an objective appraisal of that person. Couples drawn from the clients of the Marriage Council of Philadelphia constituted the sample. Fifty-five couples had received pre-marital counseling; 116 had received post-marital counseling. The two groups can be accepted as more- and less-happily married subjects. Using a personality rating scale of 17 items—selected from those used by Kelly (1941) and Burgess and Cottrell (1939)—Kelly's results were substantially verified, except that the less-happily married men judged their wives much more severely than themselves. This discrepancy seems in principle to conform with Kelly's formulation. The difference in range of happiness to be expected between the samples of the two studies would seem to account for this disparate finding.

Further results are as follows:

1. Self-ratings of spouses show positive correlations of the same order as those of the classic studies with a tendency for greater congruence in happier than in unhappy couples. (Medians = .19 and .30, respectively.)

2. Higher correlations occur, however, between ratings-of-self and ratings-of-spouse. This tendency is likewise stronger with more happily-marrieds.

Concerning the question of objectivity of perception, Preston et al. (1952) comment as follows:

> The correlations between the self-ratings of the spouses are uniformly much less than the correlations between the ratings of self and partner no matter which spouse is studied. Further,

the data of the experiment indicate conclusively that the happily married group exhibit a larger discrepancy between the relevant correlation coefficients. From these two facts the conclusion is inescapable that the happily married groups show more evidence of lack of realism in their personality appraisals than the unhappily married group (p. 335).

This conclusion becomes quite escapable when one realizes that the self as seen by the self, and the self as seen by the spouse, necessarily constitute different stimulus patterns; there is no reason to expect total agreement. Further, it is somewhat risky to invoke "realism" as a consideration when none of the variables concerned are externally validated. Rather, these data indicate a perceived similarity of self and spouse *as they interact,* such similarity increasing with marital happiness.

Dymond's (1954) data seem to support this view. She concludes: "Married love is not blind . . . the better each partner understands the other's perceptions of himself and his world, the more satisfactory the relationship" (p. 171). Her subjects were 15 couples well known to her, with a mean length of marriage of 10.4 years. One hundred MMPI items, pertaining to interaction with others, were administered to each of the 30 subjects. After answering for the self, each subject predicted the spouse's answers. In order to control for stereotypy of reply, all items which were answered uniformly by more than two-thirds of the group were eliminated, leaving 55 items exhibiting a reasonable degree of difference. Since the yes-or-no probabilities of these items were roughly equal, predictive ability ("understanding") would be uncontaminated by knowledge of group norms. Scores were then related to the happiness of the marriage, as rated by the subjects themselves and validated by Dymond's rating. The usual finding occurred: happily married spouses resembled each other more than unhappily marrieds. Dymond's principal hypothesis was verified also; happys predict spouse replies significantly better than do unhappys. Further, there is significantly less association between similarity of self-spouse and accuracy of prediction in the happy than in the unhappy group.

It can be seen from the foregoing studies that with increases in self-similarity, increases of perceived self-similarity and increases in predictive ability, happiness is greater. But all research indicates that, presumably due to patterns of assortative mating, the two selves of the partners—happy or no—exhibit similarity. The inference seems, therefore, that happiness increases as does congruence between self-as-self and self-as-spouse. Put differently, when the self as seen by the self and the self as seen by the spouse become more nearly equal stimulus configurations; that is, when the self, acting as spouse, does no violence to self-identity, then, either causatively or concomitantly, happiness increases. Considerations such as these will be expounded more fully under the section on role theory below.

Corsini's (1956a, 1956b) important and startling results allow further generalizations. Twenty volunteer students and their spouses, from the University of Chicago, participated. Marital happiness was assessed by the Burgess-Wallin scale. A 50-item adjective Q sort was sorted four times by each subject: (*a*) for self, (*b*) for spouse, (*c*) prediction for spouse, and—adding a new dimension to previous research—(*d*) prediction of the spouse's description of the subject. A long-overdue experimental control was instituted by Corsini: every conclusion with respect to couples was checked by drawing random samples of noncouples, and the same operations for couples duplicated. Following previous investigators, Corsini agrees that: (*a*) understanding the mate is not related to similarity of self and mate, and (*b*) happiness is associated with similarity of self-perceptions.

However, Corsini (1956a, 1956b) discovered that although understanding can be shown to exist between husbands and wives, this understanding is related to marital happiness only in those comparisons when the *husband* is the target of Q sorts (that is, wife's prediction × husband's self-perception; and husband's prediction × wife's perception of him). In these instances, husband-wife correlations vary positively with marital happiness for both mates. This strongly suggests that the husband's role in marriage is the crucial one for the satisfaction of both partners. However, the above-stated relationship was then shown by Corsini to be no more true for husband and wife than for randomly-paired men and women who did not even know each other! This led him to suggest that the relevant relationship may exist between marital happiness and a *stereotyped* conception of the husband. He then demonstrated that the greater "conformity" of male self-perception (measured by the mean correlation for each male against all other males) is positively correlated with happiness for both husband and wife. None of these relationships hold when perceptions of the female is the variable considered.

It seems, therefore, that our prior generalization can be expanded. The congruence, necessary for happiness, between self-perception and perception by the spouse is particularly crucial for the male; further, this agreement as to male-as-husband most often partakes liberally of widely-shared expectations of husbandly qualities.

Luckey (1959, 1960a, 1960b), in her careful and impressive study, contributes to this emerging formulation. Eighty-one couples, all of some education at the University of Minnesota, were selected from a much larger subject-pool in order to provide two groups highly differentiated on the Locke and Terman marital happiness scales. The Leary Interpersonal Check List (ICL) was completed by each subject for self, spouse, ideal self, mother, and father. Congruence or divergence between a respondent and these "significant others" could be estimated on each of four scales provided by the ICL. Luckey's results support Corsini's. Satisfaction in marriage is related to the congruence of the husband's self-concept and that held of him by the wife. The relation does not hold for concepts of wives. Happiness is also related to (*a*) congruence of the husband's self and ideal concepts. (*b*) congruence of husband's self-concept and his concept of his father, and (*c*) congruence of the wives' concepts of their husbands and concepts of their fathers.

It seems, therefore, that the maximally happy marital situation can be described as follows: husband and wife agree that he is as *he* wishes to be, namely, like his father; and as *she* wishes him to be, namely, like hers. Surely this broad area of agreement is the culturally defined male sex-role—more specifically, the male subrole of husband.

Identification

The mechanism whereby appropriate sex-typical behaviors are transmitted from one generation to another has long been labeled "identification." The psychoanalytic account of the process involved is the most elaborate: the boy renounces a direct libidinal claim upon the mother in favor of vicarious gratification through the father, with whom he thus "identifies"; thereby establishing congruent values and behaviors between boy and specific father, and also between the boy and the general male gender. The process for the girl is held to be similar, though more gradual, and culminating not in a preschool climax, but in a diffused struggling until late adolescence or early marriage, when the female identity crisis must be met.

In any case, the child renounces strong libidinal cathexes upon the opposite-sex parent. The obvious inference for mate selection has been repeatedly drawn: the courtship quest is for the opposite-sex parent image (Dreikurs, 1930; Fluegel, 1926; Hamilton & McGowan, 1930). Sporadic and generally unsuccessful efforts to test this hypothesis have been made. Hamilton and McGowan (1930) reported that only 17% of men studied did marry women bearing physical resemblances to their mothers. Of these men, however, 94% were happy, whereas only 33% of the men were happy when mates did not resemble mothers. A similar, though only slight, relationship held between happiness and wife's similarity to mother's temperament.

If men marry mother's images, would not sons of younger mothers marry younger women than sons of older mothers? Commins (1932), using 1,075 subjects of the English *Who's Who,* reported statistically significant younger age at marriage for oldest sons as compared to other-than-oldest sons. Kirkpatrick (1937), using 768 cases from the *Compendium of American Genealogy,* found no relationship between sibling position and mean age at marriage. Mangus (1936), using 600 college women as subjects, found that, on matters of interests and personality traits, women rate their ideal-as-husband more similarly to their current most intimate male companion than to their fathers. We may conclude, with Sears (1942), that there are as yet no statistical investigations which are adequate for purposes of verifying the mate-opposite sex parent resemblances notion.

The more recent investigation by Strauss (1946a, 1946b), though, did give new life to the issue. A group of 373 engaged, informally engaged, or recently married persons (200 women, 173 men) participated. Strauss reports greater resemblances between men's mothers and mates than between women's fathers and mates, but this information was garnered by simply asking the subjects how much resemblance existed—"very much" to "not at all." Responses less subject to bias, fortunately, were obtained on 25 personality traits, rated by each subject separately for self, mate, and parents. These data give evidence for something more than chance congruence between personalities of mate and parent, *but not necessarily of the opposite sex parent.* On the basis of interviews conducted with some female subjects, Strauss suggests that childhood affectional experiences with parents are linked with adult love choices.

The precise nature of this link seems to be the processes of identification. The Burgess-Wallin (1953) data, studied by Lu (1952c), indicate that parental authority-domination, as reported by the offspring, is positively related to the childhood conflict with the parent, and negatively related to adult attachment to that parent, irrespective of the sex of parent or child. These conclusions were based on the several items in the Burgess-Wallin questionnaire which bore face validity to the dimensions investigated. This limitation, plus the evident opportunity for the subjects to respond with halo, would lead a reader to withhold judgment on Lu's hypotheses. However, precisely this relationship is being demonstrated in current developmental-longitudinal studies of identification processes (Kagan, 1958; Payne & Mussen, 1956). Apparently it is affectional bonds which leads the boy to identify with the father, not fear of his castrating ire.

Earlier, we proposed that identification with the father leads to happier marriage. Assuming that early affectional relationships with the father lead to stronger identification, we would expect that such an affectional relationship would affect marital happiness.

Luckey's results are pertinent here (Luckey, 1960a, 1960b). In the unhappy marriages which she studied; men saw their fathers as more dominant and less loving than themselves on each of the ICL scales. Lu's further work suggests one of the consequences of conflict with parents (Lu, 1952b). By the use of a 16-item dominance-submission scale, he divided marriages into husband-dominant, equalitarian, and wife-dominant groups. Dominant roles are associated with conflict with parents, equalitarian roles associated with affectional attachment to parents. Further, there is good evidence for equalitarian roles' positive association with marital adjustment, and dominant roles', by either spouse, negative association with marital adjustment (Lu, 1952a).

Obviously, so few studies have been done in this area that only the most tentative general hypotheses can be extracted. But it does not seem untoward to propose the following. Solid affectional father-son bonds lead to the adoption, by the youth, of the ways of the male. This allows him, as husband, to be thoroughly himself while enacting the expected male role as husband. This satisfactory performance of husband role satisfies the expectations of the wife; the husband too is happy, for the self-as-self and the self-as-spouse produce no conflict. Under such circumstances, no submissive or compensating-dominating patterns of relationship need be instituted. The possible permutations of the few variables used here lead to a myriad of predictions, none of which could be checked by data now available. (Though it should be mentioned that a pattern of early affectional relationships leading to a predominantly cross-sexual identification—at least in the male—would be expected to lead to results opposite to those outlined above.)

Complementary Needs

A new and vigorous dissident entered the homogamy-heterogamy issue in the person of R. F. Winch, who with his associates has elaborated the theory of complementary needs. Briefly stated, the theory holds that though homogamy of social characteristics establishes a "field of eligibles," mate selection within this field is determined by a specific kind of *heterogamy of motives*—complementarity. This complementarity may be of two kinds: (*a*) that in which partners differ in *degree* of the same need, or (*b*) differ in *kind* of need. That mate is selected who offers the greatest probability of providing maximum need satisfaction, as the partners act according to their complementary pattern of motives:

> So that if individuals A and B have complementary need patterns, B's resulting behavior will be a greater source of gratification to A than will be the case with the behavior of C, who is psychically similar to A (Winch, Ktsanes, & Ktsanes, 1954, p. 242).

In marriage research, no other hypothesis produced in the last decade has been as influential:

> (Winch's) work represents a valuable entree to an extremely complex and subtle problem area . . . not only to family

studies, but to many other problem areas as well, notably personality types and the division of labor, cohesion in small groups, stable marginal adjustments, etc. (Rosow, 1957, p. 232). "It is through this fulfillment-of-complementary needs approach that further sociological studies should bear fruit" (Kephart, 1957). Application of the CN approach is being made to the field of marital counseling and social work (Meyer, 1957; Winch, Martha, 1958). The Winch group has amassed some 11 separate publications treating complementarity; several dissertations; engendered four critical articles; and numerous derivative studies, at least four of which have been published.

Yet no thorough appraisal of the data on which the theory of CN is based has appeared.[2] That will be the next task of this review. Now let us examine Winch's procedures.

The sample is described as:

> 25 married undergraduate students in selected schools of Northwestern University of white race, middle class background, 19–26 years of age, second or later generation native-born of Christian or no specified religion; and their spouses (Winch et al., 1954).

Twelve "needs" from Murray's well-known list, as well as three "general traits" were studied. Most of these variables were "double-dichotomized," that is, rated separately for being operative *within* or *without* the marriage, and separately for operating *overtly* or *covertly*, yielding 44 subvariables.

Three techniques were employed to garner information from which the 44 subvariables could be quantified. First came the need interview, a structured interview from which the following are the published sample questions: "how do you feel when someone steps in front of you in a queue in a crowded restaurant"; and "how do you feel when you see your name in print" (Winch, 1958).

Second, a case-history interview was conducted. This (Winch, 1958),

---

[2] Several of the assessments to be made here have adumbrations scattered through the literature and acknowledgements will be made below.

began with the subject's earliest memories, covered his percepts and experiences with key familial and other figures, and brought him through his various developmental stages to the present moment (p. 110).

Thirdly, eight TAT cards were administered. (It should be noted that the Cattell 16 PF, Form A, was also included, but of this we hear only a 1958 footnote characterizing the results as "largely negative" (Winch, 1958, p. 110).

Each subject was given a separate rating on each variable for the need interview (NI-1); for the case history (CH), and for the TAT (TAT-O). The quantifying techniques for each should be noted. For NI-1, two judges rated each subvariable on a 1–5 scale. Interjudge reliability is reported as .60. Ratings were summed and normalized (Winch et al., 1954).

For the TAT, the same procedure—content analysis—was followed. Interrater reliabilities were reported as in the range of .20 (Winch & More, 1956a, 1956b). "This procedure was undertaken with essentially negative results" (Winch, 1958, p. 110). Following this (Winch, 1958)

> we undertook a mode of analysis on the need-interview, the case-history interview, and the TAT which might be called "global" or "molar" or "clinical" or "projective" or "holistic." A different analyst worked on each of these three sources of information and sought, as far as the data would allow, to create a complete dynamic analysis of each subject . . . after writing such a report and on the basis of the analysis he had prepared, each analyst would then rate the subject on the 44 sub-variables" (pp. 110–111);

thus, NI-2; CH; and TAT-C.

Still another set of ratings was to come—the FC (full-case conference).

> In order to arrive at a psychodynamic interpretation and a set of ratings for each subject in which we could place our greatest confidence, we formed a clinical conference of five persons . . . each analyst read and criticized all three written reports . . . inconsistencies were discussed, and relevant evidence was exam-

ined . . . after arriving at what might be called "diagnostic" consensus, all 5 analysts agreed on a final set of ratings of the subjects' needs (Winch, 1958, p. 111).

Thus, six sets of ratings are available. Five are subsequently reported.[3]

The FC was used as the criterion for validity of the other indices. The general range of correlations between FC ratings and other sets are as follows: NI-1, .60; NI-2, .80; CH, .74; and TAT-C, .00 (Winch & More, 1956).

The hypotheses to be tested with these data were derived from the theory of CN. The statistical technique was the inter-spousal product-moment correlation, i.e., husband's subvariable scores times their respective wives subvariable scores. Of 1,936 possible interspousal correlations, 388 were hypothesized as to direction of sign: 344, involving *different* needs or traits, would be *positive* in sign; 44 involving the *same* need or trait, would be *negative* (Winch et al., 1954). The specific relationships hypothesized have not been published. The general validity of the CN theory was staked on a chi square test for greater-than-chance occurrence of signs of correlations in the hypothesized directions.

The results of interspousal correlational distributions NI-1, NI-2, and FC met this chi square test. CH did not. For TAT-C, the directionality of the distribution was reversed. Winch (1955a) concludes that "the bulk of the evidence, therefore, supports the hypothesis that mates tend to select each other on the basis of complementary needs" (p. 554).

A further analysis followed. Constructing a Q-type matrix, the correlations for variables could be compared for married pairs versus non-married pairs. In this matrix of 625 male-female correlations, 25 were of the former, 600 of the latter group. Testing for same-variable correlations, CN theory would predict lower (and presumably negative) correlations for marrieds, and higher for nonmarried. In addition to comparing the 25 to the 600, Winch also randomly matched each man with a woman not his wife and compared these correlations

[3] TAT-O disappears.

with the 25 husband-wife coefficients. In both cases, the NI-1 data demonstrate statistically significant difference between mates' and nonmates' mean correlations and in the hypothesized directions. The FC data do not show such differences. The NI-1 results are as follows: mean husband-wife correlation, .1016; mean man-woman correlation, .2316. The range of the husband-wife coefficients is from $+.52$ to $-.32$. Nine of these were negative, 16 positive.

Cluster analyses (Winch et al., 1955), R-type factor analysis (Roos, 1957), and Q-type factor analysis (Ktsanes, 1955) have been performed on the Winch data. All results have been summarized in *Mate Selection: A Study of Complementary Needs* (Winch, 1958). This volume also contains speculative elaboration of CN theory, detailed case reports, etc.

Now certain exceptions must be taken when it is maintained that the case for complementary needs theory has been demonstrated:

1. Sample—Of what population can 25 married undergraduate couples be taken as representative?

2. Ratings—"(Of the correlations) an indeterminate number could actually have been spurious reflections of the raters' implicit theories of trait organization" (Katz, Glucksberg, & Krauss, 1960, p. 205). This appraisal by Katz et al. was earlier voiced by Strodtbeck (1959). Bowman (1955) and Kernodle (1959) have complained that sociologists, by the nature of their training, are not qualified to undertake psychological analyses such as an investigation of complementary needs requires. Perhaps; but researches are to be judged by their fruit rather than their roots. Yet this psychologist cannot but wish that more account had been taken of the problems of rater subjectivity—bias, projection, halo; as well as the issues of reliability and validity: in short, all the concerns of those who deal in objective psychological assessment.

3. Statistics—Aside from the probable nonindependent nature of the variables, built in by the rating technique, there is the question of statistical nonindependence. In a distribu-

tion of intercorrelations, when Variables A and B are positively related, and likewise B and C, the relation between A and C cannot be taken as an independent event. In a matrix of 1,936 correlations which are positively related throughout (Winch & More, 1956a, 1956b), the 388 "tests" were not selected on a basis of posited independence of event, but without regard to this issue. Winch (1958) has recognized this problem, but commented that, "Just how many independent events there are is a very complex question" (p. 115). We agree.

4. Results—The data, taken as they have been rated, analyzed, and reported do not support the CN hypothesis. Winch concludes that he is upheld by the bulk of the evidence—NI-1, NI-2, and FC; and not supported by only CH and TAT-C. Are not, however, NI-1 and NI-2 in reality two ratings on only one datum? And are they not correlated an average of .60 and .80 with the third supporting set, FC? Rather than winning by 3 to 2, complementarity appears to have lost by 3 to 1. (And if one is to consider TAT-O and the 16 PF results, the score becomes even more embarrassing.)

5. Research Philosophy—Almost any set of data, if sufficiently badgered, can be exhausted into submission.

6. Other Research—Bowerman and Day (1956), using 60 couples who were either formally engaged or regular dating partners and who were drawn as volunteers from college sociology classes, attempted to test the CN hypothesis. Their intrument was the Edwards Personal Preference Schedule (EPPS); this offered an objective measurement of 10 of the needs used by Winch, as both Edwards and Winch drew from Murray's need list. On same-need matching, more evidence for homogamy than for complementarity was found; on different-need matchings, no evidence for either principle of organization was unearthed.

Winch (1957) insisted that this constitutes no replication, on the following grounds: (a) The EPPS, "though ingeniously conceived—has no known validity for measuring needs." Two other objections smack less of the pot and the kettle: (*b*) the Bowerman and Day subjects were not yet married; and (*c*) the variables used were not identical (p. 336). These objections have been answered by Schellenberg and Bee (1960). One hundred college couples were investigated. Sixty-four were recently married, 18 engaged, and 18 were going steady. The EPPS was again the measuring device. Considering the marrieds and unmarrieds separately, and the 100 couples severally, all evidence was for homogamy, not complementarity. This direction of association was statistically significant for marrieds and for the total group.

But were they indeed measuring the same things as was Winch? Seven of the variables in the two studies were conceptually identical. The intervariable correlations as reported by Winch were rank ordered; ranks were also derived for the Schellenberg and Bee variables from the EPPS manual. The rank-order correlations between them were in the range .70–.78. Half the remaining variance was attributable to the single need Nurturance, which was much more closely related to Succorance in the EPPS than in Winch.

More recently, Katz, Glucksberg, and Krauss (1960), using 56 couples with a mean marriage length of 5 years, incorporated EPPS data into Winch's husband-wife versus random pairs design. The results were overwhelmingly opposed to complementarity.

It is our judgment, in view of the foregoing discussion, that the complementary-need hypothesis as now stated is not tenable.

Due to cluster and factor analyses of his data (Ktsanes, 1955; Roos, 1957; Winch, Ktsanes, & Ktsanes, 1955), Winch believes at least two basic dimensions operate in marital patterning. He has labeled these *dominant-submissive* and *nurturant-receptive*. (One cannot fail to note the correspondence between the polarities and marital sex roles as ordinarily conceived.) Applying these dimensions to his case histories, he discovers the following generalizations which he then submits as hypotheses for verification. For example, irrespective of gender, individuals who are high in Nurturance tend to mate with those who are highly Receptive and relatively non-Nurturant; individuals who are high in Dominance mate with those who are high in Submissiveness and relatively non-Dominant. Schellenberg and Bee (1960) tested these hypotheses with what appear to be the relevant EPPS variables; the hypotheses were not confirmed. Yet Winch's case reports (Winch, 1958) are certainly convincing; and further, in analyzing his 25 couples, he reports the following distribution: marriages in which the husband is dominant, 13; in which the wife is dominant, 9; mixed dominance, 3. Not only Schellenberg and Bee, but also Lu (1952c) report a far greater proportion of equalitarian matings than Winch's couples exhibit.

A further consideration strikes the reader of Winch's case histories. "One is impressed with the degree to which it is the recollections the subject has of his parents (as he knew them between, say, 6 and 18) which either directly, or as a counter-process, shapes his needs" (Strodtbeck, 1959). And most impressive is the extent to which it is *both,* or the *cross*-sex rather than the like-sex parent who is emulated.

The suspicion grows that Winch's subjects are simply not typical of mate-selecting individuals. That they should be exceptional seems entirely reasonable, when one considers that they were drawn from a postwar, early marrying, GI Bill of Rights supported, campus group. Certainly one can take some exception to any researcher's subjects, and this review cannot stand on psychosocial speculations concerning these individuals. However, any reader of Winch's case histories must be impressed with how far these individuals veer from the generalizations proposed in this review as predictive of marital success. One would therefore predict an unusual degree of disharmony and unhappiness in these marriages. Perhaps follow-up data will some day be available by which the accuracy of these remarks may be judged.

Now if it be granted that the complementary-needs approach has not met with undue success, though making valuable contributions as to level of approach and research orientation, where has it gone awry? The answer to this question lies in developments observable in the entire enterprise of behavior analysis. The marriage relationship can be considered as a stimulus situation comprised of expectations specific to marriage. These marriage roles can thus be expected to order (or even assign) the operative needs of the individuals concerned. Assessment of needs not specific to marriage is clearly not the logical entree to predictive study.[4]

Role Theory

The role-analysis approach to marriage research has had its advocates for many years.

> What the Freudians fail to recognize, and Mead left undeveloped, is the notion of multiple patterns of role-taking in response to the varied demands of the groups in which the individual aspires to membership (Mowrer & Mowrer, 1951, p. 30).

Kargman (1957) has argued for the efficacy of role analyses, as opposed to the intrapsychic approach, in enabling both counsellor and client to appreciate marriage-relationship problems. Earlier, Mangus has offered an elaboration of role theory as it may be applied to marriage counselling. He offers sample hypotheses, e.g., the integrative quality of a marriage is a function of role perception, role expectation, and role performance

---

[4] In a stimulating article, Rosow characterizes Winch's dichotomizations as "the operational assumption that people do not have *general* personality needs, but segregate these according to different social roles and gratify them on a role-specific basis; that is, some needs in one role and others in another" (Rosow, 1957). However, there is nothing in published accounts of the interviews which demonstrate that they were adequate for (or even conceived so as to provide) marriage-role-specific assessment of needs; further, neither hypotheses nor results are reported which give any evidence of a within-without patterning or effect. We must agree, however, to the extent that Winch's work contains the ungerminated seed of the theoretical tree which we hope shall fructify in the following section.

of marital partners. This paper, along with that of Sarbin, may well be read for expositions of general role theory (Mangus, 1957; Sarbin, 1954). Research in marriage roles was active by at least 1950.

The most sophisticated psycho-social treatment of marriage relationships now available is that of Parsons and Bales (1955), which consequently deserves a brief resume here. Parsons demonstrates that in the processes of development, need dispositions, object relations, and identifications are inextricably related; so that although needs may certainly be considered as relatively enduring, as an individual finds himself engaged in a given social interaction, or assuming a given social role, this situation *organizes* (by differential orderings, rankings, and valences) the enduring need units. Any theory of action must deal not with the isolated units but with the role-ascribed organization of these units. Thus, "The role expectation . . . *is* itself also a motivational unit" (Parsons & Bales, 1955, p. 107).

Parsons (Parsons & Bales, 1955) offers this pretty metaphor:

> . . . highly differentiated need-dispositions constitute a kind of "key-board." A given role-orientation is a "tune" played on that keyboard. Many different tunes will strike the same notes but in different combinations, and some will be altogether omitted from some tunes . . . the pattern of the tune is not deducible from the structure of the keyboard (p. 171).

The two dominant *leit-motifs* are the male and female sex roles. Following an analysis of child socialization in terms of family structure, Parsons (Parsons & Bales, 1955) concludes:

> If this general analysis is correct, then the most fundamental difference between the sexes in personality type is that, relative to the total culture as a whole, the masculine personality tends more to the predominance of instrumental interests, needs and functions, presumably in whatever social system both sexes are involved, while the feminine personality tends more to the primacy of expressive interests, needs and functions. We would expect, by and large, that other things being

equal, men would assume more technical, executive, and "judicial" roles, women more supportive, integrative and "tension-managing" roles (p. 101).

These principles he then applies to marriage roles. In Parsons' system, there are two primary axes of personality differentiation, *power* and *instrumental-expressive*. In marriage, power equalization is the norm.[5] As to the instrumental-expressive axis,

> . . . the husband has the primary adaptive responsibilities, relative to the outside situation, and that internally he is in the first instance "giver-of-care," or pleasure, and secondarily the giver of love, whereas the wife is primarily the giver of love and secondarily the giver of care or pleasure (Parsons & Bales, 1955, p. 151).

The husband-wife relationship is, of course, a subsystem of the family collectivity, which involves the performance of many roles. For example, the woman as mother must adopt instrumental primacy vis-a-vis her child, while the child in his role functions with expressive primacy. Obviously, the number, sex, and temperament of children which come to a couple must affect profoundly all dimensions of marital patterning and outcome. The limitations of this essay, however, allow no more than briefly noting this important caution (see Farber & Blackman, 1956).

Parsons' formulations are not simple, yet the level of complexity is appropriate to that of the phenomena. The theory has, however, outstripped research verification. It is our next task to review marriage-role researches, comparing their results to our own and to Parsons' generalizations.

[5] Research seems to substantiate this assertion. Most marital partners see power equality in their roles. As to the effects on power distribution of extramarital role variations, e.g., working wives versus housewives, there is disagreement (see Heer, 1958 versus Blood & Hamblin, 1958). But the relationship between power-as-need and power-as-influence is unresolved in the literature. This is unsurprising, since the relationship of motive to behavior constitutes a key dilemma in psychology. This situation also highlights the importance of role-specified needs as a construct, offering as it does a potential solution to this basic theoretical issue.

In the first place, McGinnes (1958) repeated the study of Hill (1945) on campus values in mate selection. Subjects rated the importance to mate selection of 18 personal characteristics (emotional stability, good health, chastity, etc.). Remarkable consistency was demonstrated between the two studies, separated in time by 17 years. Shifts occurred principally in those items most clearly related to "companionate" marriages, and thus predictable from the generally-accepted view that marriages are shifting from "traditional" to "companionate" structuring. Role expectations, then, may be held to exhibit reasonable stability over time.

Shifts do, however, occur in individuals over time. Different patterns of traits—both those desired in the partner, and those believed to be important by the partner—are evident when subjects have reference to marriage partners than when reference is to dating partners (Hewitt, 1958). Marriage role expectations are held to differ according to courtship stage (Hobart, 1958).[6]

Occurring within a context of basic similarity, then, an individual's expectation shows differences according to the mate role in which he operates. The courtship is *somewhat* different than the marriage role. Parsons has predicted this difference, and suggests that it springs from need achievement, which operates forcefully through date selection and courtship, then much less saliently in marriage roles. It is impossible to verify this explanation with data now available, but the phenomenon of difference within basic similarity stands. It will be recalled that many dimensions, demonstrably involved in assortative mating, are found to occur intensified in more satisfactory marriages. A hypothesis for further investigation therefore offers itself; the greater the concordance between courtship and marriage role—that is, the less salient during courtship are those variables nonrelevant to marriage-roles

6 Langhorne and Secord (1955) do not find ideal-mate conceptions differing by age or marital status. But their variables are need units (see below), and do not appear comparable to these studies, which deal with specific traits.

(e.g., need achievement)—the greater the probability of marital success.

Investigations have been made of the effect of role disagreement on marriages. Jacobsen (1952) found that divorced couples exhibit a greater disparity in their attitudes toward the roles of husband and wife in marriage than do married couples. But Hobart and Klausner (1959) found no relationship between marital-role disagreement and marital satisfaction. The published examples from the questionnaires used in these two studies offer no opportunity for comparison as to equivalence. Neither study, however, used a random man-woman pairing control (or its equivalent) as should certainly be done following Corsini (1956a, 1956b). Couch (1958) found concensus on husband and wife roles to increase with length of marriage, as did accuracy in assuming the role of the other mate. The study, however, was cross sectional rather than longitudinal. Couch offers it principally for its methodological and conceptual interests, which it indeed possesses.

The most ambitious attempt to test Parsons' hypotheses has been that of Farber (1957). The questions raised by this study are many and important; adequate consideration requires a somewhat detailed examination. Parsons and Bales (1955) make the broad assignment of task-oriented roles to the husband, and socioemotional roles to the wife (each role being subordinate to the common value system). Farber notes that for the home-centered woman, and especially for the wife with children, less opportunity for variation from the socioemotional matrix is possible than is the case for the more mobile husband. Therefore, marriage integration is more dependent on the husband's conformity to the wife's values than vice versa. Farber uses three variables:

1. Marital Integration: measured by the number of times husband and wife rate self or spouse as stubborn, gets angry easily, feelings easily hurt, nervous or irritable, moody, jealous, dominating or bossy, easily excited, easily depressed, and self-centered.

2. Perceived Similarity between Self and Other: (husband and
   wife, husband and child, wife and child, etc.) measures for
   this variable are derived from the same ratings of the 10
   traits listed for Variable 1.
3. Socioemotional Valuation in Interaction: measured by the
   following five values, which, along with others, were ranked
   by subjects in order of importance: (a) "companionship,"
   the family members feeling comfortable with each other
   and being able to get along together; (b) "personality
   development," continued increase in family members' ability to understand and get along with people and to accept
   responsibility; (c) "satisfaction" of family members "with
   amount of affection shown," and of the husband and wife
   in their sex life; (d) "emotional security," feeling that the
   members of the family really need each other emotionally
   and trust each other fully; and (e) "a home," having a place
   where the family members feel they belong, where they feel
   at ease, and where other people do not interfere in their
   lives.

From the foregoing, Farber hypothesizes:

1. The ranking of items relating to socioemotional aspects of
   interaction by wives tends to be higher than the ranking by
   their husbands.
2. The degree of marital integration varies directly with the
   ranks assigned by the husband to domestic values pertaining to socioemotional aspects of interaction.

Then, using 99 couples, trained interviewers, and ending in
a dazzling (indeed sometimes blinding) display of mathemati-
cal manipulation, he accepts all four hypotheses as confirmed
at the .05 level. But this study requires scrutiny. As for Hypothesis 1, Parsons' prediction of husband-wife differentiation
in marriage roles along an instrumental-expressive axis is confirmed. But as for Hypothesis 2, when one examines the instru-
ments used to measure the two variables involved, one concludes that it is demonstrated only that "husbands who are

dedicated to getting along well in the family tend to occur in families which get along well." That is, marital integration is indexed by the same concept used to index socio-emotional role taking. Small wonder that they coincide.[7] But this exception taken to Farber's design can also be taken to the majority of marital studies in the literature.

For all the objective measures of marital satisfaction now current are heavily weighted with indices of togetherness, of agreement, of interpersonal smooth sailing. As a typical example, on the recently published Locke-Wallace short test (Locke & Wallace, 1959), 11 of the 15 items seem related to social emotional integration via agreement and togetherness. Certainly less friction in marriage may produce greater durability. Buerkle, Anderson, and Badgley (1961) have factor analyzed responses to Yale Marital Interaction Battery, composed of endorsements of alternative solutions to marital conflict situations. Factor scores were computed, and differences between adjusted marital groups and nonadjusted groups reported. The nonadjusted marriages were at that time being counseled for marital difficulties. The adjusted were marriages drawn from religion-affiliated groups. (The authors recognize the problem of accepting this group as adjusted.) At any rate, adjusted husbands were more likely to submit to wife domination and to grant the wife greater deference and respect. Adjusted wives were more likely to defer to the husband's judgment, and to expect less deference and respect from their husbands.

This study does not, however, speak to the issue of marital happiness. And, if considerations of "socioemotional integration" are less salient for the man in his marital role, it would seem that his marital happiness and success must be assessed by indices more pertinent to the satisfaction of his own peculiar motives.

[7] Farber also investigates other hypotheses. Inspection of the measuring devices again demonstrates conceptual nonseparation of the independent and dependent variables. Farber maintains that statistically, the indices need not covary. However, identical thermometers may also vary independently; our point is that Farber has placed two thermometers in a single solution.

We turn now to the important work of Langhorne and Secord (1955). When role expectations are analyzed separately for men and for women, in terms of *motivational units,* an impressive difference occurs; that is to say, women need different things from husbands than husbands need from wives. Langhorne and Secord have performed the service of describing, empirically, this difference. In six states (Virginia, Georgia, Mississippi, Ohio, Kansas, & Wyoming) 5,000 college and university students were asked to list, on blank paper, those traits which were desired in a mate. The authors then categorized (arbitrarily, but rather convincingly) the traits into need units adapted from Murray's list. Significant differences in need patterns did *not* occur by age, marital status, or geographical region. Differences by *sex* were significant both statistically and theoretically.

> Women are more concerned than men with receiving affection, love, sympathy, and understanding from their spouse, although it should be recalled that (this) need is one of the strongest of both sexes. Secondly, males are more desirous of having a spouse who is neat and tidy about the home, and who will adjust to a routine, avoid friction, be even-tempered, home-loving, reasonable and dependable, than are females. . . . Another category with a relatively large absolute difference is (*Social stimulus value*). Men are more concerned about the impression their future wife will make upon their friends and acquaintances than are women about the impression their future husband makes upon other persons. Women also stress (*Achievement*) more than males: in the present group not a single male listed an achievement trait as desirable in his future wife, whereas 6.8 per cent of the traits listed by women were in this category. Included here are such traits as getting ahead, ambitious, enjoys working, energetic, has high status profession, etc. (Langhorne & Secord, 1955, p. 32).

It is obvious that analysis is needed to determine if such grouped traits do indeed covary. However, Langhorne and Secord's groupings do no violence to customary conceptions of the need units employed. And their results are provocative. Not only does an individual wish the spouse to conform to the appropriate sex role, but notice particularly that heavily emphasized are those attributes which implement performance of the respondent's *own* role. The wife, whose role responsibility is socioemotional, wishes a husband who will work with her in an atmosphere of loving intimacy; the "instrumental" husband wishes a wife, who through her attractiveness and efficiency, implements his responsibility for instrumental success. This does not contradict the concomitant desires, respectively, for an achieving husband and for a loving wife.

Thus, following Parsons and Farber, we might indeed expect marital satisfaction to increase as the husband's socioemotional valuation increases. But for the wife, not necessarily for the husband whose marital satisfaction might be more reliably forecast by the degree to which his mate assists the performance of the male-instrumental expectations.

The obvious extension of this emerging generalization was made a decade ago by Ort (1950). His basic hypothesis is:

> the amount of self-judgment of "happiness" or "unhappiness" in marriage depends upon, or is at least related to, the number of conflicts between role expectations and roles played by the subject, and role expectation for the subject's mate, and the roles played by the subject's mate, as the subject sees it.

Fifty married couples were verbally queried on 22 issues, for example: Should a husband kiss his wife when he leaves for work? Should a husband expect to win most arguments? Both expectations concerning these roles and the subjects perception of the performances of them in the marriage were recorded. The number of conflicts between expectation and performance (for self and for mate) were totaled for each individual. Conflict totals correlated $-.83$ with subject's self-rating on a 10-point happiness scale.

Ort concludes that happiness lies in the individual playing the role he expects, and in having the spouse play the role expected of him or her, regardless of what these roles might be.

> The author interviewed certain couples who entered marriage expecting to be sexually promiscuous and with those expectations fulfilled, their self-evaluation was number one. Likewise

the author interviewed couples who had expected fidelity for
the self and the mate and were fulfilling these expectations
and they also gave themselves a happiness rating of number
one (Ort, 1950, p. 697).

As noted above, Hobart and Klausner (1959) found no relation between marital-role disagreement and marital satisfaction. In their study, 70 items of a role inventory (a mailed
questionnaire) were endorsed from one thru five, and role disagreement calculated through the sum of the 70 differences
between spouses. These authors interpret their results as refut-
ing Ort. Note however, that they did not investigate expectations *satisfied,* which is central to Ort's thinking.

Hurwitz (1959) has pursued the issue of expectation and
satisfaction with his Index of Strain. Ten role items (e.g., "I
am a companion to my wife") were ranked twice by each husband and each wife, first for the subject's performance, and
second for the expectations of the spouse's behavior. The
Index of Strain is the cube root of the sum of the cubes of the
differences between the ranks the subjects assign to each role.
Hurwitz reports the following results.

The Index of Strain is significantly higher for husbands
than for wives. That is, wives conform more to husbands'
expectations than husbands do to wives'. The husbands' and
wives' Index of Strain correlate +.20. The correlation of the
Index of Strain with the Locke-Burgess-Cottrell Marital Adjustment Scale are as follows: the husbands' Index of Strain is
−.22 with their own marital adjustment, and −.23 with the
wives' marital adjustment. Yet the wives' Index of Strain is
significantly correlated with neither their own nor their husbands' adjustment!

This is another demonstration that the husband's is the key
role in marital success. Though the relationships between expectation and satisfaction, even for husbands, are not as strong
as in Ort's study, this must be in part attributable to the difference in the sample of role items.

Certainly satisfaction now seems related to happiness, perhaps tautologically. But satisfaction of what? Ort suggests role

expectations. Katz, Glucksberg, and Krauss (1960) investigated some aspects of need satisfaction. Subjects rate the satisfaction provided by the mate on each of 11 EPPS variables. These satisfactions were also totaled for each subject. For wives, the totals were positively related to their own scores on Nurturance and Succorance; positively related to their husbands' scores on Nurturance and Achievement; and negatively to husbands' scores on Abasement and Autonomy. The totals for husbands were positively related to wives' scores on Succorance and Nurturance, and negatively to wives' Autonomy and Dominance. If any generalization can be drawn from these complex results, it would seem that individuals' needs are best satisfied within the marriage when both husband and wife operate with something like conventionally-expected sex roles, modified by need constellations allowing companionate marriage structure.

One additional study, done early but infrequently cited, has attempted to assess need satisfaction's effect—in this case, on mate selection (Strauss, 1947). Three-hundred seventy-three engaged or recently married subjects checked items on a questionnaire, if these items described one of their major needs. Later, they were asked if the mate, or other persons, satisfied these needs.

> Only 8.0% of the population appraised some other person as having satisfied their needs better than had the actual mate. As high a percentage as 89.2 appraised no other person of opposite sex as having filled major needs better than had the mate (Strauss, 1947, p. 333).

The distribution of needs satisfied appears to be highly skewed positively. This study deserves replication with adequate controls and an assessment technique which is less crude. But Strauss' study possesses the virtue of investigating needs appropriate to within-marriage considerations; for example, a need for "someone who shows me a lot of affection"; "who helps me in making important decisions"; "for someone who loves me."

The crucial issue now facing marriage-role researchers seems to be the identification of the crucial *dimensions* of marriage-role expectations and performances. These dimensions must be established through the observed covariation of discrete action units. The author is currently engaged in such an enterprise.

Summary and Conclusion

Let us now draw together summary generalizations from our study of existing research and theoretical materials.

Mates are selected from a field of eligibles. This field is determined by homogamy as to race, ethnic origin, social class, age, religion, and by residential propinquity. Exploration of this field is a function of unknown psychological variables. Cultural homogamys provide for a measure of similarity between mates with respect to social, value, and personality characteristics. Mate-selection (courtship) roles manifest patterns of needs and expectations which differ in content and organization from marriage roles. The greater the congruence between the two roles, the greater the likelihood of marital satisfaction. Modal role definitions exist, and are sex-differentiated. They are provided for by parental identifications. The husband role is the more instrumental, the wife role the more expressive-integrative. The wife being therefore more accommodating, the husband more rigid in role needs, the likelihood of marital success is a function of the husband's possession of the expected intrumental needs and capacities. Many individuals and marriages are not organized along these modal principles. The more general statement, therefore, is that marital satisfaction is a function of the satisfaction of needs and/or expectations specific to husband and wife roles.

The author recognizes that these are largely unverified hypotheses. They are, however, reasonably interrelated and made worthy of research effort by an existing body of data. This approach, however, has a serious limitation: it is largely restricted, by empirical data now available, to considerations of assortative mating and happiness in mating. Surely we must enlarge our view, in order, for example, to investigate developmental processes in marriage with Foote (1956), and psychological change processes with Uhr (1957).

Other reviewers might well abstract generalizations quite different from those presented here. Any analyst's eyes are focused by his own convictions, and the author's own might be made explicit here: role theory provides the best available framework for investigation of psychological phenomena in marriage; and, psychologists may well apply their skills to these issues—issues of pressing practical, ameliorative, and basic theoretical concern.

References

BLOOD, R. O., JR., & HAMBLIN, R. L. The effect of the wife's employment on the family power structure. *Soc. Forces,* 1958, **36,** 347–352.

BOWERMAN, C. E., & DAY, BARBARA R. A test of the theory of complementary needs as applied to couples during courtship. *Amer. sociol. Rev.,* 1956, **21,** 602–605.

BOWMAN, C. C. Uncomplementary remarks on complementary needs. *Amer. sociol. Rev.,* 1955, **20,** 466.

BUERKLE, J. V., ANDERSON, T. R., & BADGLEY, R. F. Altruism, race conflict, and marital adjustment: A factor analysis of marital interaction. *Marriage fam. Liv.,* 1961, **23,** 20–26.

BURCHINAL, L. G., HAWKES, G. R., & GARDNER, B. Personality characteristics and marital satisfaction. *Soc. Forces,* 1957, **35,** 218–222.

BURGESS, E. W., & COTTRELL, L. *Promoting success or failure in marriage.* New York: Prentice-Hall, 1939.

BURGESS, E. W., & WALLIN, P. *Engagement and marriage.* New York: Lippincott, 1953.

COMMINS, W. D. Marriage age of oldest sons. *J. soc. Psychol.,* 1932, **3**, 487–490.

CORSINI, R. J. Multiple predictors of marital happiness. *Marriage fam. Liv.,* 1956, **18**, 240–242.(a)

CORSINI, R. J. Understanding and similarity in marriage. *J. abnorm, soc. Psychol.,* 1956, **52**, 327–332.(b)

COUCH, C. J. The use of the concept "role" and its derivatives in a study of marriage. *Marriage fam. Liv.,* 1958, **20**, 353–357.

DREIKURS, R. The choice of a mate. *Int. J. indiv. Psychol.,* 1930, **1**, 103.

DYMOND, ROSALIND. Interpersonal perception and marital happiness. *Canad. J. Psychol.,* 1954, **8**, 164–171.

FARBER, B. An index of marital integration. *Sociometry,* 1957, **20**, 117–133.

FARBER, B., & BLACKMAN, L. S. Marital role tensions and number and sex of children. *Amer. sociol. Rev.,* 1956, **21**, 596–601.

FLUEGEL, J. C. *Psychoanalytic study of the family.* London: Hogarth, 1926.

FOOTE, N. Matching of husband and wife in phases of development. In, *Transactions of the third world congress of sociology.* Vol. 4. London: International Sociological Association, 1956. Pp. 24–34.

FREUD, S. Three essays on sexuality. *Complete psychological works.* Vol. 7. London: Hogarth, 1953.

HAMILTON, G. V., & MC GOWAN, C. *What is wrong with marriage?* New York: Albert & Charles Boni, 1930.

HEER, D. M. Dominance and the working wife. *Soc. Forces,* 1958, **36**, 341–347.

HEWITT, L. E. Student perceptions of traits desired in themselves as dating and marriage partners. *Marriage fam. Liv.,* 1958, **20**, 344–349.

HILL, R. Campus values in mate selection. *J. home Econ.,* 1945, **37**, 554–558.

HOBART, C. W. Some effects of romanticism during courtship on marriage role opinions. *Sociol. soc. Res.,* 1958, **42**, 336–343.

HOBART, C. W., & KLAUSNER, W. J. Some social interactional correlates of marital role disagreement, and marital adjustment. *Marriage fam. Liv.,* 1959, 21, 256–263.

HOLLINGSHEAD, A. B. Cultural factors in the selection of marriage mates. *Amer. sociol. Rev.,* 1950, 15, 619–627.

HURWITZ, N. The index of strain as a measure of marital satisfaction. *Sociol. soc. Res.,* 1959, 44, 106–111.

JACOBSEN, A. H. Conflict of attitudes toward the roles of husband and wife in marriage. *Amer. sociol. Rev.,* 1952, 17, 146–150.

KAGAN, J. The concept of identification. *Psychol. Rev.,* 1958, 65, 296–305.

KARGMAN, MARIE W. The clinical use of social system theory in marriage counseling. *Marriage fam. Liv.,* 1957, 19, 263–269.

KATZ, A. M., & HILL, R. Residential propinquity and marital selection: A review of theory, method, and fact. *Marriage fam. Liv.,* 1958, 20, 27–335.

KATZ, I., GLUCKSBERG, S., & KRAUSS, R. Need satisfaction and Edwards PPS scores in married couples. *J. consult. Psychol.,* 1960, 24, 203–208.

KELLY, E. L. Psychological factors in assortative mating. *Psychol. Bull.,* 1940, 37, 576.

KELLY, E. L. Marital compatibility as related to personality traits of husbands and wives as rated by self and spouse. *J. soc. Psychol.,* 1941, 13, 193–198.

KEPHART, W. M. Some knowns and unknowns in family research. A sociological critique. *Marriage fam. Liv.,* 1957, 19, 7–15.

KERNODLE, W. Some implications of the homogamy-complementary needs theories of mate selection for sociological research. *Soc. Forces,* 1959, 38, 145–152.

KIRKPATRICK, C. A statistical investigation of psychoanalytic theory of mate selection. *J. abnorm. soc. Psychol.* 1937, 32, 427–430.

KTSANES, T. Mate selection on the basis of personality type: A study utilizing an empirical typology of personality. *Amer. sociol. Rev.,* 1955, 20, 547–551.

KTSANES, T., & KTSANES, VIRGINIA. The theory of complementary needs in mate-selection. In R. F. Winch (Ed.), *Selected studies in marriage and the family*. New York: Holt, 1953. Pp. 435–453.

LANGHORNE, M. C., & SECORD, P. F. Variations in marital needs with age, sex, marital status, and regional location. *J. soc. Psychol.*, 1955, 41, 19–37.

LOCKE, H. J., & WALLACE, K. M. Short marital-adjustment and prediction tests: Their reliability and validity. *Marriage fam. Liv.*, 1959, 21, 251–255.

LU, Y.-C. Marital roles and marital adjustment. *Sociol. soc. Res.*, 1952, 36, 364–368.(a)

LU, Y.-C. Parent-child relations and marital roles. *Amer. sociol. Rev.*, 1952, 17, 357–361. (b)

LU, Y.-C. Parental role and parent-child relationships. *Marriage fam. Liv.*, 1952, 14, 294–297. (c)

LU, Y.-C. Predicting roles in marriage. *Amer. J. Sociol.*, 1952, 58, 51–55. (d)

LUCKEY, ELEANOR B. An investigation of the concepts of the self, mate, parents, and ideal in relation to degree of marital satisfaction. *Dissert. Abstr.*, 1959, 20, 396–397.

LUCKEY, ELEANOR B. Marital satisfaction and congruent self-spouse concepts. *Soc. Forces*, 1960, 39, 153–157. (a)

LUCKEY, ELEANOR B. Marital satisfaction and parent concepts. *J. consult. Psychol.*, 1960, 24, 195–204. (b)

MCGINNES, R. Campus values in mate-selection: A repeat study. *Soc. Forces*, 1958, 36, 368–373.

MANGUS, A. Relation between the young woman's conceptions of her intimate male associates and of her ideal husband. *J. soc. Psychol.*, 1936, 7, 403–420.

MANGUS, A. Role theory and marriage counseling. *Soc. Forces*, 1957, 35, 200–209.

MEYER, CAROL T. Complementarity and marital conflict. *Dissert. Abstr.*, 1957, 17, 2082.

MOTZ, ANNABELLE B. The role conception inventory: A tool of research in social psychology. *Amer. sociol. Rev.*, 1952, 17, 465–471.

MOWRER, E. R., & MOWRER, HARRIET. The social psychology of marriage. *Amer. sociol. Rev.*, 1951, 16, 27–36.

ORT, R. S. A study of role-conflicts as related to happiness in marriage. *J. abnorm. soc. Psychol.*, 1950, 45, 691–699.

PARSONS, T. & BALES, R. F. *Family, socialization and interaction process.* Glencoe, Ill.: Free Press, 1955.

PAYNE, D. E., & MUSSEN, P. H. Parent-child relations and father identification among adolescent boys. *J. abnorm. soc. Psychol.*, 1956, 52, 385–363.

PRESTON, M. G., PELTZ, W. L., MUDD, EMILY H., & FROSCHER, HAZEL B. Impressions of personality as a function of marital conflict. *J. abnorm. soc. Psychol.*, 1952, 47, 326–336.

ROGERS, C. R., & DYMOND, ROSALIND F. *Psychotherapy and personality change.* Chicago: Univer. Chicago Press, 1954.

ROOS, D. E. Complementary needs in mate selection: A study based on R-type factor analysis. *Dissert. Abstr.*, 1957, 17, 426.

ROSOW, I. Issues in the concept of need-complementarity. *Sociometry*, 1957, 20, 216–233.

SARBIN, T. R. Role theory. In G. Lindsay (Ed.), *Handbook of social psychology.* Vol. 1. Cambridge: Addison-Wesley, 1954. Pp. 223–255.

SCHELLENBERG, J. A., & BEE, L. S. A re-examination of the theory of complementary needs in mate-selection. *Marriage fam. Liv.*, 1960, 22, 227–232.

SEARS, R. *Survey of objective studies of psychoanalytic concepts.* New York: Social Science Research Council, 1942.

STRAUSS, A. The ideal and the chosen mate. *Amer. J. Sociol.*, 1946, 52, 204–208.(a)

STRAUSS, A. The influence of parent-images upon marital choice. *Amer. sociol. Rev.*, 1946, 11, 554–559. (b)

STRAUSS, A. Personality needs and marital choice. *Soc. Forces,* 1947, 25, 332–339.

STRODTBECK, F. L. A review of mate-selection: A study of complementary needs. *Amer. sociol. Rev.,* 1959, 24, 437–438.

TERMAN, L. M. *Psychological factors in marital happiness.* New York: McGraw-Hill, 1938.

TERMAN, L. M., & BUTTERWISER, P. Personality factors in marital compatibility. I. *J. soc. Psychol.,* 1935, 6, 143–171.

TERMAN, L. M., & BUTTERWISER, P. Personality factors in marital compatibility. II. *J. soc. Psychol.,* 1935, 6, 267–289.

TERMAN, L. M., & ODEN, M. H. *The gifted child grows up.* Stanford: Stanford Univer. Press, 1947.

UHR, L. M. Personality changes during marriages. Unpublished doctoral dissertation, University of Michigan, 1957.

WINCH, MARTHA. Some implications in marital counseling. In R. F. Winch (Ed.), *Mate selection.* New York: Harper, 1958. Pp. 310–329.

WINCH, R. F. *The modern family.* New York: Holt, 1952.

WINCH, R. F. The theory of complementary needs in mate-selection: Final results on the test of general hypotheses. *Amer. sociol. Rev.,* 1955, 20, 552–555. (a)

WINCH, R. F. The theory of complementary needs in mate selection: A test of one kind of complementariness. *Amer. sociol. Rev.,* 1955, 20, 52–56. (b)

WINCH, R. F. Comment on "A test of the theory of complementary needs as applied to couples during courtship" by Bowerman and Day. *Amer. sociol. Rev.,* 1957, 22, 336.

WINCH, R. F. *Mate-selection: A study of complementary needs.* New York: Harper, 1958.

WINCH, R. F., KTSANES, T., & KTSANES, VIRGINIA. The theory of complementary needs in mate-selection: An analytic and descriptive study. *Amer. sociol. Rev.,* 1954, 19, 241–249.

WINCH, R. F., KTSANES, T., & KTSANES, VIRGINIA. Empirical elaboration of the theory of complementary needs in mate-selection. *J. abnorm. soc. Psychol.,* 1955, 51, 509–513.

WINCH, R. F. & MORE, D. M. Does the TAT add information to interviews?: Statistical analysis of the increment. *J. clin. Psychol.,* 1956, **12**, 316–321. (a)

WINCH, R. F., & MORE, D. M. Quantitative analysis of qualitative data in the assessment of motivation: Reliability, congruence, and validity. *Amer. J. Sociol.,* 1956, **61**, 445–452. (b)

III

The Marriage Relationship: Clinical Views

Perhaps the richest tradition of thought that comes to bear on marriage is in the writings of psychotherapists. The clinical writers are heterogeneous with respect to conceptual schemes and points of emphasis; they divide themselves into various sub-schools and schools of thought. In this section, three modern clinical viewpoints are represented. Albert Ellis and Eric Berne are both highly individual thinkers; they constitute distinctive schools of thought unto themselves. The Jones selection is a sampler from a more numerous and varied group of writers; the central point of commonality among them is, perhaps, Gregory Bateson's concept of the double bind.

In all selections, but especially in the last two, the emphasis is on communication (and failures thereof)—overt and covert messages that pass between the married pair. Analysis of "psychodynamics," in the old Freudian fashion, has been de-emphasized. This appears to be the modern trend.

9

From THE FOLKLORE OF MARITAL RELATIONS—THE GREAT COITAL MYTH

ALBERT ELLIS

The fact is that almost all of what we call "sexual incompatibility" in marriage is quite unnecessary and is largely created and abetted by our Great Coital Myth.

Considering the hullabaloo that is made about courtship and premarital sex relations in our public prints and productions, references are surprisingly rare to the particular form of human behavior to which courtship is supposed to lead, that is, marital copulation. References to sex organs and to coitus can occasionally be found in the mass media of our culture, almost invariably in some euphemistic form. But in the hundreds of stories that are told and enacted each week in our popular magazines, over our radio airways, and on our movie and television screens, it is almost unheard of to find any allusion to what married couples do in bed.

From other sources, however, it is not too difficult to discover (a) what, according to our folklore and sexual tabus, husbands

SOURCE: Albert Ellis, *The American Sexual Tragedy* (New York: Lyle Stuart, Inc., 1962), pp. 75–82, 85–96. Reprinted by permission of the author and publisher.

and wives are *supposed* to do in the privacy of the marriage bed; and (b) what they *actually* do. What spouses should—or should not—do after they put out the television set and the cat, may, perhaps, best be gleaned from a perusal of our statute books. Almost every state in the Union, we learn, has a law against what is called sodomy or unnatural sex acts. Robert Veit Sherwin, in his book on *Sex and the Statutory Law*, tells us that a typical sodomy statute reads as follows: "Every person who shall carnally know, or shall have sexual intercourse in any manner with any animal or bird, or shall carnally know any male or female by the anus (rectum) or with the mouth or tongue; or who shall attempt intercourse with a dead body . . . is guilty of Sodomy."[1]

A few states which do not specifically legislate against sodomy, or define it as does the above statute, have other laws against unnatural sex acts. Thus, New Hampshire has a "Lascivious Acts" law which declares in effect that "whoever commits any unnatural and lascivious act with another person, is subject to a maximum term of five years, or a maximum fine of one thousand dollars or both." Vermont has a statute entitled "An Act Relating to Sexual Perverts," which states in effect "that any person participating in the act of copulating the mouth of one person with the sexual organ of another is subject to a maximum penalty of five years imprisonment."[2]

"In Georgia," Sherwin notes, "there is perhaps the most interesting distinction of all in the way of two separate statutes. The Sodomy Statute declares that sodomy is the carnal knowledge and connection against the order of nature by man with man, or, in the same unnatural manner with women. And the penalty given for said act is life at hard labor. And the cases that have followed and interpreted the statute declare further that connections *per os* and *per anum* are included in the statute's coverage. Then there is a statute entitled 'Bestiality' and it defines it as the carnal knowledge and connection againt the order of nature by a man or woman in any manner with a beast, and the penalty is five to twenty years."[3]

Harriet F. Pilpel and Theodora Zavin, in their recent book,

Your Marriage and the Law,[4] summarize our legal attitudes toward marital copulation in this way: "If there is any one policy behind our laws governing sexual conduct, it seems to be that they are directed to channelling all sex relations into so-called normal intercourse in marriage. In this sense, 'normal' intercourse . . . must be the type of sexual contact that can lead to the procreation of children . . ."

Typical penalties for violating a sodomy law or for engaging in what is termed unnatural sex practices even with one's own husband or wife, Sherwin tells us, range from one to ten years imprisonment and/or a one thousand dollar fine. Some of the harsher jail penalties may be found in Arkansas (5–21 years), Connecticut (30 years), Florida (20 years), Georgia (life at hard labor), Massachusetts (20 years), Minnesota (20 years), Nebraska (20 years), Ohio (1–20 years), Rhode Island (7–20 years), and Utah (3–20 years).

In addition, Sherwin, Pilpel and Zavin, and Judge Morris Ploscowe[5] inform us, "unnatural" sex acts are often heavily penalized in civil court cases, in that divorce and annulments are frequently granted where one spouse claims that the other cruelly mistreated him or her by insisting upon participation in oral-genital, anal, or other so-called unnatural marital acts.

In the light of these heavily censorious and legally penalizing attitudes toward certain sex practices in marriage, we might suppose that Americans would rarely engage in these acts. All the facts that have ever been gathered in this connection, however, prove the contrary. G. V. Hamilton (in *A Research in Marriage*[6]) some twenty-five years ago found that almost fifty per cent of the hundred husbands he interviewed admitted practicing fellatio, cunnilinctus, or other sex relations that are termed unnatural with their wives. Kinsey, Pomeroy, and Martin (in *Sexual Behavior in the Human Male*[7]) report that "mouth-genital contacts of some sort, with the subject as either the active or the passive member in the relationship, occur at some time in the histories of nearly sixty per cent of all males."

Since even the most liberal Americans are loathe to admit these sex practices, the figures of Hamilton and Kinsey may be taken as minimum estimates of the actual frequency of so-called perverse relations. These minimum figures would tend to show that, on the basis of this type of sex activity alone, over half our married couples deserve severe fines and/ or jail sentences.

Although they do not literally expect to be arrested, literally millions of our married couples guiltily refrain from these acts because our laws and our folklore deem them iniquitous. I had, for example, a fifty-year-old patient who, for thirty years of married life, had been avoiding everything but what he called normal intercourse (and rigidly permitting himself that but once a week, no matter how often he and his wife desired it). When, after several sessions of psychotherapy, he began, for the first time in his life, really to enjoy his marital sex relations, he came to me in a near-panic state and said: "We're doing almost everything now, doctor. But isn't it really wrong? Aren't we getting to be *perverted?*"

"Perverted?" I replied. "Actually, you've been a pervert for thirty years before you came for psychotherapy; and now, when for the first time you're becoming fairly normal, you talk of being a pervert!"

I went on to explain the following facts to this patient. From the standpoint of scientific fact it is virtually impossible to label any sex act abnormal or perverted or deviant. In the last analysis, any human act becomes abnormal because the citizens of a given community unconsciously or consciously decide to view it as abnormal, and not because we have any indubitable, invariant standard of normality which we can apply to all peoples at all times in all places.[8] When we call a sex act abnormal because it is statistically rare (as in the case of incest), we must realize that society's views and laws concerning the act have often made it rare. When we call sex behavior abnormal because it is biologically inappropriate (such as homosexuality or oral-genital relations which cannot lead to reproduction), we must remember that our concepts of biological inappropriateness—such as the concept that reproduction is more valuable than sex satisfaction—are community-made, essentially biased viewpoints. When we label sex activity as abnormal because it seems to be injurious to mental or physical health (as in the case of sadism, necrophilia, or exhibitionism), we should acknowledge that exceptionally few sex acts are dangerous or health-destroying in themselves, but that many become self-destructive because society insists on viewing them as such and making them so. (Rape, for example, actually inflicts little or no harm on adult victims if they are raised to view it lightly; but if they are raised to look upon it as a heinous attack, they may actually be seriously harmed by it.) When we call sex acts abnormal because they are illegal or "immoral" (as in the case of public nudity or adulterous sex relations), then we patently are making them abnormal by social fiat rather than by any unassailable definition.

All told, then, only the rarest of sexual activities—such as sexual murder—would be universally agreed upon, by all peoples of the world, as being indubitably abnormal. And these rare acts, we invariably find, are committed by individuals who are psychotic. Sex acts committed by non-psychotics might be labeled (from the standpoint of their statistical frequency) peculiar, strange, or bizarre; but it is almost impossible to find any universal criterion by which they may be unequivocally labelled abnormal or perverted.

From a psychological standpoint, however, there is a fairly reasonable and accurate means of describing a sexual (or a non-sexual) act as abnormal, perverted, or deviant, and that is by using the criterion of fixation, fetishism, or exclusivity. Psychologically speaking, any act is abnormal or neurotic if an individual performs these acts because he has arbitrarily narrowed down a potentially wide field of action into a very limited act which he feels that he must perform if he is to be comfortable or satisfied.

Eating habits may be taken as an example. Theoretically, any average human being can eat and enjoy a good many different kinds of food. Suppose, however, a given person, who is in good physical health and has no special allergic reactions, insists on eating nothing but meat and potatoes; or suppose he only will eat once a day, at three in the morning, and will not touch a bit of food at any other time, even if he is starving; or suppose he will only eat off a particular set of blue plates, and will absolutely refuse to eat if these are not available. In any of these instances, even though we would be hardly justified in calling this individual wrong or immoral, we may justifiably call him, from a psychological standpoint, abnormal, fetichistic, neurotic, or deviant.

Similarly, with human sexuality. Although as great a psychologist as Sigmund Freud made a serious mistake by trying to distinguish between "neurotic" behavior and sexually deviated or "perverted" behavior, it has become clear in recent years that the two are actually the same, and that sexual deviants are actually emotionally disturbed, or "neurotic," individuals who are fetichistically attached to some particular type of sex activity—and who usually, though not always, became fetichistically attached to this form of behavior because of peculiarities or fixations which arose during their childhood. Sexual neuroses are essentially the same as other forms of neurosis—except that, in our antisexual society, we emotionalize them and tend to view them in a special light.

The pychological criterion of sexual "abnormality," therefore, becomes that of fetishism or exclusivity. A brief consideration of homosexual behavior may illustrate most clearly. As I have elsewhere pointed out,[9] there is nothing "abnormal" or "deviant" about homosexual activity in itself—since the human animal is biologically plurisexed, and will (if not arbitrarily hemmed in by his culture) engage spontaneously in monosexual (masturbatory), heterosexual, and homosexual acts at different times during his life. Normally, in a sexually restrictive culture like our own, he learns to give up most monosexual and homosexual activity, and to confine himself, especially after marriage, to heterosexual behavior. But the point is that he does so because he *learns* to be heterosexual, not because he is created so by nature. Even in our own culture, which is violently opposed to homosexuality, Kinsey and his associates[10] have reported that some 37 per cent of all males exhibit homosexual behavior at some time during their lives; and the probability is that the vast majority of all males at some time desire to participate in homosexual activity, but many refrain from doing so out of guilt and fear.

If, then, a male in our culture engages in some homosexual behavior, alongside of his more socially acceptable heterosexual activities, we are hardly justified in calling him abnormal from almost any standpoint—since biologically, statistically, and psychologically he is behaving in a normal fashion. But suppose this male becomes *mainly* or *exclusively* homosexual. Then, from a psychological standpoint, there is little doubt that he is fixated, neurotic, or abnormal. For unless we believe that homosexuality is innate or inborn in some individuals— which virtually no psychologist who has kept up with the recent literature now believes—it is clear that an exclusive homosexual is neurotically afraid of heterosexuality, or is fearfully fixated on a homosexual level of behavior, or is obsessed with the idea of homosexuality, or is compulsively attached to homosexual activity, or is otherwise neurotically (or perhaps psychotically) attached to his exclusive homosexual activity. If he merely prefers homosexual to heterosexual relations (as a man may prefer blondes to brunettes), that is one thing; but if he simply cannot, under any circumstances, engage in any kind of heterosexual behavior, then he is unquestionably emotionally disturbed, and hence "abnormal" or "deviant."

Most educated individuals have little difficulty in seeing that exclusive homosexuals in our culture are psychologically disturbed or deviant, but they are loath to admit that heterosexuality, too, can also be neurotic. The fact is, however, that what is scientific sauce for the goose should also be sauce for the gander, and that exclusive heterosexuality can be just as fetichistic as exclusive homosexuality. This does not mean that all individuals in our culture who are exclusively heterosexual are neurotic—though it might be maintained, with some justification, that such individuals are afflicted with a social rather than an individual neurosis, in that their social upbringing arbitrarily induces them to abhor one perfectly natural mode

of sex activity. Assuming, though, that exclusive heterosexuals
are not necessarily neurotic, the fact remains that *some* of them
are—namely, those heterosexuals who are distinctly *afraid* of
homosexuality, who are compulsively heterosexual, and who
under no circumstances (even, say, if marooned on a desert
island with only other males for a long period of time) could
permit themselves to engage in homosexual activity.

Similarly, for other sex activities. If a human being, from
time to time, enjoys unusual sex participations, such as being
beaten while he is having sex relations, or copulation with
animals, or having intercourse with members of the other sex
who are dressed in some special way, we may justifiably call
him odd, or peculiar, or statistically unusual. But we may not,
from a psychological (or biological) standpoint, justifiably call
him abnormal, perverted, or deviant. If, however, this same
man *mainly* or *only* enjoys sex relations of some special sort,
then we may, psychologically speaking, call him fixated, neurotic, or abnormal. By the same token, if a man can *only* enjoy
one special mode of statistically prevalent sex relations, such
as having intercourse in one single face-to-face position, or
having it only when the moon is out and an orchestra is playing sweet music in the background; then we can justifiably call
him neurotic or abnormal—since it is clear that out of many
possible forms of pleasurable sex relations, he has arbitrarily
and fetichistically selected a single one, and ruled out all
others.

It may be asked whether, if certain sex acts, such as bestiality
or necrophilia, are not to be considered as being perverted as
long as they are not an individual's main or exclusive form of
sexual response, they are nonetheless to be considered undesirable. The answer, in regard to some of these acts, is obviously
yes. There is nothing, for example, necessarily neurotic or perverted about an individual's robbing a bank or picking a fist-
fight with his fellow citizens—at least, in some instances. Yet,
we would not ordinarily encourage such acts. Similarly, my
own prejudices lead me to believe that such acts as rape and

sexual assault should definitely be discouraged, although I should rarely consider a rapist as a pervert. Several kinds of sex behavior may well be considered dangerous or antisocial, and consequently banned by a given society. But these types of activity should not be confused with neurotic or perverted sex acts—which, I insist, should scientifically be conceived of as sex relations which have been fetichistically and arbitrarily singled out by an individual for his main or exclusive practice.

My patient, then, who had been for many years fearfully avoiding all kinds of sex relations except what he thought was the normal, face-to-face, position in intercourse, and who in addition had been restricting himself to copulate but once a week throughout his married life, was psychologically neurotic or abnormal; and he only began to become unneurotic and non-deviant when he began to extend the range and frequency of his sex acts. When I told him that he had actually been abnormal or perverted for many years he was, as I had intended him to be, quite shocked. Since then, he has come to see that I was right: that he is now, for the first time in his married life, becoming psychologically normal or non-perverted.

To return to the conflict between our sex statutes concerning what they interpret as unnatural sex practices and our actual participation in such practices: the situation becomes even more ridiculous when we note that many modern sex manuals are specifically recommending the very acts that they call unnatural and that are still criminally punishable in virtually all our states. Thus, the very latest edition of Hannah and Abraham Stone's authoritative and widely sold book, *A Marriage Manual*,[11] states: "I do not think that we can consider any particular method of sexual union as normal or abnormal. . . . Variety in the sexual approach is much to be desired for marital sexual satisfaction . . . There is nothing perverse or degrading, I would say, in any sex practice which is undertaken for the purpose of promoting a more harmonious sexual adjustment between a husband and wife in marriage." Presumably, for recommendations like this, the Stones and many other writers of modern sex manuals should be arrested and jailed for inciting to the commission of a felony in most of the states of the Union!

.   .   .   .   .

Another great American myth, which goes hand in hand with that of the vaginal orgasm, is that, in spite of the fact that they truly love each other, many couples are naturally sexually incompatible, and that therefore they cannot get along in marriage. Actually, if these couples thought about it instead of *just* believing this myth, it would be most difficult, and in some ways almost impossible, for them to be sexually incompatible.

Sexual incompatibility exists, usually, when a husband desires a greater frequency or a different mode of sex relations than does his wife, or when a wife desires sex relations more often or differently than does her husband. Perhaps ninety-five per cent of all such incompatibility exists because, in our culture, we make a fetich of one particular form of sex play—namely, penile-vaginal coitus—and neglect most other sex activities.

Consider, by way of illustration, the case of Mr. Jennings, as presented by his wife. "My husband," she said to me when she came to ask about getting a divorce, "is simply—well, impossible. It's not that I'm sexually cold myself; in fact, I believe that I'm perfectly normal. But he just seems to be insatiable. He *always* seems to want intercourse." ("Jennings" is a pseudonym, of course.)

"How many times a week do you actually have sex relations?" I asked.

"Oh, about two or three times a week. That's quite enough for me: plenty, in fact. But he could have it, apparently, every night—maybe two or three times a night. And I, of course, I could never do *that*."

I was sceptical: not that she couldn't, or at least shouldn't, have *coitus* with her husband two or three times a night, when she was satisfied with two or three times a week, but that she couldn't, and quite easily, have *sex relations* with him quite as often as he wanted. I explained to her, as I have to do to so many of my patients, that coitus and sex relations are by no means synonymous, and that the former is only one of the many possible ways of engaging in the latter. I showed her how, quite easily, she could have non-coital sex relations with her husband, especially employing manual manipulation, several times a night, if that is what he desired.

At first, she presented the usual objections: "But is that *right,* doctor? Isn't that just like—well, *masturbation?*"

In the first place, I replied, it is not like masturbation, in that *two* partners are being involved. But even more important, I added, masturbation, whether solitary or mutual, is a perfectly natural mode of sex activity, and is not to be sneered at or moralized about by any intelligent person. Both the normal male and female animal are (whether we like it or not) designed so that they require *some* form of phallic (clitoral or penile) friction in order to achieve satisfactory orgasm. *What* form this friction takes is essentially irrelevant; and derogatorily to designate one mode of friction as mutual masturbation while, at the same time, approvingly to designate another mode as natural or normal intercourse is ridiculous.

I continued, in this wise, to tell Mrs. Jennings (perhaps fifteen years belatedly) the facts of married love; and, fortunately, she listened attentively and was willing to learn. The upshot was that she stopped considering herself a martyr to her husband's "inordinate" sex demands, and began to satisfy him, in one way or another, every time he desired to have sex relations. He too, at first, was inclined to be somewhat disturbed about having non-coital sex relations, up to and including orgasm, with his wife; but a single session with me calmed his qualms, and gave him a new, realistic outlook on marital sex activities. In the end—as I had predicted to Mrs. Jennings might well be the case—it turned out that five or six climaxes a week, and not two or three a day, were quite sufficient for Mr. Jennings. It was just that, having fewer than the number of orgasms he normally required, he and his wife both imagined that he was almost insatiable—just as a man who

consumes fifteen hundred calories of food a day, instead of his
needed twenty-five hundred, will be hungry virtually all the
time, and will get the illusion that he could regularly consume
thirty-five hundred calories daily. It also turned out—as I had
also predicted it might—that in the course of satisfying her
husband non-coitally when she did not feel like having intercourse with him, Mrs. Jennings not infrequently became sexually aroused herself and came to desire more orgasms than she
ordinarily thought herself capable of desiring. All together,
the Jennings now have a marriage that is quite sexually, as
well as otherwise, compatible.

On the other side of the fence, consider the case of Mrs.
Robin. . . . She came to me with this problem.[12] "It's not that
I don't get aroused when my husband makes passes at me. I
always do. But then, when we have intercourse, nothing happens, and I'm just as aroused at the end as I was in the beginning. The next day I'm all tense and can hardly do anything.
Naturally, when he wants intercourse again, I start making
excuses, saying that I'm tired, or pretending that I'm still
menstruating. He's not stupid, of course, and I'm sure he often
knows what I'm doing and feels hurt. But how can I help it?"

After further questioning had elicited the information that
Mrs. Robin began masturbating at the age of thirteen, the
interview proceeded as follows:

COUNSELOR: Do you obtain a satisfactory orgasm through masturbation?

MRS. ROBIN: Oh, yes, always.

COUNSELOR: And about how long does it take you to do so—how
many minutes of active manipulation of the clitoris?

MRS. ROBIN: Oh, about fifteen to twenty minutes.

COUNSELOR: Ever less than fifteen minutes?

MRS. ROBIN: No, I don't think so.

COUNSELOR: And when you have intercourse with your husband,
does he ever manipulate your clitoris before actual entry?

MRS. ROBIN: Yes, he usually does. He knows all about that, having
read a book on it.

COUNSELOR: And how long does he manipulate your clitoris?

MRS. ROBIN: Oh, about four or five minutes I would say.

COUNSELOR: Ever any longer than five minutes?

MRS. ROBIN: No, I don't think so. No, I'd say never more than that.

COUNSELOR: Why not?

MRS. ROBIN: Well—I—well, he just seems to think that's long enough.

COUNSELOR: And have you ever talked to him about it—ever let him know that it isn't long enough?

MRS. ROBIN: I—uh—no, no we never have talked about it. I—uh—I guess we're—uh—we're ashamed to talk about things like that.

COUNSELOR: Well, if, as you say, it never takes you yourself less than fifteen minutes of active manipulation to give yourself an orgasm— and you, you know, are a better judge of your own sensations than anyone else can possibly be—how do you expect your husband to help you achieve a climax in no more than five minutes? You should tell your husband what your sex requirements are so that he can act accordingly. You cannot expect him to be a mind-reader or to figure them out for himself.

Mrs. Robin quickly got the idea. From that very night on, her sex problem with her husband began to be worked through and now they are fully sexually compatible.

The fact is that since women, in our culture, have for many centuries been sexually subservient to men, and have not been *supposed* to enjoy sex relations, a cult of coitus has arisen whose main premises are: (1) that the only proper and manly form of sex relations is penile-vaginal copulation; (2) that whenever the husband is sexually desirous, it is his right to beg, cajole, or demand coital relations with his wife and that, to keep him happy, she must acquiesce just about as frequently as he de- sires; (3) that the wife must obtain her sex satisfaction, includ- ing orgasm, through the same type of vaginal-penile intercourse that satisfies her husband; (4) that if the wife wishes to have intercourse more than her husband, that is just too bad for her; and (5) that, all told, the perfect union is one where hus- band and wife naturally and automatically desire intercourse exactly the same number of times per week or month, and where serious discrepancies exist in their desires, sexual in- compatibility is inevitable.

This, we say, is the Great Coital Myth of past and contemporary American (and Western European) culture. Actually, the facts, as revealed by modern psychosexual research, are these:

1. Although coitus is *one* of the most satisfying of human sex experiences, it is not necessarily *the* most satisfying experience for all men and women. In psychosexual research with average males, as well as in clinical contact with disturbed ones, it is continually found that, in spite of their being instilled in our culture with prejudices against sex practices that are called unnatural, almost all males can be brought to satisfying orgasms by several different kinds of sexual activity, especially by coitus, manual manipulation of the penis, and oral-genital relations. In my clinical practice, I invariably find that those males who have the idea that they can only be satisfied through coitus are literally guilty or afraid of being satisfied in other ways; and that when their fear or guilt is removed through education or psychotherapy, they find non-coital sex relations as satisfying, or almost as satisfying, as coitus. One of the main reasons why men exaggerate the importance of coitus is because they are raised to believe that this is the only "manly" method of sex relations. When they rid themselves of this arbitrary notion, their coital fetiches usually vanish, and they become much more labile as far as the range of their sex satisfactions are concerned. Men who are released from believing in the sacredness of coitus frequently find that they derive more satisfaction from some forms of non-coital relations than they do from sexual intercourse.

2. Women, to even a greater degree than men, may often be fully satisfied by non-coital relations. Many women, in fact, find it difficult or impossible to achieve orgasm during intercourse, even when there has been considerable previous sex play, but find it easy to achieve orgasm through non-coital manipulation alone. Women who do enjoy coitus, and who sometimes or often receive orgasm in the course of it, usually do not need it for orgasmic relief, but may obtain

full climax by manual, oral, or other manipulation of the clitoris, vulva, and/or introitus (entrance to the vagina). Although, in our culture, a good many women feel that they must have intercourse for full orgasmic release, this is often actually untrue: since, when they are released (through proper sex education or psychotherapy) from the idea that they must have intercourse to have full orgasm, they usually begin to have perfectly satisfactory climaxes in non-coital relations. There are many women who certainly seem to have the most pleasurable forms of sex activity when they have intercourse; but it as yet unclear whether their needs in this connection are largely physiological or psychological. One of my patients who at first swore that no sensation could possibly equal that which she obtained through coitus, was surprised to find, when she experimented without prejudice, that her husband's manipulating the inside of her vagina with his fingers gave her the most powerful orgasm she had ever experienced; and several of my patients who also swore by coitus at first were later willing to admit that, when they let themselves go sexually and surrendered their prejudices against non-coital relations, their husbands' manual or oral manipulation of their clitorises gave them a more intense and satisfying sensation than coitus ever had.

3. Although there is nothing to be lost, and often much to be gained, by a husband and wife's trying to adjust themselves sexually so that they each achieve an orgasm during intercourse, and often achieve it simultaneously, there is danger in their convincing themselves that mutual orgasm in intercourse is the only or even necessarily the best mode of sex satisfaction on all occasions. Orgasm is orgasm, however and whenever achieved, and may be thoroughly enjoyable on a non-simultaneous basis. A husband may legitimately give his wife an orgasm before or after he has one himself— or without ever having one himself. Similarly, a wife may help her husband to achieve a climax before, during, or entirely apart from her own climax(es). In many marriages,

the achievement of simultaneous orgasm in intercourse will seldom or never occur; and still the spouses may have a truly satisfying and perfectly compatible sex life.

4. There are some reasons to believe that many females, when fully released from sexual inhibitions and tabus, are biologically more sexually adequate than the average male. Sexually released women, very often, may have climaxes that are more frequent, more intense, and more lasting than those had by equally released men. Consequently, no man should in any way feel ashamed of the fact that he cannot fully satisfy his mate solely by means of penile-vaginal intercourse. It may well be only the rare male who thus can satisfy a sexually released, reasonably highly-sexed female. In the event that a given husband cannot satisfy his wife by means of coitus, he can, and certainly should, satisfy her by some other means. Similarly, if a wife cannot satisfy her husband by means of coitus, or if for some reason she does not frequently enjoy coitus, she should satisfy him in some non-coital manner.

5. Considerable more realism about marital sex relations is desirable in modern marriage. Although husbands and wives should normally not engage in coitus when both do not desire it, there is no reason whatever why they should not sexually satisfy each other in one or more non-coital ways when they do not themselves desire to be satisfied. Every wife who loves her husband does numerous things she does not enjoy doing in order to help him and keep their marriage a going partnership: for example, cooking, washing dishes, shopping, and housecleaning. To add to these chores another ten or fifteen minutes of manipulating her husband's genitals, even when she is not sexually aroused herself, is certainly more important to his, and therefore to her own, happiness than many of the other non-pleasant jobs she performs. Moreover, if she does overcome her inertia and attempts to satisfy her husband sexually whenever he wants to be satisfied, the chances are, that in the

process, she herself will often become sexually aroused, and will find considerably more pleasure in sex acts than she would otherwise find.

By the same token, although it is true that most men lose their sexual desire to satisfy their wives after they themselves have had a climax, and although it is true that it is not easy for all males to hold off their climaxes until their wives are ready for their final orgasm, there is nothing too onerous about a man's giving his wife two or three more orgasms, if she desires them, after he has had his first and/or last for the evening. Marriage involves all kinds of not too pleasant duties and responsibilities; and unless a man sufficiently loves his wife and has enough interest in satisfying her no matter what may be the number of orgasms she requires per day or week, he has no business marrying her in the first place. The sexual responsibilities of marriage are no more troublesome than many of its other responsibilities, and it is often more important that they be maturely and realistically acknowledged and fulfilled.

6. Naturally, there are exceptions to every rule. Some males or females, for example, seem to be almost continually aroused sexually, and would want an enormous amount of sex relations from their mates. Other men and women insist that their spouses satisfy them sexually in some particular way —such as through intercourse or through oral or anal relations—which the spouse is either incapable of performing or finds highly distasteful. In such cases, where the sex demands of one spouse become a real imposition on the goodwill of the other, a psychologist or marriage counselor should be consulted to determine whether the imposed-upon or imposing mate is acting in an unreasonable or emotionally disturbed manner; and, with the help of professional assistance, some adjustment usually may be made. If it cannot be, then divorce or separation may be necessary, or one of the partners (or both) may have to compromise seriously with his or her sexual needs in order for the marriage to

continue on a peaceable basis. My own marriage counseling experience shows, however, that true sexual incompatibility is quite rare in marriage, and that most of what is called sexual incompatibility is actually the result of sex ignorance and arbitrary bias, often accompanied by lack of love and by emotional disturbance.[13]

7. There are various techniques of prolonging coitus, such as those outlined in Edwin Hirsch's *The Power to Love* and *Modern Sex Life*[14] and in G. Lombard Kelly's *Sexual Feeling in Married Men and Women*.[15] There are also various emotional and physiological reasons why some males suffer from premature ejaculation, and many cases of this type of sex disturbance may be cured or alleviated by proper psychological or medical treatment. The average male in our culture, however, as Kinsey and his associates have shown in *Sexual Behavior in the Human Male*,[16] takes less than five minutes of active copulation to reach a climax; and many women simply cannot be brought to their climaxes in less than ten minutes of coitus, while many other women apparently can never, or at best can rarely, reach a climax solely through coitus. The obvious solution, therefore, to the problem of the relatively short-timed climax of many men and the relatively long-timed climax of many women is to have some of the husbands of the long-timed women resort to extra-coital methods of bringing their wives to orgasm. In the case of those women (who are probably relatively few) who require actual intromission for sexual satisfaction, husbands who are not sufficiently potent to meet this requirement by means of penile-vaginal intercourse may still effectively do so in many instances by using their fingers to massage the inside of the wife's vagina (while, preferably, using the fingers of the other hand to massage the clitoris). The chances are that those women who cannot, under any circumstances, be satisfied with manipulation of the clitoris, vulva, and/or vagina, but who specifically require penile-vaginal coitus, are fetichistically attached to the idea of

coitus, and should undergo some form of pychotherapy or counseling in order to release themselves from their fetichistic attachments. Similarly, any men who cannot be sexually satisfied with any other form of sex activity but coitus are probably fetichistically attached to this idea, and should undergo psychotherapy to help them overcome their fetich.

Because of the discrepancies existing between the Great American Coital Myth and the actual facts of human sexuality, many sexually incompatible marriages do, in fact, exist, and do give rise, every year, to literally hundreds of thousands of divorces, annulments, separations, desertions, twin beds, twin bedrooms, and widespread marital starvation in the midst of plenty. Not only are innumerable wives and husbands sexually starved because, as a result of the ignorance encouraged by this Great Coital Myth, their mates do not know how to satisfy them, but—even greater tragi-comedy!—countless other mates are sexually frustrated because, although they and their spouses know full well what the techniques of full sex satisfaction are, they stoutly refuse to employ them because they consider these techniques unnatural, immature, or unmanly.

(It may be parenthetically noted, as well, that in the area of premarital and extramarital relations, where non-coital sex relations are particularly desirable because they eliminate virtually all possibility of pregnancy or disease, numberless males and females refuse to employ these techniques, and instead insist on either coitus or abstinence: because, like their married confreres and consoeurs, they consider petting to climax to be immature, unmanly, or perverted. Among all the modern moralists who attempt to prevent young people from having premarital copulation, only one current writer—Alex Comfort in *Sexual Behavior in Society*[17]—seems to go to the logical conclusion of actually advocating premarital petting, up to and including orgasm, as an intelligent and logical substitute for coitus.)

The fact is, that almost all of what we call sexual incompatibility in marriage is quite unnecessary, and is actually created and abetted by our Great Coital Myth. Likewise, probably the great majority of the literally millions of instances where wives are "frigid" and husbands "impotent," and where spouses are distressed by their mate's or their own desires for extra-coital sex play, are directly or indirectly traceable to ideas and attitudes stemming from this Great Coital Myth. Marital sex relations, in these United States, are officially and unofficially conceived of as coital sex relations; and anything over, under, or around this limited sex technique just does not count—or counts so much as to make the spouses liable to being jailed.

It is not clear, from the anthropological literature, how unique the worship of the Great Coital Myth is to Western Civilization. Many other peoples of the world permit and encourage extra-coital sex relations. Clellan S. Ford and Frank A. Beach, for example, tell us that manual stimulation of the female genitalia by the male is commonly prevalent in several societies, including the Aranda, Aymara, Azande, Chamorro, Crow, Dahomeans, Hopi, Koryak, Ponca, Siriono, and the Trobrianders. Manual stimulation of the male genitals by women normally occurs among the Alorese, Aranda, Crow, Hopi, Siriono, Tikopia, Trobrianders, and Wogeo. Oral stimulation of the genitals is also encouraged by several peoples, particularly among the Trobriand Islanders and the Alorese, Aranda, Kusaians, Marquesans, Ponapeans, and Trukese.[18]

It is not clear from anthropological reports, however, which societies encourage extra-coital sex play (a) merely as preliminaries to coitus and/or (b) as orgasm-producing techniques in their own right. It would appear that in most instances the former type of permissiveness, and not the latter, exists; and that almost none of the peoples of this globe frankly and openly abet non-coital sex relations up to and including orgasm. The human male, in almost all past and present societies, seems to have dominated the sex scene to the extent of foisting *his* desired practices on the human female, and he seems to have done so largely by promulgating the tenets of the Great Coital

Myth. As idiotic as we Americans are in this connection, we at least appear to be typical rather than unique.

References

1. ROBERT VEIT SHERWIN, *Sex and the Statutory Law.* New York: Oceana Publications, 1949, p. 36.
2. *Ibid.,* p. 36–37.
3. *Ibid.,* p. 37.
4. HARRIET F. PILPEL and THEODORA ZAVIN, *Your Marriage and the Law.* New York: Rinehart, 1952.
5. MORRIS PLOSCOWE, *Sex and the Law.* New York: Prentice-Hall, 1951.
6. G. V. HAMILTON, *A Research in Marriage.* New York: Boni, 1929.
7. ALFRED C. KINSEY, WARDELL B. POMEROY, and CLYDE E. MARTIN, *Sexual Behavior in the Human Male.* Philadelphia: Saunders, 1948.
8. ALBERT ELLIS, "What Is Normal Sex Behavior?" *Complex,* 1952, 8, 41–51.
9. ALBERT ELLIS, "On the Cure of Homosexuality," *Internat. J. Sexology,* 1952, 5, 135–38.
10. ALFRED C. KINSEY and others, *op. cit.*
11. HANNAH STONE and ABRAHAM STONE, *A Marriage Manual.* New York: Simon & Schuster, 1952.
12. ALBERT ELLIS, "Marriage Counseling With Couples Indicating Sexual Incompatibility," *Marriage and Family Living,* 1953, 15, 53–59.
13. ALBERT ELLIS, *ibid.*
14. EDWIN HIRSCH, *The Power to Love.* New York: Knopf, 1952. Edwin Hirsch, *Modern Sex Life.* New York: Permabooks, 1949.

15. G. LOMBARD KELLY, *op. cit.*
16. ALFRED C. KINSEY and others, *op. cit.*
17. ALEX COMFORT, *Sexual Behavior in Society.* New York: Viking, 1950.
18. CLELLAN S. FORD and FRANK A. BEACH, *Patterns of Sexual Behavior.* New York: Harpers, 1951.

10

ADULTERY: PROS AND CONS

ALBERT ELLIS

We have now considered the pros and cons of premarital sex
relations and come to the conclusion that it is exceptionally
difficult to see why well-informed, bright, and reasonably well-
adjusted young people in our society may not justifiably engage
in ante-nuptial affairs.

The question now before us is: Should the same conclusion
be reached about adultery? More specifically: Granted that,
for a variety of reasons, adultery was a hazardous venture in
preceding centuries, and that the Sixth Commandment *once*
made sound sense, is the case against extramarital relations still
valid *today?*

Let us admit, at the outset, that many of the old grounds for
opposing adultery are just as senseless, in today's world, as
many similar grounds for combatting premarital sex affairs.
For example:

Intelligent and informed modern men and women do not
consider adultery intrinsically wicked and sinful and therefore
often commit it with little or no guilt or anxiety.

SOURCE: Albert Ellis, *Sex Without Guilt* (New York: Lyle Stuart, Inc.,
1958), pp. 51–65. Reprinted by permission of the author and publisher.

They are well able, with use of up-to-date contraceptive techniques, to avoid the dangers of illegitimate pregnancy and abortion; and with the employment of prophylactic measures and the selection of appropriate partners, they can easily avoid venereal infection.

They often need not worry about loss of reputation, since in many segments of modern society they are likely to gain rather than lose reputation by engaging in extramarital affairs.

They need not commit adultery under sordid conditions, or on a non-loving basis, as they frequently can arrange to have highly amative and affectional, and sometimes exceptionally rewarding, affairs.

They need not jeopardize their marriages: because, as the Kinsey research group has shown, adulterous affairs which are not known to one's mate can actually help enhance and preserve one's marriage rather than serve to sabotage or destroy it.

In view of these facts of modern life, it is most doubtful whether many of the old telling arguments against adultery still hold too much water. At the same time, several of the indubitable advantages of premarital sex relations, which we examined in the previous chapter, also hold true for adultery.

Thus, it may be said with little fear of scientific contradiction, that literally millions of men and women who engage in adulterous affairs thereby gain considerable adventure and experience, become more competent at sexual pursuits and practices, are enabled to partake of a high degree of varietism, and have substantial amounts of sexual and non-sexual fun that they otherwise would doubtlessly be denied. These, in a world that tends to be as dull and drab for the average man as our own, are no small advantages.

Should, then, the informed and intelligent husband and wife in our society blithely go about committing adultery? The answer, paradoxically enough, seems to be: In most cases, no. Why so? For several reasons:

1. Although, in some ideal society, it is quite probable that husbands and wives could be adulterous with impunity, and might well gain more than lose thereby, ours is definitely

not such an ideal society. For better or worse, we raise individuals to *feel* that their marriages are in jeopardy and that they are unloved if their mates have extramarital affairs. Whether, under these circumstances, adultery actually *does* destroy marriages or *does* prove lack of love, is beside the point. Once one is raised to *feel* that these things are true, they tend to *become* true; and, under adulterous circumstances, damage often *is* therefore done to marriage.

2. Because people in our culture *believe* adultery to be inimical to marriage, husbands and wives who engage in extramarital relations generally have to do so secretly and furtively. This means that they must be dishonest with their mates; and, although their adultery, in itself, might not harm their marriages, their *dishonesty* about this adultery (as about any other major issue) may well prove to be harmful.

3. Because, in our society, married couples are supposed to achieve sex satisfaction only with each other, if one mate is an adulterer he will often tend to have less sex interest in the other mate than he normally would have; and, in consequence, she may very well become sexually deprived and maritally discontent.

4. By the same token, since most individuals in our society are limited as to their financial resources, time, energy, etc., an adulterous mate by devoting efforts to his (or her) inamorata may well deprive his mate in these non-sexual respects.

5. If an individual has a good all-around marriage, in terms of the satisfaction of his love, sex, companionship, familial, and other needs; and if his mate might well be quite unhappy and might possibly divorce him if he were discovered to be engaging in an adulterous affair; he would then be jeopardizing his marriage for additional satisfactions which might hardly be worth the risk.

Under these circumstances, any individual who has a good or an excellent marriage, is foolish to risk the breakup of this relationship largely for the opportunity of having additional sex pleasures—which are often likely to be his main gain from adultery. On the other hand, individuals who have poor marriages take no such risks, and often might just as well be caught in adulterous affairs.

6. In general, the risks one takes in committing adultery behind one's mate's back are the same risks one takes in making any major move behind her back. Thus, if one invests the family savings in a new Cadillac, or accepts a job in Alaska, or decides to discontinue the use of contraceptives without informing one's mate, one is hardly being maritally cooperative, and risks his or her severe displeasure.

By the same token, if one is secretly adulterous, one is usually not being too cooperative with one's mate, and therefore risks her eventually discovering this fact and being highly displeased (not to mention hysterical) because of it. Quite aside, then, from the sexual aspects of adultery, which are highly emphasized and exaggerated in our particular society, the secret commission of any major act with which one's mate is concerned is bound to affect one's relationship with this mate, and usually to affect it adversely.

This, then, would seem to be the major issue here: not adultery itself and its so-called moral consequences, but the consequences of being dishonest with one's mate, and through this dishonesty risking an impedance or destruction of mutual trust, confidence, and working partnership.

In view of these facts, it is questionable whether a well-adjusted, rational individual in our society should normally commit adultery—at least, if he wants to perpetuate a presumably good marriage. If he is not himself married (but is committing adultery through having sex relations with someone who is), or if he is already unhappily married, then he may have nothing to lose by engaging in extramarital affairs.

If he is married happily enough, and he and his wife honestly and mutually believe that adultery is a good thing, and are not at all disturbed by the knowledge of each other's infidelities, then again he may have nothing to lose. But the chances of his and his mate's having such a liberal attitude toward adultery if they were both raised in our culture are exceedingly slim.

Otherwise stated: It does not appear to be very difficult for intelligent and informed men and women in our civilization to accept fully the fact that premarital sex relations are a good thing and to become entirely guilt-free in this connection. But, as yet, it does appear to be most difficult for them to accept the fact that they and their mates may be adulterous without sabotaging their marriages. Several past and present societies other than our own have condoned adultery; and it is possible that we, too, may do so sometime in the future. For the present, however, adultery, except under certain limited circumstances (such as an individual's being away from home for a long time), would appear to be impractical rather than sinful for most people.

Today's adulterer need not feel evil or wicked. But, from the standpoint of impairing his own marriage, he may well be acting irrationally and neurotically. If he thinks of adultery not in terms of sin but in terms of the possible *adulteration* of his own marital happiness, he should be able to make wiser choices in this connection.

After publishing the foregoing remarks in *The Independent*, I received a remarkable letter from a middle-aged psychologist which raises some interesting questions in relation to adultery. My psychological correspondent, whom I shall call Dr. X, states that he married a childhood sweetheart when he was 25, had a so-so marriage with her, managed to have satisfactory sex relations, and was a faithful, most respectable husband and father (of five children) for 22 years. Finally, in his late forties, he had his first extramarital affair with "a handsome and attractive woman with a divine bell-like voice."

About this affair, Dr. X writes: "For the first time I was in love, and even more, for the first time I learned what passion could be. Very early I became sure it could not last—I was scared of my own inadequacy to keep pace with my lover's passion and with her genuine acceptance of what could be called free love.

"I was still pretty fiercely monogamous, though to my surprise I found no difficulty in having sexual relations with my lover and two days later, with my wife at home. My family obligations also kept me from even considering a divorce at this time."

Dr. X insists that this relationship "did tremendous things for me" and even made his marriage better for awhile.

A year later, after the first affair had ended, he contracted a love affair with the widow of a cherished friend while he was away from home for six months. He says that "nothing in the whole affair is remembered with regret—just steady, warm satisfaction. There was sorrow but no hurt in the parting. And as before, the effect on my marriage was to make me for a time more affectionate, more undertanding of my wife, better able to put up with the difficulties of our basic incompatibility."

Dr. X then had an unsatisfactory affair with a woman much younger than he; and notes that "this relation did *not* help my marriage. Curious, isn't it? that when I find satisfaction elsewhere, my relation to my wife improves; when I fail elsewhere, it does not."

When his youngest child finished school, Dr. X received a divorce from his wife and later married a woman with whom he had for some time been having an adulterous affair. Both this woman and her former husband had been having, by mutual agreement, extramarital affairs since the first year of their marriage. As long as they felt that their own marriage was solid they did not mind each other's infidelities.

On one occasion, the second Mrs. X and her first husband swapped partners with a couple with whom they were friendly, and all four lived amicably together under the same roof for several months. Finally, however, Mrs. X's first husband permanently took up with still another woman; and Dr. X's adulterous affair with her began, and later led to their marrying.

At this time, Dr. X reports, "I was still a bit more inclined to the monogamous point of view. She insisted that a non-restricting attitude was a necessity for love, that one could not fully love while denying what might be a rewarding experience for the partner. I know that I grew in my understanding not of sex but of love, as we worked our way through this problem. I'd have given anything to have got some part of these insights before my earlier marriage.

"But I still wasn't sure. So one day, learning that my wife's first love, Carl, was passing through our city, suggested that she invite him to stop over for a visit. I deliberately courted the trial. Could I take it if she were to renew her old and sweet intimacy?

"I slept with her the night before Carl was to make an early arrival; then, before dawn, went away to give him a clear field. And I did find it in me to say to myself and deeply to feel: 'I want my darling to be happy with Carl whatever form that happiness takes.' I think I really wanted them to have sex intimacy. At any rate, I went home full of a kind of pride in myself and a joyful loving peace. That was a high point in my whole life.

"Later, I joined Carl and my beloved for breakfast, and we had a fine time till his train arrived. It would be good to be able to say that I don't know nor care whether they had been intimate. I didn't ask but was told: she felt that our relation was still too absorbing and rejected Carl's gentle inquiry. So in perfect honesty I said, 'Perhaps later you may feel otherwise. You know that if you do, I shall not be concerned.' Nor shall I."

Later, with another old lover of his wife's Dr. X's newly gained attitude was actually tested. Mrs. X comforted and slept with this old lover and told Dr. X what she had done. He notes; "I can say quite certainly that I was *glad* for her, and felt no loss of anything."

Dr. X concludes his letter with these observations: "Love is not a quantum that is lessened when divided. It is a growing system that increases with activity, like a living organism. True, it is subject, to use Gardner Murphy's term, to some degree of canalization. Constant adultering might divert love away from one person.

"In any kind of social arrangement there are grave problems regarding the management of love and sex. In our own society, adultery no doubt takes more intelligent thoughtfulness than is usually available. But I think we ought to keep in mind the *values* of multiple sex and love relations. Not just sex satisfaction alone, but love.

"That makes adultery dangerous. But it can mean great personal growth. I could not possibly love my wife as I do if it had not been for my adulterous love affairs. And she would not have been my beloved if she had not been able to open her love as she did to several men."

Dr. X's letter—the whole of which is ten pages long and has other pertinent things to say besides those quoted here—is most sincere and persuasive. In considering stories like his, and many more I have heard which are similar, I am compelled, once again, to be skeptical of all sweeping generalizations about human conduct.

Granted that a tabued and legally penalized mode of behavior, such as adultery, has its distinct disadvantages, it must also be admitted that it has real advantages.

Granted that it is silly, childish, and self-defeating under one set of circumstances, it can also be inordinately valuable and ennobling under other circumstances.

Granted that certain individuals in our anti-adulterous communities could never tolerate their own or their partners' extramarital affairs, it is clear that certain other individuals— such as Dr. and Mrs. X—can not only stoically bear, but actually find genuine satisfactions, in their own cuckoldry.

If we wish to be psychologically smug here, we may insist that people like Dr. and Mrs. X, who are originally raised with the prevalent puritanical notions of our society, cannot possibly *really* accept their own or their spouses' adulterous affairs. We may say that, unconsciously if not consciously, their liberal and permissive attitudes toward sex are underlain by more resentful and guilty attitudes, and that therefore they cannot receive *genuine* happiness from accepting or engaging in adultery.

This kind of psychological analysis, however, borders on the unscientific, since it gets you going and coming. If you say that you like white, it insists that you really, unconsciously prefer black but are afraid to admit this. And if you say that you like black, it says that you really, unconsciously prefer white. It leaves, this kind of "thinking," no room for *conscious* preferences.

Moreover, it is unconstructive and defeatist in that it denies all possibilities of basic human change. Admitting that human beings, once they have learned that white is good and black is bad, *have difficulty* in convincing themselves otherwise, this is not to say that they find changing their convictions *impossible*. If this were true, virtually no human progress would ever occur.

It is my firm conviction, therefore, that Dr. X *has,* in spite of his original puritanical upbringing, significantly changed his attitudes toward adultery, and that he *is* now able not merely resentfully to tolerate but actually to enjoy some of his wife's infidelities. And not, I would be willing to wager, because he is masochistic, repressive, or perverse—but because he is now more civilized, humane, and loving.

So much for Dr. X. The rest of us are actually the heart of the matter. Are *we* able to be happier, emotionally healthier, and more loving by being adulterous? In the main, considering what our (horrible) upbringing has been, I am afraid not. But even this is not the full answer.

The full answer, I think, is: Some of us are able to benefit from adultery and some of us are not. Had we dare, then, make an invariant rule for all?

11

From GAMES PEOPLE PLAY

E R I C   B E R N E

> Editor's Note: *A bit of preface is in order here, to*
> *acquaint the reader with a few of Dr. Berne's terms.*
> *Child, Adult and Parent denote distinctive parts or*
> *subsystems within the personality. They are roughly*
> *analogous to Freud's Id, Ego and Superego. The par-*
> *allel is least close for Child—Id.*
> *Mr. or Mrs. White is a person who initiates a game.*

Games

Definition

A game is an ongoing series of complementary ulterior transactions progressing to a well-defined, predictable outcome.
Descriptively it is a recurring set of transactions, often repeti-
tious, superficially plausible, with a concealed motivation; or,
more colloquially, a series of moves with a snare, or "gimmick."
Games are clearly differentiated from procedures, rituals, and
pastimes by two chief characteristics: (1) their ulterior quality
and (2) the payoff. Procedures may be successful, rituals ef-

SOURCE: Eric Berne, *Games People Play* (New York: Grove Press, Inc.,
1964), pp. 48, 49–51, 52–53, 54–55, 56–58, 61, 62, 123, 126–28, 129–31, 92,
95–97, 98–101, 101–8, 108–9. Reprinted by permission of Grove Press, Inc.
Copyright © by Eric Berne.

fective, and pastimes profitable, but all of them are by definition candid; they may involve contest, but not conflict, and the ending may be sensational, but it is not dramatic. Every game, on the other hand, is basically dishonest, and the outcome has a dramatic, as distinct from merely exciting, quality.

It remains to distinguish games from the one remaining type of social action which so far has not been discussed. An *operation* is a simple transaction or set of transactions undertaken for a specific, stated purpose. If someone frankly asks for reassurance and gets it, that is an operation. If someone asks for reassurance, and after it is given turns it in some way to the disadvantage of the giver, that is a game. Superficially, then, a game looks like a set of operations, but after the payoff it becomes apparent that these "operations" were really *maneuvers;* not honest requests but moves in the game.

In the "insurance game," for example, no matter what the agent appears to be doing in conversation, if he is a hard player he is really looking for or working on a prospect. What he is after, if he is worth his salt, is to "make a killing." The same applies to "the real estate game," "the pajama game" and similar occupations. Hence at a social gathering, while a salesman is engaged in pastimes, particularly variants of "Balance Sheet," his congenial participation may conceal a series of skillful maneuvers designed to elicit the kind of information he is professionally interested in. There are dozens of trade journals devoted to improving commercial maneuvers, and which give accounts of outstanding players and games (interesting operators who make unusually big deals). Transactionally speaking, these are merely variants of *Sports Illustrated, Chess World,* and other sports magazines.

As far as angular transactions are concerned—games which are consciously planned with professional precision under Adult control to yield the maximum gains—the big "con games" which flourished in the early 1900's are hard to surpass for detailed practical planning and psychological virtuosity.

What we are concerned with here, however, are the unconscious games played by innocent people engaged in duplex

transactions of which they are not fully aware, and which form
the most important aspect of social life all over the world. Because of their dynamic qualities, games are easy to distinguish
from mere static *attitudes,* which arise from taking a position.
The use of the word "game" should not be misleading. As
explained in the introduction, it does not necessarily imply
fun or even enjoyment. Many salesmen do not consider their
work fun, as Arthur Miller made clear in his play, *The Death
of a Salesman.* And there may be no lack of seriousness. Foot-
ball games nowadays are taken very seriously, but no more
so than such transactional games as "Alcoholic" or "Third-
Degree Rapo."

The same applies to the word "play," as anyone who has
"played" hard poker or "played" the stock market over a long
period can testify. The possible seriousness of games and play,
and the possibly serious results, are well known to anthropologists. The most complex game that ever existed, that of
"Courtier" as described so well by Stendhal in *The Charter-
house of Parma,* was deadly serious. The grimmest of all, of
course, is "War."

A Typical Game

The most common game played between spouses is colloquially
called "If It Weren't For You," and this will be used to illustrate the characteristics of games in general.

Mrs. White complained that her husband severely restricted
her social activities, so that she had never learned to dance.
Due to changes in her attitude brought about by psychiatric
treatment, her husband became less sure of himself and more
indulgent. Mrs. White was then free to enlarge the scope of
her activities. She signed up for dancing classes, and then discovered to her despair that she had a morbid fear of dance
floors and had to abandon this project.

This unfortunate adventure, along with similar ones, laid
bare some important aspects of the structure of her marriage.

Out of her many suitors she had picked a domineering man for a husband. She was then in a position to complain that she could do all sorts of things "if it weren't for you." Many of her women friends also had domineering husbands, and when they met for their morning coffee, they spent a good deal of time playing "If It Weren't For Him."

As it turned out, however, contrary to her complaints, her husband was performing a very real service for her by forbidding her to do something she was deeply afraid of, and by preventing her, in fact, from even becoming aware of her fears. This was one reason her Child had shrewdly chosen such a husband.

But there was more to it than that. His prohibitions and her complaints frequently led to quarrels, so that their sex life was seriously impaired. And because of his feelings of guilt, he frequently brought her gifts which might not otherwise have been forthcoming; certainly when he gave her more freedom, his gifts diminished in lavishness and frequency. She and her husband had little in common besides their household worries and the children, so that their quarrels stood out as important events; it was mainly on these occasions that they had anything but the most casual conversations. At any rate, her married life had proved one thing to her that she had always maintained: that all men were mean and tyrannical. As it turned out, this attitude was related to some daydreams of being sexually abused which had plagued her in earlier years.

. . . . .

THESIS. This is a general description of the game, including the immediate sequence of events (the social level) and information about their psychological background, evolution and significance (the psychological level). In the case of "If It Weren't For You" Marital Type, the details already given will serve. For the sake of brevity, this game will henceforth be referred to as IWFY.

ANTITHESIS. The presumption that a certain sequence constitutes a game is tentative until it has been existentially validated. This validation is carried out by a refusal to play or by undercutting the payoff. The one who is "it" will then make more intense efforts to continue the game. In the face of adamant refusal to play or a successful undercutting he will then lapse into a state called "despair," which in some respects resembles a depression, but is different in significant ways. It is more acute and contains elements of frustration and bewilderment. It may be manifested, for example, by the onset of perplexed weeping. In a successful therapeutic situation this may soon be replaced by humorous laughter, implying an Adult realization: "There I go again!" Thus despair is a concern of the Adult, while in depression it is the Child who has the executive power. Hopefulness, enthusiasm or a lively interest in one's surroundings is the opposite of depression; laughter is the opposite of despair. Hence the enjoyable quality of therapeutic game analysis. The antithesis to IWFY is permissiveness. As long as the husband is prohibitive, the game can proceed. If instead of saying "Don't you dare!" he says "Go ahead!" the underlying phobias are unmasked, and the wife can no longer turn on him, as demonstrated in Mrs. White's case.

For clear understanding of a game, the antithesis should be known and its effectiveness demonstrated in practice.

. . . . .

TRANSACTIONAL PARADIGM. The transactional analysis of a typical situation is presented, giving both the social and psychological levels of a revealing ulterior transaction. In its most dramatic form, IWFY at the social level is a Parent-Child game.

MR. WHITE: "You stay home and take care of the house."
MRS. WHITE: "If it weren't for you, I could be out having fun."

At the psychological level (the ulterior marriage contract) the relationship is Child-Child, and quite different.

MR. WHITE: "You must always be here when I get home. I'm terrified of desertion."

MRS. WHITE: "I will be if you help me avoid phobic situations."

. . . . .

ADVANTAGES. The general advantages of a game consist in its stabilizing (homeostatic) functions. Biological homeostasis is promoted by the stroking, and psychological stability is reinforced by the confirmation of position. As has already been noted, stroking may take various forms, so that the *biological advantage* of a game may be stated in tactile terms. Thus the husband's role in IWFY is reminiscent of a backhanded slap (quite different in effect from a palmar slap, which is a direct humiliation), and the wife's response is something like a petulant kick in the shins. Hence the biological gain from IWFY is derived from belligerence-petulance exchanges: a distressing but apparently effective way to maintain the health of nervous tissues.

Confirmation of the wife's position—"All men are tyrants" —is the *existential advantage*. This position is a reaction to the need to surrender that is inherent in the phobias, a demonstration of the coherent structure which underlies all games. The expanded statement would be: "If I went out alone in a crowd, I would be overcome by the temptation to surrender; at home I don't surrender: he forces me, which proves that all men are tyrants." Hence this game is commonly played by women who suffer from feelings of unreality, which signifies their difficulty in keeping the Adult in charge in situations of strong temptation. The detailed elucidation of these mechanisms belongs to psychoanalysis rather than game analysis. In game analysis the end product is the chief concern.

Internal psychological advantage of a game is its direct effect on the psychic economy (libido). In IWFY the socially acceptable surrender to the husband's authority keeps the woman from experiencing neurotic fears. At the same time it satisfies masochistic needs, if they exist, using masochism not in the sense of self-abnegation but with its classical meaning of sexual excitement in situations of deprivation, humiliation or pain. That is, it excites her to be deprived and dominated.

External psychological advantage is the avoidance of the feared situation by playing the game. This is especially obvious in IWFY, where it is the outstanding motivation: by complying with the husband's strictures, the wife avoids the public situations which she fears.

Internal social advantage is designated by the name of the game as it is played in the individual's intimate circle. By her compliance, the wife gains the privilege of saying "If it weren't for you." This helps to structure the time she must spend with her husband; in the case of Mrs. White, this need for structure was especially strong because of the lack of other common interests, especially before the arrival of their offspring and after the children were grown. In between, the game was played less intensively and less frequently, because the children performed their usual function of structuring time for their parents, and also provided an even more widely accepted version of IWFY, the busy-housewife variation. The fact that young mothers in America often really are very busy does not change the analysis of this variation. Game analysis only attempts to answer this question without prejudice: given that a young woman is busy, how does she go about exploiting her busyness in order to get some compensation for it?

External social advantage is designated by the use made of the situation in outside social contacts. In the case of the game "If It Weren't For You," which is what the wife says to her husband, there is a transformation into the pastime "If It Weren't For Him" when she meets with her friends over morning coffee. Again, the influence of games in the selection of social companions is shown. The new neighbor who is invited for morning coffee is being invited to play "If It Weren't For Him." If she plays, well and good, she will soon be a bosom friend of the old-timers, other things being equal. If she refuses to play and insists on taking a charitable view of her husband, she will not last long. Her situation will be the same as if she kept refusing to drink at cocktail parties—in most circles, she would gradually be dropped from the guest lists. This completes the analysis of the formal features of IWFY.

.   .   .   .   .

The Function of Games

Because there is so little opportunity for intimacy in daily life, and because some forms of intimacy (especially if intense) are psychologically impossible for most people, the bulk of the time in serious social life is taken up with playing games. Hence games are both necessary and desirable, and the only problem at issue is whether the games played by an individual offer the best yield for him. In this connection it should be remembered that the essential feature of a game is its culmination, or payoff. The principal function of the preliminary moves is to set up the situation for this payoff, but they are always designed to harvest the maximum permissible satisfaction at each step as a secondary product. Thus in "Schlemiel" (making messes and then apologizing) the payoff, and the purpose of the game, is to obtain the forgiveness which is forced by the apology; the spillings and cigarette burns are only steps leading up to this, but each such trespass yields its own pleasure. The enjoyment derived from the spilling does not make spilling a game. The apology is the critical stimulus that leads to the denouement. Otherwise the spilling would simply be a destructive procedure, a delinquency perhaps enjoyable.

.   .   .   .   .

Beyond their social function in structuring time satisfactorily, some games are urgently necessary for the maintenance of health in certain individuals. These people's psychic stability is so precarious, and their positions are so tenuously maintained, that to deprive them of their games may plunge them into irreversible despair and even psychosis. Such people will fight very hard against any antithetical moves. This is often observed in marital situations when the psychiatric improvement of one spouse (i.e., the abandonment of destructive games) leads to rapid deterioration in the other spouse, to whom the games were of paramount importance in maintaining equilibrium. Hence it is necessary to exercise prudence in game analysis.

Fortunately, the rewards of game-free intimacy, which is or should be the most perfect form of human living, are so great that even precariously balanced personalities can safely and joyfully relinquish their games if an appropriate partner can be found for the better relationship.

On a larger scale, games are integral and dynamic components of the unconscious life-plan, or script, of each individual; they serve to fill in the time while he waits for the final fulfillment, simultaneously advancing the action. Since the last act of a script characteristically calls for either a miracle or a catastrophe, depending on whether the script is constructive or destructive, the corresponding games are accordingly either constructive or destructive. In colloquial terms, an individual whose script is oriented toward "waiting for Santa Claus" is likely to be pleasant to deal with in such games as "Gee You're Wonderful, Mr. Murgatroyd," while someone with a tragic script oriented toward "waiting for *rigor mortis* to set in" may play such disagreeable games as "Now I've Got You, You Son of a Bitch."

.   .   .   .   .

Sexual Games

Some games are played to exploit or fight off sexual impulses. These are all, in effect, perversions of the sexual instincts in which the satisfaction is displaced from the sexual act to the crucial transactions which constitute the payoff of the game. This cannot always be demonstrated convincingly, because such games are usually played in privacy, so that clinical information about them has to be obtained secondhand, and the informant's bias cannot always be satisfactorily evaluated. The psychiatric conception of homosexuality, for example, is heavily skewed, because the more aggressive and successful "players" do not often come for psychiatric treatment, and the available material mostly concerns the passive partners.

The games included here are: "Let's You and Him Fight," "Perversion," "Rapo," "Stocking Game" and "Uproar." In most cases, the agent is a woman. This is because the hard forms of sexual games in which the man is the agent verge on or constitute criminality, and properly belong in the Underworld section. On the other side, sexual games and marital games overlap, but the ones described here are readily available to unmarried people as well as to spouses.

Let's You and Him Fight

THESIS. This may be a maneuver, a ritual or a game. In each case the psychology is essentially feminine. Because of its dramatic qualities, LYAHF is the basis of much of the world's literature, both good and bad.

1. As a maneuver it is romantic. The woman maneuvers or challenges two men into fighting, with the implication or promise that she will surrender herself to the winner. After the competition is decided, she fulfills her bargain. This is an honest transaction, and the presumption is that she and her mate live happily ever after.

2. As a ritual, it tends to be tragic. Custom demands that the two men fight for her, even if she does not want them to, and even if she has already made her choice. If the wrong man wins, she must nevertheless take him. In this case it is society and not the woman who sets up LYAHF. If she is

willing, the transaction is an honest one. If she is unwilling or disappointed, the outcome may offer her considerable scope for playing games, such as "Let's Pull A Fast One on Joey."

3. As a game it is comic. The woman sets up the competition, and while the two men are fighting, she decamps with a third. The internal and external psychological advantages for her and her mate are derived from the position that honest competition is for suckers, and the comic story they have lived through forms the basis for the internal and external social advantages.

Perversion

THESIS. Heterosexual perversions such as fetishism, sadism and masochism are symptomatic of a confused Child and are treated accordingly. Their transactional aspects, however, as manifested in actual sexual situations, can be dealt with by means of game analysis. This may lead to social control, so that even if the warped sexual impulses remain unchanged, they are neutralized as far as actual indulgence is concerned.

People who are suffering from mild sadistic or masochistic distortions tend to take a primitive kind of Mental Health position. They feel that they are strongly sexed, and that prolonged abstinence will lead to serious consequences. Neither of these conclusions is necessarily true, but they form the basis for a game of "Wooden Leg" with the plea: "What do you expect from someone as strongly sexed as I am?"

ANTITHESIS. To extend ordinary courtesy to oneself and one's partner; that is, to refrain from verbal or physical flagellation and confine oneself to more conventional forms of coitus. If White is a true pervert, this will lay bare the second element of the game, which is often clearly expressed in his dreams: that coitus itself has little interest for him, and that his real satisfaction is derived from the humiliating foreplay. This is something that he may not have cared to admit to himself. But it will now become clear to him that his complaint is: "After all this work, I have to have intercourse, yet!" At this point the position is much more favorable for specific psychotherapy, and much of the pleading and evasiveness has been nullified. This applies to ordinary "sexual psychopaths" as seen in practice, and not to malignant schizophrenic or criminal perversions, nor to those who confine their sexual activities to fantasy.

The game of "Homosexuality" has become elaborated into a subculture in many countries, just as it is ritualized in others. Many of the disabilities which result from homosexuality arise from making it into a game. The provocative behavior which gives rise to "Cops and Robbers," "Why Does This Always Happen to Us," "It's the Society We Live In," "All Great Men Were" and so forth, is often amenable to social control, which reduces the handicaps to a minimum. The "professional homosexual" wastes a large amount of time and energy which could be applied to other ends. Analysis of his games may help him establish a quiet ménage which will leave him free to enjoy the benefits that bourgeois society offers, instead of devoting himself to playing his own variation of "Ain't It Awful!"

Rapo

THESIS. This is a game played between a man and a woman which might more politely be called, in the milder forms at least, "Kiss Off" or "Indignation." It may be played with varying degrees of intensity.

1. First-Degree "Rapo," or "Kiss Off," is popular at social gatherings and consists essentially of mild flirtation. White signals that she is available and gets her pleasure from the man's pursuit. As soon as he has committed himself, the game is over. If she is polite, she may say quite frankly "I appreciate your compliments and thank you very much,"

and move on to the next conquest. If she is less generous, she may simply leave him. A skillful player can make this game last for a long time at a large social gathering by moving around frequently, so that the man has to carry out complicated maneuvers in order to follow her without being too obvious.

2. In Second-Degree "Rapo," or "Indignation," White gets only secondary satisfaction from Black's advances. Her primary gratification comes from rejecting him, so that this game is also colloquially known as "Buzz off, Buster." She leads Black into a much more serious commitment than the mild flirtation of First-Degree "Rapo" and enjoys watching his discomfiture when she repulses him. Black, of course, is not as helpless as he seems, and may have gone to considerable trouble to get himself involved. Usually he is playing some variation of "Kick Me."

3. Third-Degree "Rapo" is a vicious game which ends in murder, suicide or the courtroom. Here White leads Black into compromising physical contact and then claims that he has made a criminal assault or has done her irreparable damage. In its most cynical form White may actually allow him to complete the sexual act so that she gets that enjoyment before confronting him. The confrontation may be immediate, as in the illegitimate cry of rape, or it may be long delayed, as in suicide or homicide following a prolonged love affair. If she chooses to play it ¬ a criminal assault, she may have no difficulty in finding me. ¬ary or morbidly interested allies, such as the press, the police, counselors and relatives. Sometimes, however, these outsiders may cynically turn on her, so that she loses the initiative and becomes a tool in their games.

In some cases outsiders perform a different function. They force the game on an unwilling White because they want to play "Let's You and Him Fight." They put her in such a position that in order to save her face or her reputation she has to cry rape. This is particularly apt to happen with girls under the legal age of consent; they may be quite willing to continue a liaison, but because it is discovered or made an issue of, they feel constrained to turn the romance into a game of Third-Degree "Rapo."

In one well-known situation, the wary Joseph refused to be inveigled into a game of "Rapo," whereupon Potiphar's wife made the classical switch into "Let's You and Him Fight," an excellent example of the way a hard player reacts to antithesis, and of the dangers that beset people who refuse to play games. These two games are combined in the well-known "Badger Game," in which the woman seduces Black and then cries rape, at which point her husband takes charge and abuses Black for purposes of blackmail.

One of the most unfortunate and acute forms of Third-Degree "Rapo" occurs relatively frequently between homosexual strangers, who in a matter of an hour or so may bring the game to a point of homicide. The cynical and criminal variations of this game contribute a large volume to sensational newspaper copy.

The childhood prototype of "Rapo" is the same as that of "Frigid Woman," in which the little girl induces the boy to humiliate himself or get dirty and then sneers at him, as classically described by Maugham in *Of Human Bondage* and, as already noted, by Dickens in *Great Expectations*. This is Second Degree. A harder form, approaching Third Degree, may be played in tough neighborhoods.

ANTITHESIS. The man's ability to avoid becoming involved in this game or to keep it under control depends on his capacity to distinguish genuine expressions of feeling from moves in the game. If he is thus able to exert social control, he may obtain a great deal of pleasure from the mild flirtations of "Kiss Off." On the other hand it is difficult to conceive of a safe antithesis for the Potiphar's Wife maneuver, other than checking out before closing time with no forwarding address. In 1938 the writer met an aging Joseph in Aleppo who had checked out of Constantinople thirty-two years previously, after one of the Sultan's ladies had cornered him during a business visit to the Yildiz harem. He had to abandon his shop, but took time to pick up his hoard of gold francs, and had never returned.

RELATIVES. The male versions of "Rapo" are notoriously found in commercial situations: "Casting Couch" (and then she didn't get the part) and "Cuddle Up" (and then she got fired).

·   ·   ·   ·   ·

The Stocking Game

THESIS. This is a game of the "Rapo" family; in it the most obvious characteristic is the exhibitionism, which is hysterical in nature. A woman comes into a strange group and after a very short time raises her leg, exposing herself in a provocative way, and remarks, "Oh my, I have a run in my stocking." This is calculated to arouse the men sexually and to make the other women angry. Any confrontation of White is met, of course, with protestations of innocence or counter-accusations, hence the resemblance to classical "Rapo." What is significant is White's lack of adaptation. She seldom waits to find out what kind of people she is dealing with or how to time her maneuver. Hence it stands out as inappropriate and affects her relationships with her associates. In spite of some superficial "sophistication," she fails to understand what happens to her in life because her judgment of human nature is too cynical. The aim is to prove that other people have lascivious minds, and her Adult is conned by her Child and her Parent (usually a lascivious mother) into ignoring both her own provocativeness and the good sense of many of the people she meets. Thus the game tends to be self-destructive.

This is probably a phallic variant of a game whose content depends on the underlying disturbance. An "oral" variant may be exhibited by women with deeper pathology and well-developed breasts. Such women often sit with their hands behind their heads so as to thrust their breasts forward; they may draw additional attention to them by remarking about their size or some pathology such as an operation or a lump. Some types of squirming probably constitute an anal variant. The implication of this game is that the woman is sexually available. Thus it may be played in a more symbolic form by bereaved women who "exhibit" their widowhood insincerely.

ANTITHESIS. Along with the poor adaptation, these women show little tolerance for antithesis. If the game is ignored or countered by a sophisticated therapy group, for example, they may not return. Antithesis must be carefully distinguished in this game from reprisal, since the latter signifies that White has won. Women are more skillful at counter-moves in "Stocking Game" than men, who indeed have little incentive to break up this game. Antithesis, therefore, is best left to the discretion of the other women present.

Uproar

THESIS. The classical game is played between domineering fathers and teen-age daughters, where there is a sexually inhibited mother. Father comes home from work and finds fault with daughter, who answers impudently; or daughter may make the first move by being impudent, whereupon father finds fault. Their voices rise, and the clash becomes more acute. The outcome depends on who has the initiative. There are three possibilities: (a) father retires to his bedroom and slams the door (b) daughter retires to her bedroom and slams the door (c) both retire to their respective bedrooms and slam the doors. In any case, the end of a game of "Uproar" is marked by a slamming door. "Uproar" offers a distressing but effective solution to the sexual problems that arise between fathers and teen-age daughters in certain households. Often they can only live in the same house together if they are angry at each other, and the slamming doors emphasize for each of them the fact that they have separate bedrooms.

In degenerate households this game may be played in a sinister and repellent form in which father waits up for daughter whenever she goes out on a date, and examines her and her clothing carefully on her return to make sure that she has not had intercourse. The slightest suspicious circumstance may give rise to the most violent altercation, which may end with the daughter being expelled from the house in the middle of the night. In the long run nature will take its course—if not that night then the next, or the one after. Then the father's suspicions are "justified," as he makes plain to the mother, who has stood by "helplessly" while all this went on.

In general, however, "Uproar" may be played between any two people who are trying to avoid sexual intimacy. For example, it is a common terminal phase of "Frigid Woman." It is relatively rare between teen-age boys and their female relatives, because it is easier for teen-age boys to escape from the house in the evening than for other members of the family. At an earlier age brothers and sisters can set up effective barriers and partial satisfactions through physical combat, a pattern which has various motivations at different ages, and which in America is a semi-ritualistic form of "Uproar" sanctioned by television, pedagogic and pediatric authorities. In upper-class England it is (or was) considered bad form, and the corresponding energies are channeled into the well-regulated "Uproar" of the playing fields.

ANTITHESIS. The game is. not as distasteful to the father as he might like to think, and it is generally the daughter who makes the antithetical move through an early, often premature or forced marriage. If it is psychologically possible, the mother can make the antithetical move by relinquishing her relative or absolute frigidity. The game may subside if the father finds an outside sexual interest, but that may lead to other complications. In the case of married couples, the antitheses are the same as for "Frigid Woman" or "Frigid Man."

Under appropriate circumstances "Uproar" leads quite naturally into "Courtroom."

.   .   .   .   .

Marital Games

Almost any game can form the scaffolding for married life and family living, but some, such as "If It Weren't for You," flourish better or, like "Frigid Woman," are tolerated longer, under the legal force of contractual intimacy. Marital games, of course, can only be arbitrarily separated from sexual games, which are treated in a separate section. Those games which characteristically evolve into their most full-blown forms in the marital relationship include "Corner," "Courtroom," "Frigid Woman" and "Frigid Man," "Harried," "If It Weren't for You," "Look How Hard I've Tried" and "Sweetheart."

Corner

THESIS. Corner illustrates more clearly than most games their manipulative aspect and their function as barriers to intimacy. Paradoxically, it consists of a disingenuous refusal to play the game of another.

1. Mrs. White suggests to her husband that they go to a movie. Mr. White agrees.

2a. Mrs. White makes an "unconscious" slip. She mentions quite naturally in the course of conversation that the house needs painting. This is an expensive project, and White has recently told her that their finances are strained; he requested her not to embarrass or annoy him by suggesting unusual expenditures, at least until the beginning of the new month. This is therefore an ill-chosen moment to bring up the condition of the house, and White responds rudely.

2b. Alternatively: White steers the conversation around to the house, making it difficult for Mrs. White to resist the temptation to say that it needs painting. As in the previous case, White responds rudely.

3. Mrs. White takes offense and says that if he is in one of his bad moods, she will not go to the movie with him, and he had best go by himself. He says if that is the way she feels about it, he will go alone.

4. White goes to the movie (or out with the boys), leaving Mrs. White at home to nurse her injured feelings.

There are two possible gimmicks in this game:

A. Mrs. White knows very well from past experience that she is not supposed to take his annoyance seriously. What he really wants is for her to show some appreciation of how hard he works to earn their living; then they could go off happily together. But she refuses to play, and he feels badly let down. He leaves filled with disappointment and resentment, while she stays at home looking abused, but with a secret feeling of triumph.

B. White knows very well from past experience that he is not supposed to take her pique seriously. What she really wants is to be honeyed out of it; then they would go off happily together. But he refuses to play, knowing that his refusal is dishonest: he knows she wants to be coaxed, but pretends he doesn't. He leaves the house, feeling cheerful and relieved, but looking wronged. She is left feeling disappointed and resentful.

In each of these cases the winner's position is, from a naive standpoint, irreproachable; all he or she has done is take the other literally. This is clearer in (B), where White takes Mrs. White's refusal to go at face value. They both know that this is cheating, but since she said it, she is cornered.

The most obvious gain here is the external psychological. Both of them find movies sexually stimulating, and it is more or less anticipated that after they return from the theater, they will make love. Hence whichever one of them wants to avoid intimacy sets up the game in move (2a) or (2b). This is a particularly exasperating variety of "Uproar." The "wronged" party can, of course, make a good case for not wanting to make love in a state of justifiable indignation, and the cornered spouse has no recourse.

ANTITHESIS. This is simple for Mrs. White. All she has to do is change her mind, take her husband by the arm, smile and go along with him (a shift.from Child to Adult ego state). It is more difficult for Mr. White, since she now has the initiative; but if he reviews the whole situation, he may be able to coax her into going along with him, either as a sulky Child who has been placated or, better, as an Adult.

"Corner" is found in a somewhat different form as a family game involving the children, where it resembles the "double-bind" described by Bateson and his associates. Here the child is cornered, so that whatever he does is wrong. According to the Bateson school, this may be an important etiological factor in schizophrenia. In the present language, then, schizophrenia may be a child's antithesis to "Corner." Experience in treating adult schizophrenics with game analysis bears this out—that is, if the family game of "Corner" is analyzed to demonstrate that the schizophrenic behavior was and is specifically undertaken to counter this game, partial or total remission occurs in a properly prepared patient.

An everyday form of "Corner" which is played by the whole family and is most likely to affect the character development of the younger children occurs with meddlesome "Parental" parents. The little boy or girl is urged to be more helpful around the house, but when he is, the parents find fault with what he does—a homely example of "damned if you do and damned if you don't." This "double-bind" may be called the Dilemma Type of "Corner."

"Corner" is sometimes found as an etiological factor in asthmatic children.

.   .   .   .   .

Closely allied to "Corner" on the one hand, and to "Threadbare" on the other, is the marital game of "Lunch Bag." The husband, who can well afford to have lunch at a good restaurant, nevertheless makes himself a few sandwiches every morning, which he takes to the office in a paper bag. In this way he uses up crusts of bread, leftovers from dinner and paper bags which his wife saves for him. This gives him complete control over the family finances, for what wife would dare buy herself a mink stole in the face of such self-sacrifice? The husband reaps numerous other advantages, such as the privilege of eating lunch by himself and of catching up on his work during lunch hour. In many ways this is a constructive game which Benjamin Franklin would have approved of, since it encourages the virtues of thrift, hard work and punctuality.

Courtroom

THESIS. Descriptively this belongs to the class of games which find their most florid expressions in law, and which includes "Wooden Leg" (the plea of insanity) and "Debtor" (the civil suit). *Clinically* it is most often seen in marital counseling and marital psychotherapy groups. Indeed, some marital counseling and marital groups consist of a perpetual game of "Courtroom" in which nothing is resolved, since the game is never broken up. In such cases it becomes evident that the counselor or therapist is heavily involved in the game without being aware of it.

"Courtroom" can be played by any number, but is essentially three-handed, with a plaintiff, a defendant and a judge, represented by a husband, a wife and the therapist. If it is played in a therapy group or over the radio or TV, the other members of the audience are cast as the jury. The husband begins plaintively, "Let me tell you what (wife's name) did yesterday. She took the . . ." etc., etc. The wife then responds defensively, "Here is the way it really was . . . and besides just before that he was . . . and anyway at the time we were both . . ." etc. The husband adds gallantly, "Well, I'm glad you people have a chance to hear both sides of the story, I only want to be fair." At this point the counselor says judiciously, "It seems to me that if we consider . . ." etc., etc. If there is an audience, the therapist may throw it to them with: "Well, let's hear what the others have to say." Or, if the group is already trained, they will play the jury without any instruction from him.

ANTITHESIS. The therapist says to the husband, "You're absolutely right!" If the husband relaxes complacently or triumphantly, the therapist asks: "How do you feel about my saying that?" The husband replies: "Fine." Then the therapist says, "Actually, I feel you're in the wrong." If the husband is honest, he will say: "I knew that all along." If he is not honest, he will show some reaction that makes it clear a game is in progress. Then it becomes possible to go into the matter further. The game element lies in the fact that while the plaintiff is overtly clamoring for victory, fundamentally he believes that he is wrong.

After sufficient clinical material has been gathered to clarify the situation, the game can be interdicted by a maneuver which is one of the most elegant in the whole art of antithetics. The therapist makes a rule prohibiting the use of the (grammatical) third person in the group. Thenceforward the members can only address each other directly as "you" or talk about themselves as "I," but they cannot say, "Let me tell you about him" or "Let me tell you about her." At this point the couple stop playing games in the group altogether, or shift into "Sweetheart," which is some improvement, or take up "Furthermore," which is no help at all. "Sweetheart" is described in another section (page 236). In "Furthermore" the plaintiff makes one accusation after the other. The defendant replies to each, "I can explain." The plaintiff pays no attention to the explanation, but as soon as the defendant pauses, he launches into his next indictment with another "furthermore," which is followed by another explanation—a typical Parent-Child interchange.

"Furthermore" is played most intensively by paranoid defendants. Because of their literalness, it is particularly easy for them to frustrate accusers who express themselves in humorous or metaphorical terms. In general, metaphors are the most obvious traps to avoid in a game of "Furthermore."

In its *everyday* form, "Courtroom" is easily observed in children as a three-handed game between two siblings and a parent. "Mommy, she took my candy away." "Yes, but he took my doll and before that he was hitting me, and anyway we both promised to share our candy."

. . . . .

Frigid Woman

THESIS. This is almost always a marital game, since it is hardly conceivable that an informal liaison would present the required opportunities and privileges over a sufficient length of time, or that such a liaison would be maintained in the face of it.

The husband makes advances to his wife and is repulsed. After repeated attempts, he is told that all men are beasts, he doesn't really love her, or doesn't love her for herself, that all he is interested in is sex. He desists for a time, then tries again with the same result. Eventually he resigns himself and makes no further advances. As the weeks or months pass, the wife becomes increasingly informal and sometimes forgetful. She walks through the bedroom half dressed or forgets her clean towel when she takes a bath so that he has to bring it to her. If she plays a hard game or drinks heavily, she may become flirtatious with other men at parties. At length he responds to those provocations and tries again. Once more he is repulsed, and a game of "Uproar" ensues involving their recent behavior, other couples, their in-laws, their finances and their failures, terminated by a slamming door.

This time the husband makes up his mind that he is really through, that they will find a sexless *modus vivendi*. Months pass. He declines the negligee parade and the forgotten towel maneuver. The wife becomes more provocatively informal and more provocatively forgetful, but he still resists. Then one evening she actually approaches him and kisses him. At first he doesn't respond, remembering his resolution, but soon nature begins to take its course after the long famine, and now he thinks he surely has it made. His first tentative advances are not repulsed. He becomes bolder and bolder. Just at the critical point, the wife steps back and cries: "See, what did I tell you! All men are beasts, all I wanted was affection, but all you are interested in is sex!" The ensuing game of "Uproar" at this point may skip the preliminary phases of their recent behavior and their in-laws, and go right to the financial problem.

It should be noted that in spite of his protestations, the husband is usually just as afraid of sexual intimacy as his wife is, and has carefully chosen his mate to minimize the danger of overtaxing his disturbed potency, which he can now blame on her.

In its *everyday* form this game is played by unmarried ladies of various ages, which soon earns them a common slang epithet. With them it often merges into the game of indignation, or "Rapo."

ANTITHESIS. This is a dangerous game, and the possible antitheses are equally dangerous. Taking a mistress is a gamble. In the face of such stimulating competition, the wife may give up the game and try to initiate a normal married life, perhaps too late. On the other hand, she may use the affair, often with the help of a lawyer, as ammunition against the husband in a game of "Now I've Got You, You Son of a Bitch." The outcome is equally unpredictable if the husband undertakes psychotherapy and she does not. The wife's game may collapse as the husband grows stronger, leading to healthier adjustment; but if she is a hard player, improvement on his part may result in divorce. The best solution, if available, is for both parties to go into a transactional marital group, where the underlying advantages of the game and the basic sexual pathology can be laid bare. With this preparation both spouses may become interested in intensive individual psychotherapy. That may result in a psychological remarriage. If not, at least each of the parties may make a more sensible readjustment to the situation than they might have otherwise.

The decent antithesis for the *everyday* form is to find another companion. Some of the shrewder or more brutal antitheses are corrupt and even criminal.

RELATIVES. The converse game, "Frigid Man," is less common, but it takes much the same general course with some variations in detail. The final outcome depends upon the scripts of the parties involved.

The crucial point of "Frigid Woman" is the terminal phase of "Uproar." Once this has run its course, sexual intimacy is out of the question, since both parties derive a perverse satisfaction from "Uproar" and have no need of further sexual excitement from each other. Hence the most important item in anti-"Frigid Woman" is to decline "Uproar." This leaves the wife in a state of sexual dissatisfaction which may be so acute that she will become more compliant. The use made of "Uproar" distinguishes "Frigid Woman" from "Beat Me Daddy," where "Uproar" is part of the foreplay; in "Frigid Woman," "Uproar" substitutes for the sex act itself. Thus in "Beat Me Daddy," "Uproar" is a condition of the sexual act, a kind of fetish which increases the excitement, while in "Frigid Woman," once "Uproar" has taken place, the episode is finished.

An early analogue of "Frigid Woman" is played by that type of prissy little girl described by Dickens in *Great Expectations*. She comes out in her starched dress and asks the little boy to make her a mud pie. Then she sneers at his dirty hands and clothing and tells him how clean she is.

.   .   .   .   .

Harried

THESIS. This is a game played by the harried housewife. Her situation requires that she be proficient in ten or twelve different occupations; or, stated otherwise, that she fill gracefully ten or twelve different roles. From time to time semi-facetious lists of these occupations or roles appear in the Sunday supplements: mistress, mother, nurse, housemaid, etc. Since these roles are usually conflicting and fatiguing, their imposition gives rise in the course of years to the condition symbolically known as "Housewife's Knee" (since the knee is used for rocking, scrubbing, lifting, driving and so forth), whose symptoms are succinctly summarized in the complaint: "I'm tired."

Now, if the housewife is able to set her own pace and find enough satisfaction in loving her husband and children, she will not merely serve but enjoy her twenty-five years, and see the youngest child off to college with a pang of loneliness. But if on the one hand she is driven by her inner Parent and called to account by the critical husband she has chosen for that purpose, and on the other unable to get sufficient satisfaction from loving her family, she may grow more and more unhappy. At first she may try to console herself with the advantages of "If It Weren't For You" and "Blemish" (and indeed, any housewife may fall back on these when the going gets rough); but soon these fail to keep her going. Then she has to find another way out, and that is the game of "Harried."

The thesis of this game is simple. She takes on everything that comes, and even asks for more. She agrees with her husband's criticisms and accepts all her children's demands. If she has to entertain at dinner, she not only feels she must function impeccably as a conversationalist, chatelaine over the household and servants, interior decorator, caterer, glamor girl, virgin queen and diplomat; she will also volunteer that morning to bake a cake and take the children to the dentist. If she already feels harassed, she makes the day even more harried. Then in the middle of the afternoon she justifiably collapses, and nothing gets done. She lets down her husband, the children and their guests, and her self-reproaches add to her misery. After this happens two or three times her marriage is in jeopardy, the children are confused, she loses weight, her hair is untidy, her face is drawn and her shoes are scuffed. Then she appears at the psychiatrist's office, ready to be hospitalized.

ANTITHESIS. The local antithesis is simple: Mrs. White can fill each of her roles in succession during the week, but she must refuse to play two or more of them simultaneously. When she gives a cocktail party, for example, she can play either caterer or nursemaid, but not both. If she is merely suffering from Housewife's Knee, she may be able to limit herself in this way.

If she is actually playing a game of "Harried," however, it will be very difficult for her to adhere to this principle. In that case the husband is carefully chosen; he is an otherwise reasonable man who will criticize his wife if she is not as efficient as he thinks his mother was. In effect, she marries his fantasy of his mother as perpetuated in his Parent, which is similar to her fantasy of her mother or grandmother. Having found a suitable partner, her Child can now settle into the harassed role necessary to maintain her psychic balance, and which she will not readily give up. The more occupational responsibility the husband has, the easier it is for both of them to find Adult reasons to preserve the unhealthy aspects of their relationship.

When the position becomes untenable, often because of official school intervention on behalf of the unhappy offspring, the psychiatrist is called in to make it a three-handed game. Either the husband wants him to do an overhaul job on the wife, or the wife wants him as an ally against the husband. The ensuing proceedings depend on the skill and alertness of the psychiatrist. Usually the first phase, the alleviation of the wife's depression, will proceed smoothly. The second phase, in which she will give up playing "Harried" in favor of playing "Psychiatry," is the decisive one. It tends to arouse increasing opposition from both spouses. Sometimes this is well concealed and then explodes suddenly, though not unexpectedly. If this stage is weathered, then the real work of game analysis can proceed.

It is necessary to recognize that the real culprit is the wife's Parent, her mother or grandmother; the husband is to some extent only a lay figure chosen to play his role in the game. The therapist has to fight not only this Parent and the husband, who has a heavy investment in playing his end, but also the social environment, which encourages the wife's compliance. The week after the article appears about the many roles a housewife has to play, there is a *How'm I Doing?* in the Sunday paper: a ten-item test to determine "How Good A Hostess (Wife) (Mother) (Housekeeper) (Budgeteer) Are You?" For the housewife who plays "Harried," that is the equivalent of the little leaflet that comes with children's games, stating the rules. It may help to speed up the evolution of "Harried," which, if not checked, may end in a game of "State Hospital" ("The last thing I want is to be sent to a hospital").

One practical difficulty with such couples is that the husband tends to avoid personal involvement with the treatment beyond playing "Look How Hard I'm Trying," because he is usually more disturbed than he cares to admit. Instead he may send indirect messages to the therapist, through temper outbursts which he knows will be reported by the wife. Hence "Harried" easily progresses to a third-degree life-death-divorce struggle. The psychiatrist is almost alone on the side of life, assisted only by the harried Adult of the patient which is locked in combat that may prove mortal against all three aspects of the husband, allied with her own inner Parent and Child. It is a dramatic battle, with odds of two against five, which tries the skill of the most game-free and professional therapist. If he quails, he can take the easy way out and offer his patient on the altar of the divorce court, which is equivalent to saying "I surrender—Let's you and him fight."

If It Weren't For You

THESIS. The detailed analysis of this game has already been given. . . . It was historically the second game uncovered, after "Why Don't You—Yes But," which up to that point had been regarded merely as an interesting phenomenon. With the additional discovery of IWFY, it became clear that there must be a whole department of social action based on ulterior transactions. This led to a more active search for such goings-on, and the present collection is one outcome.

Briefly, a woman marries a domineering man so that he will restrict her activities and thus keep her from getting into situations which frighten her. If this were a simple operation, she might express her gratitude when he performed this service for her. In the game of IWFY, however, her reaction is quite the opposite: she takes advantage of the situation to complain about the restrictions, which makes her spouse feel uneasy and gives her all sorts of advantages. This game is the internal social advantage. The external social advantage is the derivative pastime "If It Weren't For Him," which she plays with her congenial lady friends.

Look How Hard I've Tried

THESIS. In its common *clinical* form this is a three-handed game played by a married couple with a psychiatrist. The husband (usually) is bucking for a divorce, despite loud protestations to the contrary, while the spouse is more sincere in wanting to continue the marriage. He comes to the therapist under protest and talks just enough to demonstrate to the wife that he is cooperating; usually he plays a mild game of "Psychiatry" or "Courtroom." As time passes he exhibits either increasingly resentful pseudo-compliance or belligerent argumentativeness toward the therapist. At home he initially shows more "understanding" and restraint, and finally behaves worse than ever. After one, five or ten visits, depending on the skill of the therapist, he refuses to come any longer and goes hunting or fishing instead. The wife is then forced into filing for divorce. The husband is now blameless, since his wife has taken the initiative and he has demonstrated his good faith by going to the therapist. He is in a good position to say to any attorney, judge, friend or relative, "Look how hard I've tried!"

ANTITHESIS. The couple is seen together. If one—let us say the husband—is clearly playing this game, the other is taken into individual treatment and the player is sent on his way, on the valid ground that he is less ready for therapy. He can still get a divorce, but only at the expense of abandoning his position that he is really trying. If necessary, the wife can start the divorce, and her position is much improved since she really has tried. The favorable, hoped-for outcome is that the husband, his game broken up, will go into a state of despair and then seek treatment elsewhere with genuine motivation.

In its *everyday* form this is easily observed in children as a two-handed game with one parent. It is played from either of two positions: "I am helpless" or "I am blameless." The child tries, but bungles or is unsuccessful. If he is Helpless, the parent has to do it for him. If he is Blameless, the parent has no reasonable grounds for punishing him. This reveals the elements of the game. The parents should find out two things: which of them taught the child this game; and what they are doing to perpetuate it.

An interesting, though sometimes sinister, variant is "Look How Hard I Was Trying," which is usually a harder game of the second or third degree. This can be illustrated by the case of a hard-working man with a gastric ulcer. There are many people with progressive physical disabilities who do the best they can to cope with the situation, and they may enlist the help of their families in a legitimate way. Such conditions, however, can also be exploited for ulterior purposes.

First Degree: A man announces to his wife and friends that he has an ulcer. He also lets them know that he is continuing to work. This elicits their admiration. Perhaps a person with a painful and unpleasant condition is entitled to a certain amount of ostentation as a poor recompense for his suffering. He should be given due credit for not playing "Wooden Leg" instead, and deserves some reward for continuing to assume his responsibilities. In such a case, the courteous reply to "Look How Hard I'm Trying" is, "Yes, we all admire your fortitude and conscientiousness."

Second Degree: A man is told that he has an ulcer, but keeps it a secret from his wife and friends. He continues working and worrying as hard as ever, and one day he collapses on the job. When his wife is notified, she gets the message instantly: "Look How Hard I Was Trying." Now she is supposed to appreciate him as she never has before, and to feel sorry for all the mean things she has said and done in the past. In short, she is now supposed to love him, all previous methods of wooing her having failed. Unfortunately for the husband, her manifestations of affection and solicitude at this point are more apt to be motivated by guilt than by love. Deep down she is likely to be resentful because he is using unfair leverage against her, and has also taken unfair advantage of her by keeping his illness a secret. In short, a diamond bracelet is a much more honest instrument of courtship than a perforated stomach. She has the option of throwing the jewelry back at him, but she cannot decently walk out on the ulcer. A sudden confrontation with a serious illness is more likely to make her feel trapped than won over.

This game can often be discovered immediately after the patient first hears that he has a potentially progressive disability. If he is going to play it, the whole plan will very likely flash through his mind at that point, and can be recovered by a careful psychiatric review of the situation. What is recovered is the secret gloating of his Child at learning that he has such a weapon, masked by his Adult concern at the practical problems raised by his illness.

Third Degree: Even more sinister and spiteful is the sudden unheralded suicide because of serious illness. The ulcer progresses to cancer, and one day the wife, who has never been informed that anything serious is amiss, walks into the bathroom and finds her husband lying there dead. The note says clearly enough, "Look How Hard I Was Trying." If something like this happens twice to the same woman, it is time for her to find out what she has been playing.

.   .   .   .   .

Sweetheart

THESIS. This is seen in its fullest flower in the early stages of marital group therapy, when the parties feel defensive; it can also be observed on social occasions. White makes a subtly derogatory remark about Mrs. White, disguised as an anecdote, and ends: "Isn't that right, sweetheart?" Mrs. White tends to agree for two ostensibly Adult reasons: (a) because the anecdote itself is, in the main, accurately reported, and to disagree about what is presented as a peripheral detail (but is really the essential point of the transaction) would seem pedantic; (b) because it would seem surly to disagree with a man who calls one "sweetheart" in public. The psychological reason for her agreement, however, is her depressive position. She married him precisely because she knew he would perform this service for her: exposing her deficiencies and thus saving her from the embarrassment of having to expose them herself. Her parents accommodated her the same way when she was little.

Next to "Courtroom," this is the most common game played in marital groups. The more tense the situation, and the closer the game is to exposure, the more bitterly is the word "sweetheart" enunciated, until the underlying resentment becomes obvious. On careful consideration it can be seen that this is a relative of "Schlemiel," since the significant move is Mrs. White's implicit forgiveness for White's resentment, of which she is trying hard not to be aware. Hence anti-"Sweetheart" is played analogously to anti-"Schlemiel": "You can tell derogatory anecdotes about me, but please don't call me 'sweetheart.'" This antithesis carries with it the same perils as does anti-"Schlemiel." A more sophisticated and less dangerous antithesis is to reply: "Yes, *honey!*"

In another form the wife, instead of agreeing, responds with a similar "Sweetheart" type anecdote about the husband, saying in effect, "You have a dirty face too, dear."

Sometimes the endearments are not actually pronounced, but a careful listener can hear them even when they are unspoken. This is "Sweetheart," Silent Type.

12

BINDS AND UNBINDS

DOROTHY M. JONES

Revolving, spiralling, mushrooming processes cannot be described in linear fashion, and there lies one of the major problems in explicating the pivotal variables which comprise the field of interaction in a family. In an attempt to develop a testable hypothesis about interaction systems in families with a schizophrenic child, I conducted a series of pilot interviews to determine the nature and content of the rules in the family. It became apparent, however, that it was not the existence of the rule which caused the disorder, but rather the way in which the rule was implemented and incorporated into a system of interaction. There was a patterned process in gyrating motion of which the components fed, reinforced and derived from a particular system of interaction. This paper will present an excerpt from a family interview which dramatizes the family's characteristic habits of behavior and interaction. The theoretical frame of reference derives from social systems concepts (4, 10, 15) and from recent studies in the interaction field in families (3, 8, 9, 11, 12, 13, 14).

SOURCE: Dorothy M. Jones, "Binds and Unbinds," *Family Process* (1964), 323–31. Reprinted by permission of the author and publisher.

The specific system of interaction in this type of family will be described here as a process of binds and unbinds. This is not a reference to simple binds but to the double bind described by Bateson et al. (1, 2, 5, 6, 7). This is a communication mode in which contradictory injunctions are expressed on different levels of abstraction, and where something is shifted from one level of abstraction to another in order to conceal or disguise its meaning. When one member of a family places a reciprocal in such a bind, the reciprocal attempts to remove himself from the bind—to unbind himself. There are various ways in which this can be accomplished, but in the process being described, the reciprocal unbinds himself by placing the binding member in another bind, and in this process of binding and unbinding, the family members place themselves in a convoluting series of more and more confused binds, increasingly distant from their sources of origin, and increasingly disguised. The result is a process in which meaninglessness is effected in a context of contending to be meaningful; ambiguity and equivocation in a context of professing to be clear cut and explicit; concealment in a context of ostensible openness; and disguise in a context of revelation. It is both implicit and explicit, subtle and crude. The multiple sources of this process include the life history of each family member, the life history of the family group, the family's network of connections and cultural setting, and the family's particular manner of interaction and relationship. Despite the manifold dimensions of this process, its nature is persistent, consistent and ubiquitous.

The systematic manner in which a particular family embraces this process will be demonstrated with an excerpt from a recorded family interview of the "Crane" family. The members include Herman, forty-seven year old father, Betty, forty-three year old mother, and Lilly, their one child of eleven.

Lilly was hospitalized in August 1962 at a children's psychiatric unit in a small psychiatric hospital connected with one of the major West Coast universities. She was initially referred by her school because of her inability to relate to peers, her use of a private language, social withdrawal and bizarre behavior. She was diagnosed as childhood schizophrenia. Lilly was discharged as a day patient in August, 1963. This paper does not deal with those aspects of Lilly's treatment administered by the resident and other hospital staff but focuses primarily on those family processes revealed in the course of casework with the parents.

Although the life history of both parents provides a plethora of relevant material, the striking characteristic of each individual is a deeply entrenched fear of conflict and differences, and a total commitment to the illusion of family togetherness. Herman, himself an only child, perceives his early life as a series of potentially devastating conflicts which he avoided by quiet submission and compliance. He lived in a series of eight foster homes between the ages of five and thirteen, after his parents divorced and dispersed to other cities. Throughout the remainder of his adolescent years, he lived with his mother and a contentious and alcoholic stepfather. When he was thirty-two years old, he married, anticipating the fulfillment of a lifelong dream of a closely-knit family. Never having experienced close, interpersonal relations he aspired to a utopian image which found fruition in the partnership with a woman so specialized in creating images that her adumbrated reality was barely accessible to her.

Betty also views her past life as one lurking with potential clashes which she shunned with a honey-mouthed, ingratiating, unctuous attitude. Fearful lest the expression of a strong feeling might lead to disaster, Betty developed a communication mode intended to disguise and neutralize her expressions. She accomplishes this by over-elaboration, over-explaining, contradicting, denying what she affirms and vice versa so that the listener is lost in a maze of detail. Betty was the baby and the pet of her parents and four siblings, the closest of whom was ten years her senior. Her father's occupation required frequent moves so that she never lived in one place for more than a year. She had neither close friends nor relationships during her life, and expended her energies in creating the appearance of friendship and closeness. She selected a husband who seemed able to play the complimentary role in the game of creating illusions.

These parents manifested a seemingly impenetrable defense against knowing or being known intimately by others. Father's defenses crumbled somewhat when his daughter was defined as psychotic and he manifested a growing capacity for meditation, examination and revelation. But mother, throughout the major part of casework, and after five years of prior psychotherapy, persistently produced a rich variety of tenacious defenses against interpersonal closeness.

The excerpt which follows was selected from a recorded interview that took place nine months after Lilly's hospitalization.

FATHER: For example, yesterday I had to do something I didn't want to. I wasn't even consulted until the die was cast almost. Betty decided and talked to Lilly about it and

MOTHER: Well, I talked to Lilly about it before I took my cue.

FATHER: And then came to me and told me what was up and even though I didn't want to, why, I went along with it. I was tired. I had spent several hours working out in the back yard and I thought the way it was handled, why I certainly had to go along with it whether I wanted to or not.

CASEWORKER: How did you feel about that?

FATHER: Well, I was resentful about it except I thought it was basically a good idea and under ordinary circumstances I would have been more wholeheartedly in favor of it than I was yesterday.

CASEWORKER: How did it come about?

MOTHER: Well, Herman and I had been seated on the back porch steps. This was something I had wondered about our talking about today anyway. Because I was wondering if I had handled it wrong and I was wondering about Herman's reaction to it when it developed later and he said to me, um, oh, what was it? I don't know whether you used the word pressured or what, but anyway, I was wondering if you felt that way and if therefore I had handled it incorrectly. And I had conflicts about it because I thought this advice to me to make decisions on my own, and uh, I thought, well, gosh, if he doesn't want to, he should let us know. It's nothing that's definite. Speak up. It started out on the back porch while he was having a cool drink. We were commenting on the fact that we had, well, we had discussed before the possibility of a barbecue depending on the weather and this was early afternoon and we were just commenting that the weather didn't look too good. We might as well have our ground beef patties indoors, you know, at dinner, indoors, without the bun, and we sort of let it go at that. Well, I got to thinking. This little gal was kinda going back to her younger play habits and so forth a bit yesterday, weren't you dear, and . . . So we just sort of mentioned this. The weather wasn't too good and we would just have our plain hamburgers inside. And he said he didn't care to have the buns with them and so forth. And I got to thinking of Lilly and her day; that she hadn't uh had anything special. She wasn't about to have a friend over. She wasn't doing anything particularly constructive that was fun, and, uh, the sun began to seep through a little bit, and all this put together, I got to thinking, well, uh, why don't Herman and I ask her about this, and then I thought, no, here we go putting a responsibility where it doesn't belong the way we did one Sunday morning with putting the decision to her, so what I did was to say to Lilly, "Well, Lilly, daddy and I have about decided that maybe the weather isn't quite good enough to, uh, have a barbecue outside. Maybe we'll just have our ground meat inside." And, uh, then I got to thinking, well sharp as she is in her feelings, she's going to know maybe why I'm saying this, so I'll, to be clear cut and unconfused about it, I'll just say it. I said, "Of course you know I'm saying this to get your reaction." And she said, "Aw, aw, let's have a barbecue, aw c'mon. I'd want to barbecue outside if it weren't either snowing or raining." And, uh, so I said, "Do you very much want it or just kinda want it," and she said, "Very much, please."

So I went out and told Herman. I didn't have time to tell him all the details of how this took place, but that I had felt her out on this and she seemed anxious to have a barbecue and that the weather was a little bit better and maybe could we, after all, and, uh, he said something, right at that point, spontaneously, that, uh, made me think—oh, did I handle it wrong, because he said—do you remember exactly what you said?

FATHER: Well, I think I said something to the effect that I was sort of put in a position where I had to go along with it because I hadn't been consulted and I was being pressured to go through with it and uh, by that time, I had been working in the back yard about three or four hours and I was ready to drop. I was in the middle of doing a difficult job of trimming an overgrown hedge and when a barbecue is held, it means that I do quite a bit of the work and I just wasn't in the mood to go through all that work after having put in a hard physical afternoon out there, and it seemed to me that two things were wrong with this picture; one that she had gone ahead and put this idea in Lilly's head and of course Lilly would want to go ahead and do it then, without first having discussed it with me at all, so that it was sort of a *fait accompli*, as it were. And number two, if she couldn't see how tired I was, well, I thought it was kind of, uh, uh, inconceivable that she couldn't tell I was about ready to drop. And it made me mad that she was kinda blind to my situation, so I was rather blunt in my remarks and so finally she went off after I had expressed my feeling in no uncertain terms I thought. And then, later on, it was as though I hadn't told her, as though she hadn't gotten the message, how I felt about it. I sorta felt that she made up her mind to do it and wanted to do it, and

MOTHER: Well, I told you right that very minute, after your very first response that if you were too tired, we wouldn't do it, but then you insisted—no, that we go on with it.

FATHER: Well, because I thought it was useless to do anything else.

MOTHER: (*Sighing*) We weren't communicating.

FATHER: Well, I'm sure that there wasn't full communication, or if there was, it was too late.

CASEWORKER: (To father) If you didn't want to do it, why didn't you make the decision not to?

FATHER: Well, I didn't want to be arbitrary about it and say no, I won't do it because I'm tired, but I wanted her to know I was doing it because the die was cast as it were, and she had sort of committed herself to doing it with Lilly, and Lilly would like to do it, and I thought, well, I'll do it even though I'm doing it under protest.

MOTHER: Oh, it wasn't a hundred per cent sure with Lilly, and I thought I made that clear too. I just came out to tell you she would very much like it and so, could we? But you didn't give me a No answer.

FATHER: Well, I did everything but come out and say No in so many words. I thought there was no mistaking how I felt about it. How did you think I felt about it?

MOTHER: Well, I got the message that you didn't like the way I handled it and then I was a little bit confused because I thought, here I was supposed to be making some decisions more on my own, and I make one and do the wrong thing, darn it (laugh). And, uh, the decision was to broach the subject to Lilly. The decision was not to have the barbecue because that was still up to you, but, uh, the decision was to find out how she felt about it, and how strongly and so forth. And, uh, then I thought that you felt though that the decision to have it absolutely had been made and that you felt you'd been railroaded or something, but when I urged you to say no if you were very much against it, after all (laugh), you have as much say as she does. More. Well, then you wouldn't say no, I just really rather we wouldn't today or no

FATHER: You got the feeling I was strongly against it though.

MOTHER: Uh, that you would rather not, but that you were going along because she wanted it apparently. But I thought if you were very, very strongly against it, that you would say, no, let's not.

FATHER: You didn't feel that I was strongly against it?

MOTHER: Well, not strongly enough to say no.

FATHER: In other words, I would have to say no, to make it formal. There'd be no other way for me to change the decision other than to come out and say, to formally say, to express my feelings, in spite of all the other things I had done to get my message through I thought.

MOTHER: Well, just say, well, no, really, I don't want to go along with that this afternoon. I, uh, the weather is not right, or, uh, I don't want us to do it. Cause later on, when I asked you about it again, even later, I said, "Well, look, we still don't have to go through with it if you're too tired," and you said "Oh, no, it's not that I'm too tired, it's just that I wasn't particularly in the mood this afternoon." Remember that?

FATHER: I also remember when we discussed it, I said "Apparently all the hints I dropped didn't get to you. You didn't get the message."

CASEWORKER: (To Lilly) What do you think, are your parents arguing?

LILLY: I think sort of they are.

CASEWORKER: What do you think about that?

LILLY: It's kind of strange. It makes me feel kind of puzzled. If somebody loves each other, why should they argue?

CASEWORKER: (To Parents) Maybe the two of you don't want to be sure it's an argument either.

LILLY: How much does a tape recorder cost?

The discussion will deal with some of the major dimensions that comprise this family's interaction system; a system which produces the deeply entrenched, self perpetuating, self enforcing system of binds and unbinds.

Pseudo-mutuality, used in the sense that Lyman Wynne (16) intended, appears as the superordinate value in the family. This central value is safeguarded and defended by a number of methods, some of which involve avoidance of conflict at all costs, avoidance of defined differences and differentiations, basing action on assumptions made about one another rather than on actual information, and a communication style which renders interchanges meaningless or neutralizes them so that their meaning cannot be discerned. Pseudo-mutual families seem to fear that the momentary loss or appearance of close mutuality results in disaster, thus much of the family's energy store is directed towards maintaining this illusion. In the excerpt, mother's attempt to avoid conflict with father resulted in a tangle of ambiguous messages, one of which was the explicit statement to Lilly of the vague decision not to have the barbecue, immediately followed by an implicit adjuration to Lilly to formulate the decision.

The inability to differentiate the feelings of one from the other in the family seems interwoven with the entire process.

Both parents respond to Lilly on the basis of assumptions they make about her feelings and thoughts and not on information about them. These assumptions usually consist of projections of the parents' thoughts and feelings. This provides them with an escape valve for problems and frustrations threatening to burst into the open, and a safe arena in which to express their unresolved, albeit disguised, conflicts. At the same time, it protects their image of the conflict-free family. When Lilly requests impersonal information, mother often assumes that this is a message intended to disguise feeling unloved. Mother responds to Lilly with a reassurance that she is loved. Lilly, confused by the irrelevancy of mother's response, will herself respond with irrelevant and often bizarre behavior. Mother then assumes that Lilly is feeling increasingly insecure and continues to reassure her that she is loved and wanted. By this time, Lilly usually hugs mother so tightly she bruises her. When father complains, mother effectively denies the meaning of his complaint by countercomplaining about the lack of togetherness in the family. Thus, in the context of a complaint, mother demands an absence of complaint.

It appears that one of the chief derivative sources for the process of binding and unbinding lies in internal binds of the individual members, e.g. father's resentment of mother's flagrant ineptitude to perform routine household chores is in conflict with his need for mother to provide him with the image of the well-functioning, ideally harmonic family. To make an unequivocal demand for efficiency from mother would be tantamount to a demand that she grow up. The fear that mother's growing up or away from him will constitute a loss of the relationship, coupled with his need for her to provide him with the image of the stable, well-run home presents him with an internal bind which expresses itself in a contradictory injunction to mother. On one level of abstraction, he encourages her childlike behavior for fear that growth will lead to destruction of the relationship, and on another level of abstraction he discourages her childlike behavior by refusing to play a role complementary to it.

This is gross oversimplification. Only a slice of this family's vast network of binds and unbinds has been extracted to indicate the manner in which this self perpetuating process may lead to the disorganization of one of the family members. Professional standards of "healthy" functioning appeared to the Cranes, throughout the course of casework, as a malignant intruder threatening to destroy the only mode of relationship that existed in their range of experience. Yet the family actively participated and resisted in an examination of their habits of behavior. This basic interaction pattern continued, but in a way which included occasional thrusts into new, unfamiliar ways of relating and communicating.

References

1. BATESON, G., JACKSON, D. D., HALEY, J. and WEAKLAND, J., "Toward a Theory of Schizophrenia," *Behav. Sci.*, 1, 251–264, 1956.

2. BATESON, G., "Minimal Requirements for a Theory of Schizophrenia," *Arch. Gen. Psychiat.*, 2, 477–491, 1960.

3. BOWEN, M., "Family Psychotherapy," *Am. J. Orthopsychiat.*, 31, 40–60, 1961.

4. BRIM, O., "The Parent-Child Relation as a Social System: Parent-Child Roles," *Child Devel.*, 28, 343–365, 1957.

5. HALEY, J., "An Interactional Description of Schizophrenia," *Psychiatry*, 22, 321–332, 1959.

6. HALEY, J., "The Family of the Schizophrenic: A Model System," *J. Nerv. Ment. Dis.*, 129, 357–374, 1959.

7. JACKSON, D. D. and WEAKLAND, J. H., "Conjoint Family Therapy: Some Considerations on Theory, Technique and Results," *Psychiatry*, 24, 30–45, 1961.

8. LIDZ, T., FLECK, S., CORNELISON, A. and TERRY, D., "The Intrafamilial Environment of the Schizophrenic Patient," *Am. J. Orthopsychiat.*, 28, 764–776, 1958.

9. LIDZ, T., "Schizophrenia and the Family," *Psychiatry*, 21, 21–27, 1958.

10. PARSONS, T. and BALES, R. F., *Family Socialization and Interaction Process*, Glencoe, Ill., Free Press, 1954.

11. ROSENBAUM, C. P., "Patient-Family Similarities in Schizophrenia," *Arch. Gen. Psychiat.*, 5, 120–126, 1961.

12. SPIEGEL, J. P. and BELL, N. W., "Families of the Schizophrenic Patient," in Arieti, S. (ed.), *American Handbook of Psychiatry*, New York, Basic Books, 1959.

13. STRINGER, J., "Case Studies of the Families of Schizophrenics," *Smith College Studies in Social Work*, 32, 118–149, 1962.

14. STRODTBECK, F. L., "The Family as a Three Person Group," *Am. Soc. Rev.*, 19, 23–29, 1954.

15. WEINER, N., *The Human Use of Human Beings*, New York, Doubleday, 1950.

16. WYNNE, L. C., RYCKOFF, I. M., DAY, J. and HIRSCH, S. I., "Pseudo Mutuality in the Family Relations of Schizophrenics," *Psychiatry*, 21, 205–220, 1958.

IV

*Marriage in the Social
Matrix*

The first three selections, here, treat roles as they are influenced by forces from the social milieux. Rainwater *et al.* and Whyte discuss the wife's role, as it is played at opposite ends of the social hierarchy. The former describe, in the main, the wives of workingmen: the daily round of tasks and activities, and the associated attitudes. Whyte writes of the corporation executive's wife: what is expected of her; how she feels about this; and how her performance may affect her husband's career. David Riesman offers an analysis in depth of changing sex roles; young people, especially college students, are the prime focus of attention.

In the final article, Slater interprets marriage (along with other customs) as a mechanism which opposes a profound human tendency toward withdrawal, the atomizing of society, and the dissolution of social bonds.

13

DAY IN, DAY OUT

LEE RAINWATER, RICHARD COLEMAN,

AND GERALD HANDEL

We have discussed briefly the social position in the American
social hierarchy which is called "working class," and have noted
that the women whose lives are being described belong to this
class by virtue of their husbands' blue collar jobs, their own
and their husbands' modest educational attainments (mostly
high school graduation, sometimes less) and their similarly
modest housing and residential acquisitions. In this chapter
we shall concern ourselves with the way in which these women
live their daily lives within such a social context. In our research, we have asked working class women to tell us what
their day-to-day activities are and how they feel about these by
asking: "What is a typical day like?", "How does the week go?",
"How are the weekends different from weekdays?", "What
happens at vacation time?", "Which holidays are celebrated?",
and "How does winter differ from summer, or spring from
fall?".

SOURCE: Lee Rainwater, Richard Coleman and Gerald Handel, *Working-
man's Wife* (Dobbs Ferry, New York: Oceana Publications, Inc., 1952),
pp. 26–41. Copyright © 1959 by Social Research, Inc. Reprinted by permission of Oceana Publications, Inc.

The way working class and middle class women talk in response to such questions provides us with insight into the variety of activities in which they engage, and indicates the hierarchy or importance of time consumption for them. We learn about the "daily rhythm" in these women's lives and come to some understanding of the "annual round of life"— the adjustments made to the changing seasons and the ways holidays and vacations interrupt the normal routine. Finally, we gain insight into their emotional response to the content of their daily lives.

The working class wife's daily life is centered upon the tasks of homemaking, child-rearing, and husband-servicing. When these women describe a "typical day" they devote most of their reportorial attention to three aspects of the day: their housework, their children, and their husbands. The attention devoted to their children is only partially affected by the age of these children—the mothers of very young children quite naturally believe their "typical days" are consumed by both nurturant and policeman-like attention to these children; however, the mothers of older children seem to be equally wrapped up in the activities of these not-so-necessarily-dependent children. The working class women whose lives seem to contain any other important foci are those who hold jobs. In the following description we occasionally differentiate between the "working women" and the "homemakers only." And, of course, we also find it useful to separate the mothers of older children from those of very young children. However, it is this latter group which we have taken as our main model.

We will let some of these women speak for themselves about their days. These samples are rather typical in the range and kind of daily activity mentioned even though these particular women are more articulate than many in the richness of detail they provide. The first description was given by a 24-year old woman from Trenton, New Jersey. She lives in one of Levittown's modest new houses:

> Well, naturally, I get up first, make breakfast for my husband and put a load of clothes in my washer while breakfast

cooks. Then I wake him up, give him his breakfast and he's off to work. Then I make breakfast for the children. After the children eat I dress them and they go out to play. Then I hang the clothes up and clean lightly through the house. In between times I do the dishes—that's understood, of course. Then I make lunch for the children and myself and I bring them in, clean them up, and they eat. I send them out to play when they're done and I do the dishes, bring the clothes in, and iron them. When I'm done ironing it's usually time to make supper, or at least start preparing it. Sometimes I have time to watch a TV story for half an hour or so. Then my husband comes home and we have our meals. Then I do the dishes again. Then he goes out to work again—he has a part-time job—at his uncle's beverage company. Well, he does that two or three nights a week. If he stays home he watches TV and in the meantime I get the kids ready for bed. He and I have a light snack, watch TV awhile and then go to bed.

A 22-year old housewife from Tacoma tells much the same story:

> Ye Gods—what do I do. Well, I get up and out of bed at 6 A.M. I get my son dressed and then get breakfast. After breakfast I wash dishes then bathe and feed my baby. She's 3 months old. Then I start the procedure of house cleaning. I make beds—dust, mop, sweep, vacuum. Then I do my baby's wash. Then I get lunch for the three of us. Then I put my baby to bed, and the little boy to bed for his nap. Then I usually sew or mend or wash windows or iron and do the things I can't possibly get done before noon. Then I cook supper for my family. After supper my husband usually watches TV while I wash dishes. I get the kids to bed. Then—if I'm lucky—I'm able to sit down, watch TV or read a magazine. Then I set my hair and go to bed.

Here is a story of harassment told by a 23-year-old Louisville mother of two young children:

> Well, I fight with the children to eat for one thing. They don't want to eat. The little girl—she's 4—is hungry and then she won't eat. They usually go on outside after breakfast. I feed the baby and give him a bath and then I put him on the

floor. Then I make the bed up, dust the floors and dust the furniture and by that time it's time for dinner. Then I fix dinner and do the dishes. In between time I have to feed him and give him a bath and put him to bed. Then it's time to fix supper and Daddy comes home. After supper we just sit here and watch TV or I visit one of the neighbors. We very seldom go out during the week because he works. My husband may wash the car or something like that. Other than that he just watches TV or goes to sleep. He putters around the yard or reads maybe. He is usually too tired after he comes home from work. The children just spend the whole day playing and getting messed up. Then they watch TV after supper with me. Then they get washed and go to bed about 9 o'clock.

And finally, we have a daily-tale told by a 29-year old Trenton woman in which a mode of relaxation other than TV is mentioned:

I get up and do the dishes and make the beds and sweep the floors. I scrub the kitchen once a day, wash and iron, and then towards evening I get dinner. I do just what most everybody does. In the afternoons—well, my husband works nights—so I get his meal about 2 o'clock, and clean up after him. Then I usually have a couple of hours I spend at the neighbors yaking. This backyard takes a lot of work too because we are going to seed it over. This place was a mess when we moved in here a year ago. I usually go to the store once a day and my little boy takes a nap too. Usually I sit and sew half the evening and read the rest of the evening.

These four accounts of "my day" illustrate quite clearly how extremely busy the woman is with her housework. She fixes breakfast, washes clothes, dresses children, cleans the house, does the dishes, makes lunch, irons the clothes, makes supper, makes light snacks, makes beds, dusts, mops, sweeps, mends old clothes, washes windows, scrubs the kitchen, works out in the yard, shops for groceries, and sews on new clothes or curtains. She has no maid to help her with any of these tasks. Her children are too young to be of assistance. Her husband often has an extra income job or has his own responsibilities (such as washing the car or seeding the yard), so that he cannot be counted on to help her.

It is no wonder that with all these homemaking activities to perform, she is sometimes tempted to describe her daily life as one in which:

> I wash or iron or clean up the house or sew and that just about covers my days. I haven't ever caught up with myself since the twins were born four years ago.

or where,

> By the time I get breakfast and dishes done my morning's gone and by the time the canning I'm doing this summer is over the whole day's gone. And it's been just housework all day long.

She also views her children as a source of considerable concern in her daily life. She must feed them, clothe them, bathe them, and put them to bed, and she must keep a continual weather-eye out for them, even when she is not immediately ministering to their habitual wants and needs, lest "I spend half of my day kissing all their little hurts and bruises." Or, as another said, "What with hunting for the kids I'm running in and out most of the day."

These women frequently find that "life around little children" is one perpetual battle—either with them, or between them. When they are asked how the children spend their time —and hers, many chorused: "The children—they fight," or "The kids get up in the morning and they don't do anything but fuss all day," or "In between fights, the children play and eat and sleep." And sometimes, "They don't want to eat," so that the mother must "fight with the children to get them to eat."

Time and again working class women express the feeling that their responsibilities toward their children preclude many expeditions into the outside world of clubs or parties or travels. To these women the presence of small children in a home is an automatic definition for the busy woman: "I have three boys so you can imagine I'm busy all right."

In these descriptions of daily routines, the husbands seem to come in a poor third in the attention they get. The wives serve them breakfast, sometimes fix their lunch, prepare their suppers, wash and mend their clothes—but don't "waste" nearly as many words on them, as on the house and children. Perhaps this is because the presence of the husband is only a part-time phenomenon, while the children are a "full-time nuisance."

The principal effect of the husband's activities on these daily routines seems to be in setting the hour for breakfast, supper, and bedtime. If a husband does not work the standard eight-hour day (between 8:00 and 5:00), the working class woman regards this as upsetting her time schedule. She may have to fix her big meal at 2:00 in the afternoon, instead of at noon or in the early evening. If the husband has an extra job in the evening or on the weekends, this enlarges the amount of home and yard responsibilities she must undertake. If the husband drives the car to work, she finds herself isolated in her own immediate neighborhood while he's gone.

By the time she fulfills the tasks which arise from these three important roles as homemaker, child-rearer, and husband-servicer, she finds herself with little time for, or interest in, any other kind of activity. She rarely attends a club meeting or goes to a party—at least she doesn't mention this as being a part of her typical day. She may get time for reading, "while the children are napping," or "before going to bed." She almost never mentions playing games, such as bridge or canasta, or spending time at sports, such as bowling or swimming.

The "daily routine" of a working class wife typically includes only two activities beyond the big three of house, children, and husband. These "other two" activities are TV watching and neighbor or relative visiting. However, "casual visiting" as a daily activity is not mentioned by a majority of these women. Television, in contrast, ranks very high in their devotion: well over a majority of working class women consider their television sessions important enough aspects of their days to be included in their descriptions. Very few of these women, however, work in any TV time until the evening when they are able to sit down in front of the set with either their husbands or children. Occasionally a young housewife mentions that her family takes daily car rides in the evening, or that she chauffeurs the children to a nearby swimming pool in the summer. But such adventures beyond the realm of homemaking or TV watching are distinct exceptions.

The only "adventurers" among these young housewives are those with jobs which take them out of their homes every day. This kind of "adventure" however does not change their daily life much, except to confine it to a quadrangle instead of a triangle: the job becomes a fourth point of energy output. They do not use their jobs as an avenue toward additional adventure. Perhaps this report of "her day" from a 39-year old Chicago working wife will illustrate the typical effect of a job upon the daily routine.

> I just run from one day to the next. I get up at six, eat breakfast and fix lunch for myself and my husband. We get up at the same time, but he leaves a half-hour before me. He takes the bus to work and then later on at five I pick him up in the car and we drive home. I drive if he is tired, or else he does the driving. You see, we both work near each other—it's really only a few blocks away. I let mother keep care of my youngest daughter, and then I send Carol, who is 3, to nursery school. In the evenings I just get the supper and then do the dishes, plus maybe some ironing or cleaning. There's always enough to do: too much in fact. Mostly we just watch TV in the evening, or if it's hot like yesterday we go out and sit on the lawn. But mostly we're both tired. Our jobs just knock us out and in the evenings we just plop down.

Where the wife has no children around her house—because she is still a "young bride," or has become a "deserted mother," or was never anything other than a "childless wife," a slight increase is noted in the extent of her "visiting" or "movie going." However, the evidence leans in the direction of indicating a relatively "empty" existence for these women rather than one of equal "busyness" directed elsewhere. When asked how their days went, these women were singularly non-verbal, as if their days were not as full of meaningful activity.

A young bride related the events of her typical day in the following fashion:

> We get up at 5:45. I make my husband's breakfast and pack his lunch. I have coffee and straighten up the house, then I go to work at 8:45. Both my husband and I work all day long. My husband gets home at 4. I get home an hour later and I start supper. Afterwards, I clean the dishes. We spend our evenings either visiting or going to movies. We watch television when we get home and then retire at 10 or 11.

And a deserted mother describes her "deserted day" with these comments:

> I get up at 5:30 in the morning and make breakfast. I get my husband off to work at 6:30. He comes home about 4 o'clock and I make dinner. In between times I do some household chores and look at television maybe an hour or so. In the evening we visit friends for several hours in the neighborhood and then go to bed about 11 o'clock.

One suspects that her television set is left on for more than "an hour or so," and that she has not reported the amount of time she spends in magazine reading.

At the other extreme from the daily boredom implied by this woman's report of her day, is that given us by a "school-age mother" who is trying to expand her mental and social horizons.

> First of all I fix breakfast for everybody—We have six people in the house—then I start the wash—when there is enough to bother with. That's about three times a week. Then right away I fix my husband's lunch to take to work. I get up at 5:45 in order to get everything done. After breakfast I get the wash out and put it in the dryer, clean the dishes and fix lunch for myself and my children. They have come home from school, and I keep them home for a full hour so they will rest. Then I send them back at 1 o'clock. After lunch I straighten things up around the home and do some sewing—you see I make my own dresses and a lot of other things. I'm not a TV watcher like some people. I'd rather sew or read. By 5:45 it's time to start supper so we can all eat around 6:00. In the evenings I just read or sew or I visit with the neighbors. A lot of the time I show them how to sew. I have classes, sort of—

I taught it to myself, you know. I'm not a professional dress-maker—what I want to do now is to take some evening course so that I'll learn to sew without a pattern like a real pro-fessional.

This woman is an exception: as a rule, working class house-wives whose children are of school age do not get out of the house much more than the younger mothers. A minority of them, mostly upper working class mothers in new suburbs, mention some PTA activity or work in the scouting move-ments or attendance at Little League games.

The Working Class Wife Classifies Her Daily Routine as "Dull, Normal"

She characterizes her daily life as "busy," "crowded," "a mess," "humdrum," "dull, just dull." But she feels that this is the lot of most housewives, except, perhaps, "those society leaders you read about in the papers." The general tenor of her attitude toward what a day in her life is like is indicated by the follow-ing comments:

> Crowded, just crowded—that's what every day is like. They're all busy. They're just dull too. We just don't do much except work. They're all dull compared to those you read about in the newspapers of people who run around all the time.
>
> Oh, it's housework all day long. We really don't do very much—I would like to get out more if I weren't so isolated out here. My husband has the car all day long, so I'm sort of stuck here.
>
> All I ever seem to do is mess around. I get up at 8—I make breakfast, so I do the dishes, have lunch, do some more dishes, and then some more work in the afternoon. Then it's supper dishes and I get to sit down for a few minutes before the children have to be sent to bed. That's it—that's all there is to my day.

> My day's just like any other wife's. It's just routine. Humdrum. It's really just what every other housewife does.
>
> We don't do much of anything special. I imagine my day is spent doing what any housewife does. Just cooking and cleaning, washing the dishes and mending clothes. Then the biggest part of the time I am chasing kids.

If she feels that her own life is one of monotony or is a "humdrum" existence, she is consoled by her belief that this does not make her different from most of the other women she knows.

She usually does not know many middle class women. Since middle class women and working class women tend to live in different sections of the city, the latter are not sufficiently acquainted with the middle class mode of life to draw comparisons of self or life styles. Even if the working class woman were able to make such comparisons, she might not see her own life as so very different. After all, the "young mothers" among the middle class also spend a considerable amount of time in infant care; they also wash dishes and clothes; they also fix three meals a day for their families (as a rule). Where the middle class woman is really different is not so much in what she does (though this is different in noticeable ways, as will be described shortly), but in her reaction to her life circumstances.

The middle class woman does not see her daily life as "dull, normal." To her one day is not "just like the next." Life is not "routine," or "humdrum"—if anything, it sometimes seems not quite "routine" enough. When middle class women were asked to describe a typical day they reacted with statements such as:

> Are there any typical days? Every day there's something new! How can I possibly describe a typical day?

or,

> Each day is different. I do try to accomplish certain things each day—but my schedule usually gets upset.

or,

> Every day is different when you have two little ones around. I have a teenager and then this little child, and I can assure

you that with them coming up with something new, there are no two days alike. You can't even plan very well.

Where the working class wife finds her children "fighting every day," the middle class woman sees her children "coming up with something new." Undoubtedly both groups of children do their share of squabbling and "coming up with something new." But the working class mother is more conscious of the fights and their wearing effect upon her patience, while the middle class woman is more conscious of the "new," and this engenders pride and wonderment at her children. The difference in these women's days seems as much a matter of viewpoint as behavior.

Middle class women do not believe they have "typical days." The variety which they impute to their "days" is not solely a product of different viewpoint, however. They frequently schedule the days in the week so each has its function. The weekend is assigned its importance as a time when the whole "family can get together and do something as a unit." It is a time specifically laid aside for relaxation. The various seasons are thought of as providing opportunities for exploration of different facets of life: winter is for social pleasures, and summer is for the personal pleasures of swimming or boating or working in the garden. This is the way the middle class woman thinks of her year. When, therefore, she is asked to describe a typical day, her first thought is to ask: "Do you mean a weekday, or a Sunday?"; "Do you mean in summer or winter— we've got a different pattern, you know."

The middle class woman, despite her knowledge that it might not work out as she intends, usually assigns a function to each of her days:

> Monday is laundry; Tuesday, I shop for groceries; Wednesday, the cleaning woman comes; Thursday, I buy the meats for the weekend; and Friday, I go to the beauty parlor.

> Monday is washing and ironing; Tuesday is club meeting; Wednesday is mending and shopping; Thursday is downstairs day, and Friday is upstairs day.

She obviously homemakes just as does the working class wife. However, she does not appear to be hell-bent on doing everything every single day. Thereby she apparently makes more efficient use of her housekeeping time.

The middle class woman also child-rears and husband-tends. She fixes their meals, sews their clothes frequently, and makes sure they get to work or school on time. But that is not all she does.

> I get up at 6:45 A.M. and get every one off—my husband to work, and my daughter to school. Then I get my younger two children dressed for outside so they can play while I do up my dishes and my general housework. In the afternoons I do a lot of sewing—making things for the girls and myself. I have a lot of organizations I belong to and sometimes I attend those if I can find someone to take care of the children. Then my husband comes home—and we have a fairly late dinner, usually, unless he has to run out to attend a couple of his meetings. If he doesn't, he may work around the house, while I read or sew—and then again, we may just watch TV. Right now we're getting ready to have an open house this weekend —so my husband will probably help me get the place in ship-shape.

The middle class woman experiences more variety in her life, and less monotony, because she has a much greater number of personal, avocational and outside interests than does the working class wife. Most middle class women have a "meeting" to go to at least twice a month. And they report that every now and then one of their "typical" days might include:

> Going out for dinner and a dance,
> Getting together with another couple to play mahjongg,
> Having an open house for 40 to 50 people,
> Going to a tea today—we'll probably play bridge also,
> Doing voluntary work for the Red Cross,
> Playing volleyball down at the club with a bunch of the girls,
> Doing some backstage work at the Little Theater.

Both groups of women report with fairly considerable frequency that a typical day might include some "visiting." But when the middle class woman speaks of visiting, she is usually referring to the talking she does at one of these meetings or parties, while the working class woman usually refers to visits with a "neighbor," "relatives and in-laws," or "a girl friend" whom she's known since her childhood. Thus, even the visiting a working class wife does during a day might seem monotonous to her (as compared with that done by the middle class woman), inasmuch as she's doing it with the "same old people" she has always known.

Let us conclude this comparison of the "typical" day by noting that time and again the middle class women refused to describe a "typical day." They combined elements from several of their days into their description of one. Perhaps they were afraid a "typical day" would not really do justice to the variety of interests which occupy them during a month. Perhaps they did not want to appear to lead as dull a life as a single day, taken at random, might indicate. On the other hand, the working class women did not seem to mind describing a "typical day," though they were mindful and conscious of how routinely similar the days are.

The Weekend Routine Is Also Dull, Normal

Weekends are "not too much different from the rest of the week" for the working class wives. When these women are asked: "How are the weekends different from the rest of the week?" they are apt to curtly reply, "They're not." They may issue this judgment in a variety of ways: the chorus is different, but the tune is essentially the same.

> Nothing different about them. They're much the same except that I may go for a swim.
>
> There's really not too much to do around this town so they're pretty much the same.
>
> The only thing different about them is that my husband has a different job—he works right through Saturday and Sunday.

> The weekend is just the same as the week except the children sometimes go to Sunday School. We're pretty much the homebodies—we really lead quite dull lives.
>
> Oh well, there's hardly any difference. My husband has to work part of Saturday and Sunday, too.
>
> They are just about the same, except I refuse to do housework on weekends. They're really just like any other day. A day's a day to me.
>
> I'm a lot busier, that's what. I do the same things as I do the rest of the week, but with everybody home, I have less time to do them in.

Let it be noted that "weekend days" are not always the same: the housewife refuses to work, or else she's busier. The children may go to Sunday school, the husband may have a different job, the wife may go for a swim. But these differences seem less significant to them than the similarities. They seem surprisingly ready to believe that "every day is like every other." Perhaps the worst indictment of the weekend was rendered by a woman who reported:

> Saturday is different from Sunday because my husband brings home all his work clothes and I wash them.

In fact, it is far from true that "the weekends are no different from the rest of the week" for the majority of these women. There is one custom practiced by a great many (on either Saturday or Sunday) which is not paid such regular heed during the week. This is a visit to the relatives. Many echo the statement made by the 32-year old housewife from Tacoma:

> On Sunday we always get the family together; that's just automatic.

For some families, this weekend visit is Sunday dinner at either the mother's home or the mother-in-law's; for others it requires a drive into the country or to a nearby town to visit "the folks" or perhaps a brother and sister-in-law who still live in the "old hometown."

Other activities, which various working class women report

as characteristic of their weekends (in contrast to their weekdays), are "taking a ride out into the country," "going to the
shore," "my husband goes fishing or hunting," "taking in a
movie," or "going out to eat." For many families there is a
division between Saturday and Sunday: Saturday is for yard
work and shopping, while Sunday is for church and relaxation.
However, less than half of the women in our study sample go
to church as often as twice a month. They are not church-
going women for the most part, just as they are not club
members.

Working class women do not actually experience a weekend as it is known by most "white collar" Americans. Many of
the husbands have "extra income jobs" on Saturday or Sunday
(or perhaps in the evenings during the week). Another large
portion of the husbands, particularly those in the transporta-
tion industries or in public service as policemen or firemen,
are required by the nature of their employment, to serve the
public during the weekend as well as on weekdays.

In direct contrast, middle class women think of their weekends as entirely different from the weekdays. The weekend
theme is "doing things as a family" and "relaxing from the
ardors of mid-week." Middle class women describe their weekends in a strikingly different tone.

The difference is that I try to do things with my family
more than some housework. Sometimes I prepare a lunch or
dinner out on the lawn in summertime—and we do a little
extra entertaining in the winter.

Sunday is the day we do things together—the whole family
goes to church and then we may go visiting. We want to do it
all together if we can.

We never have a set routine for the weekend. We do whatever we feel like on the spur of the moment. I don't worry
about the work as much. I spend more time with my family—
and we just enjoy loafing around the house and get more
relaxation out of it. We may have some extra-good things to
eat.

We break out of the weekday grind. Our meals are at
different times. Sunday, we go to church, and maybe we will

shop on Saturday, or my husband will play golf, or sometimes we all go bowling. During the week, when the children are in school, I'm more or less my own boss. I do as I please— but on the weekends my family is around and we do a lot together.

We belong to a club of couples—we play cards about once a month. My husband is a Mason and we go to the Shrine Club on Saturday nights quite often. Sometimes we take the children, sometimes we don't. Sunday, after church, it's just 'mess-around.' We may go swimming or out to the beach in the afternoon during the summer. We do just what we want to do and when we want to do it. There is no really set pattern for anything.

Occasionally they visit relatives on the weekend, but most of the instances cited involved a relative who had a "beach cottage" or perhaps a horse farm where the "children can learn how to handle animals." In short, when middle class women say they do "things as a family" during the weekend, they are usually referring to the immediate family circle of their children and husband; whereas, the working class women who say that "getting the whole family together is automatic" every weekend, are talking about the extended clan of in-laws, brothers, and perhaps aunts, uncles or grandparents.

Summer Is Dull, Normal, Just Like Winter

Working class women, generally, believe that their lives are very little influenced by the changing seasons. The biggest change they envision is the invitation from summer weather to stay outside in their yards more often, while winter forbiddingly keeps them "holed up in their houses."

As with their reaction to the "weekend" or the "weekday," working class women are more conscious of the overall similarities in daily events than they are of whatever diversity and variety may be present.

> We're outside more in the summer and inside more in the winter, that's all. My husband remodelled the inside of the house this past winter. He'll paint the outside next summer. We stay inside more at night in winter. We usually sit outside in the summer time. I wouldn't really say that the time of the year makes any difference in what we do—when you have three children you've got to stay home a lot the whole year round.
>
> It's about the same in summer or winter. I'm still sewing. All we do is work no matter what month of the year it is.
>
> One thing that's different is that summer is cheaper for us. We can eat outdoors quite often, and it doesn't cost us so much. It doesn't use up so much electric power. We're confined to the inside during the winter and we watch TV all the time. (She also said: "The TV relaxes me and gives me a change from reading so many short stories," presumably Macfadden's.)

Working class husbands seem to be more affected by the changing of season, thereby eliciting varying reactions from their wives. At times it leaves the wives somewhat less than happy, as when:

> My husband fishes in summer and hunts up in the mountains in winter—but in either case I stay home.

On the other hand, the change in seasons can be a blessing when:

> My husband doesn't fish in the wintertime, so he stays home and I get to enjoy his company.

or,

> He doesn't go off playing sandlot ball in the winter.

But then, there is the woman who wishes the seasons did make a difference in her husband's life, because:

> There's no difference at all in the wintertime—my husband still makes his model cars, boats, and airplanes.

These bleak references to the lack of any difference between the seasons fortunately are not the whole picture. Though a good many of these women take this view, for others the winter is a time when they can go ice-skating, attend church more often, play cards every now and then, go bowling, take part in some of the children's school activities, or spend more time on home improvement projects. And the summer is a time when they can take more drives out into "nature," when they can garden, go on barbecues, swim, take in a baseball game every now and then, go berry picking or clam digging, watch their son's Little League games, or do some outdoor cooking.

Middle class women report many of the same differences between their summertime lives and their winter days. They also view winter as the time for indoor life and summer as the season for outdoor living. However, above and beyond these changes in the details of life, middle class women see the different seasons as having essentially different functions. Winter is the "social season," and summer is "for more purely personal pleasures":

> We do more entertaining in the winter evenings than during the summer. In the summertime so many friends are vacationing at any one time and are out of town that it's simpler to get the group together in the winter than during the summer.
>
> We have all these social activities in the winter—parties and dances, school affairs, or civic things like Community Chest drives, and then there's football games most every Saturday in the fall, and plays or concerts all through the winter. But in summer, we have our lake cottage, and we go out there more and get away from people. We just swim and relax. By the time summer is over, we're ready to pitch into our winter schedule once again.

If winter is highly active for the middle class families, then the summer's function is recuperative.

Working class wives do not usually have vacations which they can devote to travel. What they do with their vacation time is strictly influenced by the wife's age or child-rearing status. Many of the young mothers scoff at the idea of a "vacation." As one said: "Vacations, what are those? You don't ever get one when you have three little kids around." Most "older mothers" are able to report trips of one kind or another, even if their only purpose is to visit a relative in a nearby city. The "young" working class wife is unlikely to take a vacation either, because her husband is not established enough in his occupation:

> My husband hasn't always worked long enough or steady enough for a vacation—but we plan the first one he gets to go to the beach or camping and fishing.
>
> We don't have vacation time—my husband never gets a paid vacation. We're going to plan on it for next year though.
>
> My husband isn't going to get a vacation this year. Last year he got one—but it wasn't exactly a vacation. He went out to visit his sick mother. Sometime I'd like to leave the children behind and go to Mexico or Hawaii or Paris and do a lot of sightseeing.

or because her brood of children would be "too much trouble carting around the country."

> We visited my relatives in Iowa last year—but it was a nightmare taking two children along. I certainly didn't think I'd had any vacation. I'm waiting till they get a little older before I try that again.
>
> Babies are such a mess to bother with—they don't enjoy it and neither do you.

Or else, she and her husband choose to spend any vacation time on home projects:

> Last year we spent it building the house.
>
> We just stay around the house—he paints the outside of the house, and I try to keep the kids out of his way.

or perhaps on extra jobs which will eventually provide a better "home in the suburbs."

Middle class women in this same age group are also quite frequently inclined to "pass up real vacations while the kids are young." However, instead of letting the tender age of these children interfere with their own vacations, many manage to persuade forbearing grandparents to "take over the kids for a week or two." They say, in justification of their behavior, "That makes everybody happy: we get away from the kids, they get away from us . . . and then the grandparents are tickled to have them for a while, and for the kids it's a great treat too."

For many working class women the celebration of one of the big holidays (Christmas or Easter or Thanksgiving) is the nearest thing to a vacation. These holidays are usually celebrated in family-clan fashion at the grandparents' home. This, again, is somewhat different and in contrast with the middle class pattern of spending such holidays with the immediate family or with adult friends of long standing.

Overall, it appears that the lives of working class wives are relatively more constricted to the triangle of the home, children, and husband than is the case with the middle class families. Many satisfactions are found within this triangle, which often expands to include the whole circle of relatives and the family clan. However, they also respond to the life lived within this triangle by feeling it does not provide them with as much variety or relief from monotony as they might like. They see themselves as "hard working" women. They feel "tied down to the house" by their small children. They are solaced in their sometimes unhappy reaction by the recognition that their "dull" lot in life is shared by many American housewives, including most of the women they know.

The satisfactions which they do find are vested primarily in the people with whom they live so closely, and in the daily occupation of their lives as wives and mothers. We will see later the strong effect this has on their attitudes and motivations as consumers.

14

THE WIVES OF MANAGEMENT

WILLIAM H. WHYTE, JR.

There is a person, it would appear, to whom the modern corporation is beginning to pay a good bit of attention. Over the last few decades, as is now so frequently observed, the corporation has been evolving a social community able to provide its members with more and more of their basic social wants. Yet, the corporation now concedes, one of the principal members of its community remains officially almost unnoticed; to wit, the Wife. For the good of the corporation, many executives believe, it is time the matter was remedied. "We control a man's environment in business and we lose it entirely when he crosses the threshold of his home," one executive says mournfully. "Management, therefore, has a challenge and an obligation to deliberately plan and create a favorable, constructive attitude on the part of the wife that will liberate her husband's total energies for the job." Others, though they might not put it quite so badly, agree that the step is logical.

Just how to do this is a problem that has many a manage-

SOURCE: William H. Whyte, Jr., "The Wives of Management," *Fortune* (October, 1951), pp. 86–88ff. Copyright © by Time, Inc. Reprinted by permission of the publisher.

ment understandably baffled. On one very basic matter, however, management is not in the slightest baffled. It knows exactly what kind of wife it wants. With a remarkable uniformity of phrasing, corporation officials all over the country sketch the ideal. In her simplest terms, she is a wife who is: (1) highly adaptable, (2) highly gregarious, (3) realizes her husband belongs to the corporation.

Are the corporation specifications presumptuous? It would appear not. For the significant fact is not that corporations are trying to get this kind of wife. The significant fact is that her kind is precisely what our schools and colleges—and U.S. society in general—seem to be giving the corporation.

Let us define terms: we are discussing the wives of the coming generation of management, whose husbands are between twenty-five and forty, and in junior or middle management or with logical aspirations of getting there. There is, of course, no sharp dividing line between age groups, but among older executives there is a strong feeling that this younger generation of wives is the most cooperative the corporation has ever enlisted. "Somehow," says one executive, "they seem to give us so much less trouble than the older ones." "Either the girls are better or the men are marrying better," says another. "But whatever it is with these people, *they get along.*"

Perhaps it is merely that this generation of wives has not yet grown older and more cantankerous. Perhaps. But there is evidence that this group-mindedness is the result of a shift in values more profound than one might suppose. The change is by no means peculiar to the corporation wife, but by the nature of her job she may be the outstanding manifestation of it. And a preview, perhaps, of what is to come.

The Stabilizers

First, how do the wives conceive their own role? Critical literature has been answering the question rather forcefully, with the result that many Americans (and practically all Europeans) assume that the wife of the American businessman is not only the power behind the scenes but wants to become more so. The picture needs considerable revision. For the striking thing that emerges from wives' comments is the negativeness of the role they sketch. As they explain it, the good wife is good by *not* doing things—by *not* complaining when her husband works late; by *not* fussing when a transfer is coming up; by *not* engaging in any controversial activity. Moreover, they agree heartily that a good wife can't help a husband as much as a bad wife can hurt one. And the bad wife, clearly, is one who obtrudes too much—whether as a "meddler," a "climber," a "fixer," or, simply, someone who "pushes" her man around.

This conservatism is fairly recent. Slick-magazine fiction, that excellent index of accepted values, documents the shift. As late as the mid-thirties, a plot analysis indicates, stories were full of "dumb" smart girls, manipulating their amiable but often oafish husbands to business success. No longer. In affairs of commerce today's heroines are lovable nitwits, while the husbands, with tousled hair and lopsided grin, definitely run the show. It is still, in short, a man's world.

So, at least, it is to the executive wife. Resolutely antifeminist, she conceives her role to be that of a "stabilizer"— the keeper of the retreat, the one who rests and rejuvenates the man for the next day's battle. "A man gets so frustrated at the office—it's a disgrace—he should be able to come home to calmness." "I manage it so he can relax" . . . "I try to see that there are no problems left around the house."

This stabilizing calls for more than good homemaking and training the kids not to bother Daddy before dinner. Above all, wives emphasize, they have to be good listeners. They describe the job somewhat wryly—they must be "sounding boards," "refueling stations," "wailing walls"—but they speak without resentment. Nurturing the male ego, they seem to feel, is not only a pretty good fulfillment of their own ego but a form of therapy made increasingly necessary by the corporation way of life. Management psychologists couldn't agree more. "Most top executives are very lonely people," as one puts it. "The greatest thing a man's wife can do is to let him unburden the worries he can't confess to in the office."

In addition to listening, she can do some judicious talking. If she is careful about it, she can be a valuable publicity agent for the husband. "In a subtle way," says one executive, "they put in a plug for the husband, they tell things he wouldn't dare tell for fear of seeming immodest." In similar fashion they can humanize him if he's a boss. "About the time I get fed up with the bastard," says a junior executive, "here I am, going over to dinner at his house. And she's so nice—she jokes about him, kids him to his face—I figure he can't be so bad after all."

The Art of Survival

Good, low-key "stabilizing," then, the wife sees as her main task. There is another aspect to her role, however, and it is a good bit less passive. For the good corporation wife must also be a social operator—and when husbands and wives sketch out the personal characteristics of the ideal wife it is the equipment for this role that comes first to their minds. What they ask for, more than any other quality, is gregariousness—or a reasonable facsimile. Here are some of the ways in which they spell it out.

EXECUTIVE: "She should do enough reading to be a good conversationalist . . . Even if she doesn't like opera she should know something about it, so if the conversation goes that way she can hold her own. She has to be able to go with you if you're going to make a speech or get an award, and not be ill at ease."

EXECUTIVE: "The hallmark of the good wife is the ability to put people at their ease."

WIFE: "The most important thing for an executive's wife is to know everybody's name and something about their family so you can talk to them—also, you've got to be able to put people at their ease."

EXECUTIVE: "Keeping herself so she is comfortable with people on the boss's level is important. I don't think reading and music and that kind of stuff are vital."

EXECUTIVE: "The kind you want is the kind that can have people drop in any time and make a good show of it even if the baby's diapers are lying around."

WIFE: "It's a very worth-while bunch we have here. Edith Sampson down on Follansbee Road is sort of the intellectual type, but most of the gang are real people."

For the corporation wife, in short, being "sociable" is as important as stabilizing. Like the Army wife (an analogy she detests), she must be a highly adaptable "mixer." In fact, she needs to be even more adaptable than the Army wife, for the social conditions she meets are more varied. One year she may be a member of a company community, another year a branch manager's wife, expected to integrate with the local community —or, in some cases, to become a civic leader; and frequently, as the wife of the company representative, to provide a way station on the route of touring company brass.

As a rule, she is inextricably bound up in the corporation "family," often so much so that her entire behavior—including what and where she drinks—is subtly conditioned by the corporation. "It makes me laugh," says one wife in an eastern city dominated by one corporation. "If we were the kind to follow the Pattern, I'll tell you just what we would do. First, in a couple of years, we'd move out of Ferncrest Village (it's really pretty tacky there, you know). We wouldn't go straight to East-mere Hills—that would look pushy at this stage of the game; we'd go to the hilly section off Scrubbs Mill Pike. About that time, we'd change from Christ Church to St. Edwards, and we'd start going to the Fortnightlys—it would be a different group entirely. Then, about ten years later, we'd finally build in Eastmere Hills." It just makes her laugh, she says, because that would be the signal to everybody that she had become a wife of the top-brass bracket. Which she probably will.

The Rules of the Game

Few wives are as articulate as that on the social role, but intuitively they are generally superb at it; their antennae are sensitive, and the rules of the game they know by heart. Second nature to the seasoned wife, for example, are the following:

> Don't talk shop gossip with the Girls, particularly those who have husbands in the same department.
> Don't invite superiors in rank; let them make the first bid.
> Don't turn up at the office unless you absolutely have to.
> Don't get too chummy with the wives of associates your husband might soon pass on the way up.
> Don't be disagreeable to any company people you meet. You never know. . .
> Be attractive. There is a strong correlation between executive success and the wife's appearance. (Particularly so in the case of the sales wife . . . .)
> Be a phone pal of your husband's secretary.
> Never—repeat, never—get tight at a company party (it may go down in a dossier).

One rule transcends all others: *Don't be too good.* Keeping up with the Joneses is still important; but where in pushier and more primitive times it implied going substantially ahead of the Joneses, today keeping up means just that: keeping up. One can move ahead, yes—but slightly, and the timing must be exquisite. "We will have a grand piano," says one wife, "when we are ready for it"—which is quite different from "when we can afford it." Whatever the move, it must never be openly invidious. Perhaps it is for this reason that the Buick is such a preferred car; it envelops the whole executive spectrum and the jump from a Special to a Super, and from a Super to a Roadmaster, can be handled with tact.*

---

* In one eastern steel town, where cars have always been the accepted symbol of rank, this convenient arrangement has been thoroughly disrupted.

Neither must one be too outstanding in more personal ways. The good corporation wife does not make her friends uncomfortable by clothes too blatantly chic, references to illustrious forebears, or excessive good breeding. And intellectual pretensions she avoids like the plague. It is interesting to watch one wife rearrange her magazine basket as she primps for callers; almost automatically, she shuffles her *Harper's* and *Atlantic Monthly* beneath the pile. The Girls might not understand.

Are these rules of the game merely the old fact of conformity? In part, yes. But something new has been added. What was once a fact has now become a philosophy. Where people used to like to talk, at least, of "individualism," today's young couple are without hypocrisy on the matter; not only do they concede their group-mindedness, they are outspokenly in favor of it. They blend with the group not because they fear to do otherwise, but because they approve of it.

And in this, they can correctly point out, they are no more than in tune with currents in American thought and pedagogy; from the "group integration" of the progressive schools to the growing emphasis in the universities on group dynamics, human relations, and industrial psychology, the young couple have impressive material at hand with which to rationalize group living as the key to the pursuit of happiness.

Even the fiction they read has picked up the moral. To return to magazine plots a moment: Today, good people simply don't buck the system. In 1935–36 the heroine was quite likely to tell the boss off or do something equally contentious. Rarely now; if she has troubles, she solves them by patience, understanding, and compromise. She practices human relations.

The net effect is more than the mere Babbittry young couples' frankness so often makes it sound. A "real" person the wife explains, is one "whose satisfactions are not sought

---

The Chairman of the Board has a Cadillac—certainly a high enough ceiling. The President, however, has taken to buying Buick Supers, with the result that people in the upper brackets are chafing because it would be unseemly to go higher. Except for the Chairman, accordingly, only the local tradespeople drive Cadillacs and Roadmasters.

selfishly" within oneself, but "with others." Her search, to be
sure, includes popularity but it also includes civic activities,
P.T.A., and all the intangible satisfactions of *esprit de corps.*
Even her tensions are in character; for it is almost an article of
faith with her that her deepest personal desires and the values
of the group contain no conflict that a little "adjusting" can't
fix up. It does not, unfortunately, always work out that way.

The Ascendants

The corporation itself has a way of exploding her equable
world. On one very crucial question, as a result, the rules of
the game contain an inconsistency that can pose for the wife
a wrenchingly tough dilemma. *What is she to do if her husband begins moving up faster than his age group?* In advancing
the husband in the office, the corporation is quite likely to
advance him socially as well; it may, for example, put him up
for membership (when the company quota opens up) in one
of the better local clubs; or suggest to him that just by the way
there happens to be a good real-estate bargain in a suburb
favored by the brass.

There is no easy out for the couple in such cases, and for
the wife the inward tug-of-war between the social status quo
and the prospect of advancement can be extremely poignant.
As one young executive puts it, "If I go ahead as I hope, and
some of our friends progress as little as I think they will, there's
going to be friction. My wife can't see this. She thinks we'll
hold them as friends; she is nice to everyone and thinks if you
are that way, everyone will be nice to you."

The shock is not long in coming. "I must have made some
terrible mistakes," laments one wife now in mid-passage. "I
love people and I've made many intimate friends in the company, but since Charlie got his new job it's just been hell on
us. He has so much control over their lives, and it's all gotten

so complicated." In a larger community the ascendant couple would have recourse, for there exists a sort of freemasonry of success, where they can talk freely without anyone taking offense. But in the smaller community their upward course is more difficult, as, baffled and hurt, they try to hang on to their old friends and wonder why they are rebuffed.

Eventually most adjust. The price, however, is a kind of social professionalism. The wife must now learn to make "constructive" friendships, to become consciously aware of the vagaries and gradations of the social structure of business—and learn to play an entirely new role in it. "It's tough," says the wife of a thirty-five-year-old plant manager. "You have got to leave behind your old friends. You have to weigh the people you invite to parties. You have to be careful of who you send Christmas cards to and who you don't. It sounds like snobbery, but it's just something you have to do. You have to be a boss's wife."

While few young wives are aware of the sacrifice involved, the role of the boss's wife is one that they very much covet. In talking about the qualities of the ideal wife—a subject they evidently had thought over long and often—they were at no loss. In one-third of the cases, the word "gracious" came instantly to them, and in nearly all the others the descriptions spelled out the same thing. Their's is a sort of First Lady ideal, a woman who takes things as they come with grace and poise, and a measure of *noblesse oblige;* in short, the perfect boss's wife.

The Listeners

So far, not so bad. In respect to her outward, social role, at least, the wife can reflect that there is no conflict that some good, hard, adjusting can't fix up. But is the same true of her more basic role—helpmate to the husband? There is some evidence that the role of the perfect wife she so skilfully affects to herself is something of an illusion—and for her as well as others.

What, for example, of the listening job that wives take such pride in? How well *can* they listen? They bring certain natural interests to the job; they are extremely interested in the husband's salary, in his status—often, indeed, more than he is himself—and they have the normal feminine curiosity for human relationships. And though the details interest them much less, most realize that they should have a grasp of the husband's responsibilities.

Yet, granted all this, how much do they know about their husbands' work? Consensus of a cross section of U.S. executives: very little. ("And for God's sake, don't quote me.") Some wives are notable exceptions,* but the dinner conversations sketched by most executives run a highly similar course. When office politicking is involved, the lady's interest perks, and the husband who has just been chewed out by the boss can get understanding because she listened well when he told her before what a jerk the boss was. But the husband who has spent the day sweating out more involved problems gets no such solace ("she just gets restless and changes the subject"); and those that have to wrestle with tough technical problems get almost none for the simple reason that their wives haven't the faintest idea of what they are talking about.

The Children May Hear . . .

The wives get the blame—and many accept it. After the first blush of interest has worn off, some concede they can muster so little curiosity in the details of their husband's work that their listening becomes progressively more passive. There are

---

* Charles Gray's wife, for example, in John P. Marquand's *Point of No Return*—but she had been a law secretary and they are generally supposed to be very clever girls.

excuses aplenty. "If he has had a rough day," says one wife, "I don't want to hear about it. He'd only get mad and say things the children shouldn't hear." "I suppose I'm a little bit of a moral coward," says another, "after about ten minutes of listening, I find it so convenient to turn to the children and answer their questions instead."

The husband, however, may be the one chiefly to blame. He asks for active, intelligent listening, yet seldom wants advice ("She always sees everything in black and white" . . . "jumps to conclusions every time." . . . "women just don't understand."). More important, he has neither the patience nor the inclination to give his wife the exposition necessary for understanding. "It's like taking a girl to a baseball game," explains one executive. "You want her to understand the game, but you get so damned tired of her silly questions."

The baseball analogy is a little one-sided. There is another reason for the husband's reticence. Even to his wife he instinctively presents something of a doctored self-image—and as the old saw about valets goes, it is not something to stand too brilliant a light. "Automatically, we build ourselves up to them," concedes one executive. "It all comes back to the fact, I guess, that mentally anyway you really want her to stay the hell at home."

Like the coal mines in which woman must never set foot, the office can spell sanctuary. And the fact does not go unresented. "It's as if," says one wife, "he lived twice as much as I." Perhaps this is why the Christmas office party provokes such surprisingly bitter, if concealed, feeling from many wives. It dramatizes the wife's exclusion. Here, on this appointed day, is the world she can never share, and for all her brave little chuckles at the standing jokes of the office gang, she comes face to face with the fact. That is, if she's allowed to attend.

Where Is Home?

Burning though this exclusion may be to the wives, it is a topic they dislike intensely to talk about—or to think about. And for them, indeed, the waters may well be better left muddy: to peer too deeply is to uncover an underlying point even more provoking. Where, the awful question comes up, does the man find his major satisfactions?

A common feminine observation is that, of course, the man's major satisfactions come from the home; if he's happy there, why, then he can be happy in his work—and if he is happy in his work, then he is happy in his home, too. The belief is probably necessary. Is it correct as well?

ITEM: If the home is the executive's end-all, why has he become a defaulting father? As an earlier *Fortune* survey (August, 1946) indicates, the husband wants to turn over more of the child rearing to the wife than she is willing to assume. One of the most general plaints of executives' wives is summed up in a sentence: he doesn't spend enough time with the kids. In most cases, the husbands agree; if only it weren't for the treadmill . . .

ITEM: As management psychologists note, the average executive shows a remarkable ability to repress his home worries while on the job; rarely, however, can he shut out office worries at home.

ITEM: The downright fright of many executives at the prospect of imminent retirement. Here would seem to be the fulfillment of all he has worked for. Why, then, does he view it with such dismay?

ITEM: The reaction to this Hobson's choice question: "If you had to make the choice, which would you take: an increasingly satisfying work life and a proportionately souring home life— or the opposite?" The answers would surprise wives. "This business of doing it all for the family," as one husband confesses, "it's just a rationalization. If I got a windfall today I'd still knock myself out." Even those who duck the question do so on the grounds that one alternative is not realistic. They simply can't conceive, they say, of a home life being happy if the job isn't.

"Man's love is of man's life a thing apart," Byron once observed. " 'T'is woman's whole existence." So, for all the group integration and communication skills she can muster, it will probably remain.

The Elusive Plateau

The schism between Home and Office does not remain subterranean. Inevitably, it comes to the surface on those infrequent, but critical occasions when the husband and wife must weigh the question of ambition. In the earlier days the task would have been less ticklish for them; ambition was then spelled out in terms of definite, concrete goals—like making half a million, perhaps, or building the biggest skyscraper. Now, however, ambition has become relative; it floats in space and time, fixed only by the progress of the group. The young couple are no less ambitious than their predecessors, but they see no sense in constructing definite goals, what with taxes, war threats, and such; furthermore, they want to be team players, and ambition that is graphic would be no help.

The effect of this double drive is a paradox. Reduced to its simplest terms it runs like this: I want to take it easy, I want to enjoy life and yet I want to keep up. But since everyone else wants to—and we can't get together—we all end up knocking ourselves out. Thus the high frequency in the talk of younger executives of words like "treadmill," "twirl," "whirlpool," "ratrace," "merry-go-round," all implying a futile perpetual motion. In counterpoint, they speak wistfully, of settling on a "plateau" instead of continuing the climb—there is almost the suggestion of how wonderful it would be if everyone could just get together in a sort of cartel agreement on ambition. But the executive knows better; he'll never get promoted unless he's something of a rate buster, and rate busters can't park on The Plateau. The "antagonistic cooperation," to use David Riesman's phrase, must continue.

Ambition Without Ulcers

Here we come to the misunderstanding. The wife believes in The Plateau. The more philosophic wives see man's drive and ambition as the core of his being; a lot talk that way, but most see man's drive as an unnecessarily divisive factor in the home.* For the security that so preoccupies wives includes not only a good income, but a husband still alive and reasonably kicking at fifty. Thus, much more even than the husbands who may be afflicted, they think on the specters of coronary thrombosis, ulcers, and nervous breakdowns, and whatever may bar the way to The Plateau. For good reason, the "bad wives" they speak of are not the wives who hold down their husbands but those who push them—the wives, in other words, who upset the applecart.

But it is the corporation that wives see as chiefly to blame— and it is only in this respect that they exhibit any real animus towards it. Since the husband works largely for the goal of a happy home, they reason, his overwork must be due to the

---

* In the opinion of at least one psychologist, there is a vicious-circle effect that further confounds the problem. "I've had a number of executives whose job effectiveness is impaired because they are sexually frustrated. It is possible that these men have drained off their energy through worry over the job so much they are no longer any good as lovers. This makes them worry even more. One excellent man I've had to study is losing his grip fast. His wife's an outgoing, attractive gal that now finds him lacking sexually. She's now practically an alcoholic."

pressure put on him by the corporation. "There must be something wrong with industry," says one wife. "My husband doesn't think he's overworking, but he is. They must make him." With a wealth of unsettling detail, wives paint the picture of a corporation consuming their men.

It is the wife's duty, it follows, to offset this pressure with counterpressure of her own. This she does incessantly. "I've let Bob know I would sooner have him in a lower job than knocking himself out as a v.p." . . . "When Edgar's work gets so it's interfering with his health and happiness, it's not worth it. I keep telling him we're a lot better off than most—another car and things like that aren't necessary." . . . "He probably won't make the Executive Committee, and I don't want him to. It would take all of him—and what good would the extra money be then?" So, over the countless dinner tables of suburbia, is the sermon preached.

"Every Tenth Time . . ."

How effective is the sermon? In some cases it has held a husband back, for it has influenced him in one of those vital fork-in-the-road decisions. In the average case? "I'll tell you what good it does," says one executive. "Every tenth time I listen." Others agree; the badgering sometimes does have a valuable braking effect. As one man puts it, "If the wife doesn't put pressure on you to be home on the five-thirty, and the company wants you around, it's hard to back away from the office."

All of which is to the good. Unfortunately, however, the braking effect is severely limited by one simple fact. The wife constantly visualizes the cost of ambition; rarely, however, does she visualize the social cost of the lack of it. You cannot get to be a boss's wife, unfortunately, unless your husband gets to be a boss, and when the couple have to get down to cases the inconsistency blows up in her face. "The minute you put the dollar sign on your work," says one husband, "she gets ambitious quick." And again, the group resolves the problem; as another husband puts it, "If my wife gabs to you as she does to me about settling for what we have now—well, just ask her which one of her friends' husbands she would take as my boss."

Home vs. the Expense Account

In this problem of ulcers and ambition the corporation has been, at worst, no more than an exacerbating influence. It is ironic, therefore, that the wives rest their case against it on the ground of pressure. For there is one way in which the corporation has become an active, if involuntary, agent of division—and it is something quite different from what the wives suspect.

Thanks, in part, to the way the tax structure has accumulated, the corporation now provides the man with a higher standard of living in his work than in his home—and, it might be added, a higher one than his wife enjoys. From nine to five he may be a minor satrap, guiding the destiny of thousands, waited on by secretaries and subordinates; back in his servantless home, he washes the dishes. Nor is it merely the fact of his satrapy; the corporation virtually rigs it so that he can have more fun away from home.

The expense account has become a way of life. There is not only travel, there are luncheon clubs, company retreats, special conventions, parties, and perquisites, and though the wife may be thrown an occasional convention as a crumb, the expense-account world rarely encompasses her. It is primarily a man's world—and if the man is at a low salary, he is likely to find the pattern of life at 7118 Crestmere Road dull in comparison.

'The company has spoiled Jim terribly," says one wife. "Even when he was only earning $7,500 a year, he used to be sent to Washington all the time. He'd go down in a Pullman drawing room and, as J. R. Robinson of the General Company, take a two-room suite. Then he used to be asked by some of the company officers to a hunting and fishing lodge that the company kept in the north woods. When he went to New York, he'd entertain at 21, the Barberry Room, and the Chambord. Me, meanwhile, I'd be eating a 30-cent hamburger and when we went away together on vacation, we would have to go in our beat-up old car, or borrow my sister's husband's. This taste of high life gives some of these characters delusions of grandeur. Small wonder that they get to fidgeting after they have been home a couple of weeks."

Curiously, the disparity does not exercise most wives, or to put it another way, what they don't know doesn't hurt them. Of the wives *Fortune* interviewed, many mentioned, commiseratingly, how their husbands looked forward to coming home, how awful it was sleeping in hotel beds, rattling around on trains, and eating bum food. "What the hell can you say?" says one executive. "Here I am eating high off the hog, meeting interesting people, while Jo is slaving back home. I get a big bang out of all this, but I also have a sort of guilty feeling, so I say to her 'Gee, honey, I hate all this traveling, but I just have to do it.' "

The Outgrown Wife

There are some things, however, that cannot be explained away. For more than sirloins and drawing rooms are at issue; over the long pull this disparity aggravates perhaps the most subtle problem of marriage: equality of growth. If marriage, as sociologist Everett Hughes puts it, is a "mutual mobility bet," for whom are the cards stacked?

Growth can mean many things; to the younger generation of executives it seems to mean an increasing ability to handle

and mix with people. And the terms are the same for the wife.
"The wife who is not very sociable," goes a highly typical male
observation, "might not affect the husband directly, but she
can hurt him just the same. A lot of business is done weekends. If she doesn't go for this, her lack of growth can hold
the man back." Even the old idea of a wife as a sort of culture
carrier is virtually dead; she is still expected to read and things
like that, but for functional reasons. "Sure I want her to read
good books and magazines," as one executive puts it, "I don't
want her to make a fool of herself in conversation."

By this yardstick of growth, the corporation virtually forces
the progress of the man. But what, meanwhile, is happening to
the wife? "We give our young men finish and finesse because
we give them an opportunity to observe men who are ahead of
them," one company head points out. "We do nothing for
the wife." Significantly, she rarely worries over the fact. Husbands do. In most cases they seem well enough satisfied; they
speak often of a pause in her growth that occurs with the birth
of the first child and continues until the children are well into
junior high. But, they observe, leisure time opens up once
again and she can catch up.

But there is another pattern, too. Though it is much more
infrequent, it is one that corporations find anguishing because
it is highlighted by the very potential of the man. "I have
seen it happen so many times," says one executive, sadly. "He
marries the kid sweetheart, the girl next door, or a girl from
the jerkwater college he went to. They start off with a lot in
common—but then he starts going up. Fifteen years later he
is a different guy entirely; he dresses differently, talks differently, thinks differently. But she's stayed home—literally and
figuratively."

The pattern is particularly acute with the corporations that
draw their executive material from the ranks. Says a personnel
man of a large retail organization, "It's a classic problem with
us; a clerk marries the salesgirl at the notions counter. Ten
years later we may be ready to make him a store manager in a
locality where he has to move in country-club circles and up-

hold a certain position in the town—a store manager has to relate the store to the community. Some of the wives never can seem to do this. An awful lot of unhappiness comes out of it."

The effect on the marriage is profound. If the wife defends herself by enveloping her husband with home ties, he is put at an intolerable disadvantage in competing with his less enveloped associates. Some subside and try to enjoy it. Most seek escape. For them the office becomes the spiritual home, the house merely a base of operations, and the wife somebody to be kept in the background lest one's style be cramped. The effect on her? She does not always immolate herself in the home; companionship, sometimes alcoholic, is to be had with other such wives—often you may see her at the club, idly plunking quarters into the slot machines.

While the socially retarded wife has become the secret sorrow of the corporation, and partly its responsibility, there is little it believes it can do. Most corporations keep tabs on the wife's growth only as an index to the executive's availability for certain positions. As a result, the topic is generally not brought up until events force it.

It is time, some executives think, that young men were frankly told about the problem. "I generally warn the younger men," says one company president, "of this danger of their wives not keeping up with them. I suggest to them that they encourage their wives to join things, to play golf, to go on business trips with them occasionally." Many have been grateful for the advice. Says one rapidly climbing executive, "I have let my wife know that she must grow with me. Sometimes there has been a problem as to who was to baby sit when there was a community meeting. I have told her that I would stay at home—it was more important for her to go. And I think I've learned it earlier than most."

Growth Insurance

Fundamentally, of course, the problem goes back to who the executive chooses in the first place. Is the moral that he should marry a girl "superior" to him? Thanks to the commonly accepted saw that a woman can pull a man up, but not vice versa, there are many who think he should. ("My best executives," remarks one boss, "are the ones who 'outmarried' themselves.") But the pitfalls are many. Her qualities may drive the man to preoccupation with office prestige in order to prove himself to her; furthermore, unless she is excellent at hiding her superiority—or lets it rest fallow—she can hurt his chances in a close "family" community. The Bryn Mawr accent can be absolute death for a career in some Midwest corporations.

What kind of background for the woman, then, is the optimum? A serious career can be dismissed easily; there is almost universal agreement among wives, husbands, and corporations on this score. Work before marriage, however, is generally approved. "I feel the fact that I worked before marriage," says one wife, "is a help. I know what goes on in an office and can understand what Charles is up against."

College? Here is the *summum bonum.* There are some obvious reasons; because virtually all executives now go to college, the couple in such cases start off with shared values. But corporation people mention a reverse factor almost as much. It is not so important for the wife, they say, to have gone to college: but it is very important not to have *not* gone to college. If she hasn't, corporation people warn, she is prey to an inferiority complex that makes it difficult for her to achieve real poise. Some corporations, accordingly, make it their business to find out whether or not the wife has a degree.

The corporation would seem to have reason for optimism. Since more girls are going to college, the proportion of executives' wives who are college graduates has been steadily increasing. In part, as a result of this, the problem of the outgrown wife appears to be less acute among the younger wives.

And the omens in some other respects would seem as good. The younger wives are afflicted with all of the old problems of adjustment—and some new ones of the corporation's own making—but rarely has there emerged a generation of wives so dedicated to the job of grappling with them. On almost every point of contact—from entertaining to moving across the continent, their background is making them the most tractable material the corporation has ever had.

What does the corporation plan to do with it? That is another story. And one that also has implications for American life beyond the sphere of the corporation itself.

15

PERMISSIVENESS AND SEX ROLES*

DAVID RIESMAN

Cross-generational misunderstandings are, of course, no new thing in America, nor are conflicts about permissiveness and sex. Indeed, foreign observers visiting this country a hundred years ago commented about the tolerance shown children, and, while some admired the children's poise and independence, others were horrified by their insolence or bad manners. Tocqueville was greatly impressed by the fact that American young women went around what was still a rude country without chaperones, and he and his fellow traveller, Beaumont, wrote home that American girls, while very attractive and appealing, were protected, not as on the continent by ignorance,

* This paper was originally presented at the Annual Symposium of the Committee on Human Development, University of Chicago, February, 1958, and was expanded in a talk at Kenyon College, October, 1958. Work on matters discussed herein has been facilitated by a grant from the Carnegie Corporation for the study of higher education.

SOURCE: David Riesman, "Permissiveness and Sex Roles," *Marriage and Family Living*, XXI, 3, (August 1959), 211–17. Reprinted by permission of the author and the National Council on Family Relations.

but by what we might today call know-how. He was not quite sure how he felt about these emancipated women, with whom gallantry was no longer a sport for passing the time and asserting one's superiority.

Something like his complaint is echoed in the tendency for men of my own generation and older to look with dismay on the practice of going steady among young people in high school and college. This older generation compares going steady unfavorably with its own romantic and nostalgic images of the "playing the field"; correspondingly, it sees young marriages as a too early captivity avoiding frivolity and flirtation.[1]

We should note at the outset that early dating and early sex life in general is characteristic of the working class, as Kinsey documented, and of the rural population in many peasant countries. What seems to have happened in this as in so many other ways, is that the middle class has been losing its traditional orientation towards the future and inhibitions in the present, and that the permissiveness which arises from inconsistency and indifference in the lower strata has now become a matter of principle and only an occasionally unprincipled tolerance in the educated strata. Thus, even debutantes and students at the elite colleges go steady, whereas they would once have thought such practices common.

In a recent article in *Science*, Margaret Mead and Rhoda Metraux have called attention to a hitherto unnoticed consequence of this change in values.[2] They were investigating (not by means of a national sample, but rather by careful selections here and there) the attitude of high school students towards science and scientists and they made the discovery that the career choice of boys was being increasingly influenced by the

[1] Some critics, however, speak from the point of view of an older morality. Thus, Catholic priests at some parochial schools and colleges have forbidden steady dating on the ground that it is an occasion for sin. In this they reveal the protective bias the Church has always had towards women, for it could be argued that steady dating, while slightly increasing sin among young women, substantially reduces it among young men.
[2] "The Image of the Scientist among High-School Students: A Pilot Study," *Science*, 126 (August 30, 1957), pp. 384–390.

judgments of girls as to what were good careers for their boyfriends to be in. That is, if girls thought scientists would make
poor husbands, this helped shape the image of the scientist
that prevailed in high school—and helped, perhaps impercep-
tibly, to push boys towards careers that were considered compatible with decent domesticity. Of course girls were not
wholly responsible for the image of the scientist which the
researchers discovered: a person who is remote and sexless,
who has too much or too little hair, wrapped up in the laboratory and not quite human—indeed, sometimes quite in-
human like a science fiction monster. But their article suggests
that in an earlier day, when boys in the upper strata became
aware of girls at a later point in life, when the boys were already themselves committed to a career, the judgment by girls
would be less influential: the girls would have to take the
men as they had become.

Now, however, both boys and girls are talking with each
other about such serious matters as career choice, and not
merely handing out a "line" with which to impress each other
in the rating-dating game. The very fact that boys as well as
girls are willing to go steady and to marry earlier indicates a
general cultural change of emphasis towards the affective and
non-work side of life, and makes it possible for boys and girls
together to decide the kind of domestic life they will jointly
seek and the sorts of careers that will further and not interfere
with that ideal.

In these developments, we see reflected the greater prosperity
of society; the situation of virtually full employment for the
well-educated; the understandable growth, not so much of an
irresponsible hedonism (although this is often charged and
certainly does occur) as of a more relaxed view of what has to
be done to get along—and of how much has to be sacrificed
in order to get only marginally ahead. Here what might be
termed "social permissiveness" cooperates with parental facili-
tation; thus Marvin B. Sussman showed in an article in the
American Sociological Review a few years ago that middle class
parents in New Haven were willing to stake their children
to various sorts of help in the early years of marriage (even

though they may not always have been pleased with the particular marriage or with its early consummation).[3]

If one talks to the faculties of medical schools, one finds them sometimes quite concerned with these developments. For one thing, there is evidence of a general decline of applications to medical school in the last several years, and it has been suggested that this is partly due to dislike of the postponement medical education requires. At the University of Kansas Medical School, three-quarters of the students are married, and this affects how they conduct themselves as students.[4] The married students are not eager for night duty, for example, or for the surgical residencies that involve night duty; nor do they yearn to sit around talking about science, ethics, and women with their fellow students. Rather, they are quickly off after their stint in the hospital to give their spouses a hand with the children and to relax with them in the evening. Faculties of medical schools under these altered conditions tend to recall their own student days as those of bachelor asceticism (modulated by an occasional binge), and readily feel out of touch with these new men who are on the one hand so mature (in being well started on family life and choice of specialty), and on the other hand, so "mature" as not to care to talk shop. And the students, in turn, eager to end the long period in which they must be supported by their wives and families, resent the protracted training necessary for certain specialties and the arduous isolation which, if not inherently "necessary," has traditionally been considered part of the folkways of that specialty.

What men have lost in willingness to undertake arduous and highly specialized careers has not, of course, marked any commensurate gain for women. Thus, although it is a good deal easier today than a generation ago for women to enter medical school, and although they probably suffer less hazing

[3] Marvin B. Sussman, "The Help Pattern in the Middle Class Family," *American Sociological Review*, 18 (February, 1953), no. 1, pp. 22–28.
[4] I am drawing here on unpublished materials prepared by Howard C. Becker and Blanche Geer of Community Studies, Inc., in Kansas City under the direction of Professor Everett C. Hughes of the University of Chicago.

in school from their professors and from male students, they are still a tiny proportion of the students—10 per cent or less. (The situation is very different in many countries in Europe and in the Soviet Union where women play a dominant role in medicine.) The same emphasis on the affective side of life, on the family as the most important element in the good life, which has influenced the career decisions of men, has also led even the most brilliant and energetic college women to decide that they do not want to undertake long preparation for careers which might cut them off from the chance of marriage or in some subtle way defeminize them. And while that has always been true of American women, college women today seem both more universally ready to hold a job than they once were (there are fewer playgirls) and less ready to risk, on behalf of greatly ambitious career aims, the possibility of a stable marriage.

These developments are occurring at the same time that there has been a great hue and cry, stimulated by Sputnik, that we need more doctors, more scientists, more engineers, more highly trained people generally. Most of this hue and cry is based on what I regard as an exploitative concern for the state of the national labor force in the Cold War; it assumes that it is inconceivable that we might end the Cold War, and that, in a society of abundance, we might regard the talents of our young people as an opportunity to develop new sorts of careers and new relations towards work. Among some of the most sensitive and gifted young people, there has developed the tendency to withdraw altogether from the great and overriding political concerns of the elders, sometimes by choosing fields such as the humanities or the ministry which could not have a conceivable Cold War or big-project relevance, and sometimes by withdrawing any deep involvement from work in large organizations even while going through the motions.[5] As a result

---

[5] Compare the interesting article, "Beatniks in Business," *Mademoiselle* (March, 1959), pp. 74–75 and 142–145, and see, more generally, my article, "Work and Leisure in the Post-Industrial World," in Eric Larrabee and Rolf Meyersohn, Editors, *Mass Leisure,* Glencoe, Illinois: The Free Press, 1958.

of these developments, there would seem to be building up an often irrational reaction against permissiveness—sometimes in the mild forms in which we see it in the cartoons of *The New Yorker,* and sometimes in the intemperate attacks on the schools by such men as Admiral Rickover.

What is left out in this cross-generational bickering is any understanding of what is happening, of some of the positive values that are emerging, and of some of the problems for the individual as well as for society that these new emancipations bring. There can be no doubt that what many educated young men and women today are looking for in each other is not the rating-dating game of twenty years ago.[6] To be sure, there are still fraternities and sororities on the campus and still an interest in good looks, popularity, good grooming, and smoothness. But all this is more subdued and the relationships increasingly sought for are more searching, more profound, more sincere. There is more desire to share; less desire to impress. There is less desire to dazzle members of one's own sex and more to come to some sort of humane terms with the opposite sex. Moreover, it seems to me that young people are increasingly preoccupied with their capacity to love as well as to be loved. And I have the impression that sexual relations themselves when they do occur come about less frequently from a desire on the part of the boys to present trophies to their own male vanity than to secure themselves against the anxiety that they may not be truly and deeply loved, or capable of love.

Moreover, the increase in going steady that has brought about some diminution of the search for those careers which require arduous preparation has not brought about a lessened level of seriousness among students either in high school or college. In fact, it could even be argued that young people who have made themselves secure in a vital area through the practice of going steady can consequently afford to commit themselves more fully to their studies, becoming more equable

[6] Compare the study by Robert Blood, Jr., "Uniformities and Diversities in Campus Dating Preferences," *Marriage and Family Living,* 18 (February, 1956), pp. 37–45.

if sometimes less frantic students than were many in an earlier day who were constantly preoccupied as to whether or not they had a date or should have a date or what they might be missing if they did not.

At some of the more academically oriented colleges, the rise in the level of demands on students has made many students doubt their own intellectual adequacy—and then seek to prove that they are after all good for something in their relations with the opposite sex. They do not choose to go on dates rather than to study; rather they do both—and if something has to give way under this pressure, it is their sleep. (There is some evidence that students are staying up later and later and, if evidence from various student health services could be compared, it might shed interesting light on some of these problems.)

The seriousness and depth of some of these steady relationships in high school and college is such as to give young people the feeling that they really know members of the opposite sex well enough to choose a marriage partner much earlier in life than people of equivalent sensitivity would have dared to do with their eyes open in an earlier day. Talcott Parsons argues in his writings that romantic love allows a kind of leap of faith across the impossibility of making a rational choice (much as advertising encourages a similar leap of faith among equally available brand-name items). But in fact many of the young people are not "romantic" in the nineteenth century sense; they believe in love, but not in a starry-eyed way. Indeed, the danger of some of these steady relationships may be exactly like that of some marriages; that a plateau of routinization is too quickly reached, with stability quickly achieved as a platform for competent but unexciting family life and serious, if not totally demanding, work.

In our society, whatever becomes a fashion puts pressure on those whom the fashion does not readily fit. In an earlier day, when it was thought sober in the upper strata to postpone marriage, it took a certain hardihood or impulsivity to marry early, and to have more than two or three children. Today, in contrast, things are often hard on those who do not feel ready to "grow up," to date, to marry young, and to have a sizeable family. Girls, of course, are not chaperoned anymore, either in the Latin way or in the more characteristic Calvinist way in which they carried their invisible chaperone inside. Boys are, therefore, not protected from having to make advances to girls by the latters' obvious unavailability. Indeed, the availability of girls in America is an omnipresent and inescapable part of our visual esthetic—built into the widths of our cars, the reels of our movies, into the pages of our advertisements, and built into the girls themselves, I might add, in the way they carry themselves and dress. The greater, but still not sufficiently psychological, awareness has produced the phenomenon I have occasionally seen as a teacher: that students feel under pressure from adults to have "experiences" and are ashamed to be thought dull and not to have any.

Likewise, boys and girls have a new fear, one which a generation earlier was not conscious for most men no matter how sheltered, nor for most women—that is, the fear that they might be homosexual. In talking with Dr. John Spiegel about some of the men's colleges in the Ivy League, we agreed that this fear is one factor which haunts the campus, putting pressure on many young men to be guarded in their relations with each other, and also with their male teachers, while at the same time putting pressure on them to seek out relations with girls in order to convince themselves and perhaps each other that they are not.

As a concomitant development, the ribbing of sissies, at least in the middle class, is much less strong now than it once was, and in that sense, greater "femininity" is being increasingly permitted to educated men in this country. While one can still find colleges where men define themselves as men by being athletic and going in for engineering, there are many institutions throughout the country where men can without embarrassment be interested in art, in English, in dance, and in music. But this very openness, which permits men to do things which they would once (and in many parts of the coun-

try today would still) reject, has also had the curious consequence that they cannot clearly and unequivocally define
themselves as men by their roles. They have to define themselves as men, therefore, in other ways, and especially in the
one physiological way which appears irrefutable; and the girls
are under somewhat analogous pressure, possibly less out of a
fear of homosexuality, but hardly less out of a fear of not
being really a woman and responding to men as a woman
should. Whereas, in the days of the double standard, nice
boys would not molest good girls, that is college girls, now they
often use Freud to persuade the latter, and their steady dates,
that to be inhibited is bad, likely to harm the boy, if not
produce or symbolize frigidity in the girl. Thus, we see that
permissiveness in some areas, like any movement of liberation,
produces unpermissiveness in others. Boys and girls, for instance, have *less* permission than they once did to proceed in
their relations to each other and to themselves at idiosyncratic
rates.

We can see what this means when we look at high schools
in the way that my former colleague at Chicago, James Coleman, has recently been doing. He has asked high school students what they are interested in; and when boys are asked
this question they volunteer a great many concerns; they are
interested in automobiles, in high-fi, in sports, and ham radios,
and even occasionally in the curriculum. They are interested
in girls, too, but in rather a secondary way. In contrast, and
here I interpret from his data which is still being coded and
tabulated, the girls are interested in boys and in each other,
and even their interest in each other I suspect is sometimes
secondary or resonant to their interest in boys. Girls in high
school are natural sociometrists; even in the fourth grade this
is true. The boys have many defenses against being interested
in girls, but the girls have very few comparable defenses against
an interest in boys, and this is a pressure on boys as well as
on girls. We know something of what this means in terms of
age disparities. At Vassar the entering freshman girl is already
date-conscious and is likely to be picked up, let us say at Yale,

by upper classmen.[7] But the senior girl in high school is too old for the comparable boys now and is perhaps cut off by physical or psychological distance from college boys, whereas the freshman and sophomore boys in high school are thrown with girls who are not able to respond to them, or they to the girls, as our popular culture tells them that they should. If William James were to look at this situation, he would say that girls need a moral substitute for boys; and, indeed, for their own development, I think they need an alternative to sociometry as their major field of research in high school and college.

One reason why it seems to me that some people can profit from non-coeducation at some stages in their lives is that girls can be given in this way an alternative—at least a partial one —that allows them to cultivate, free from the pressure of boys and boy-minded girls, including the boy-minded parts of themselves, interests that might otherwise be thought of as unfeminine. And, by the same token, it may allow boys to cultivate an interest in such things as the student newspaper, or ballet, which are occasionally monopolized by girls in a co-ed school (to be sure, as I have already mentioned, most girls in a co-ed school will be less active and pluralistic in their interests than boys of similar background, but there may be a few who will take over certain artistic activities and thus define them in such a way that boys will feel excluded). We see here a paradox: the influence of girls on boys in high school and college can be a broadening one in that it saves the boys from a narrow vocationalism and over-intellectual or over-ambitious or over-technocratic occupation with getting ahead in conventional terms. So, too, girls can be saved by the presence of boys from the kinds of artful stuffiness and female "accomplishment" that some of the more fashionable and less intellectual junior colleges for women still advertise as their stock in trade. But at the margin, the presence of each limits rather than

7 Compare, on the general developmental sequence of college girls at Vassar, Nevitt Sanford, *et al.,* "Personality Development in the College Years," *Journal of Social Issues,* 12, no. 4 (1956), pp. 1–72.

expands the potentialities of the other—and again permissiveness imposes subtle restraints of its own.[8]

These changes in the awareness each sex has of the role of the other have a bearing on our ways of handling education of both sexes in the social sciences and in the other sciences. Every curriculum contains many implicit statements about ideas as "feminine" or "masculine"—statements which are carried in the language or texture of the discipline, and in the tone and attitudes of its professors. For instance, there are many teachers of psychology in college who resent the fact that women who are "interested in people" come into their courses, and these teachers react by turning their subject into a branch of engineering—an aggressively "male" subject from which all concrete and humane concerns of both men and women are excluded in the name of rigor, and in which precisely such considerations as we are here today discussing would not be called "psychology." Then, too, as already indicated, in many good colleges, the more sensitive students of both sexes feel themselves shut out from mathematics, physics, chemistry, and technology generally. This may, in a few cases, be because they associate these fields, understandably enough in our time, with missiles and war maneuvers, with all that they find oppressive and intractable in the modern world. But it is also because these subjects are often taught in such a way that the subtlety of their ideas is not conveyed, but only the "hardware." As I think of the great physicists and mathematicians of recent times, it seems to me that their ideas (consider Einstein, Oppenheimer, Bohr) have a quality which should not alienate sensitive and very feminine women or sensitive and very intraceptive men. But both in high school and college, these fields are often taught, mainly by men, for whom the text is a kind of cook book—an old-style cook book at that. Conversely, English and art are taught in many secondary schools and some colleges as very much prissy, traditionally female and snob-tainted subjects.

[8] Compare, for further discussion, Riesman, *Some Continuities and Discontinuities in the Education of Women,* John Dewey Memorial Lecture, Bennington College, 1956.

As a result, certain compartmentalizations remain very important in our culture in spite of greater freedom and permissiveness. Women, for instance, remain shut out, by one set of snobberies and self-imposed restrictions, from college and university teaching, while men remain shut out by another set of constrictions from elementary school teaching and from the teaching of music in secondary school. Women in this country are decreasingly charged with carrying the burdens of culture alone, including the burden of human and humane understanding, but there is still much that needs to be done before men are permitted to share more equally in these tasks, and women in the tasks of the outside world of politics and work.[9] Our ideal here would be a culture in which the interests of each would be developed on behalf of the interests of all, on the no doubt utopian assumption that the work of the world would get done through genuine relatedness (in Erich Fromm's sense) and not through the captivity of either sex or the psychological compulsions of a class.

In a way, this is already happening: the liberation of women from traditional and conventional bondages both accompanies industrialization and brings it in its wake. In these respects American women are the envy of the whole world, so that American movies, for instance, are a force for radical emancipation in Moslem countries, and men try to prevent their womenfolk from seeing them lest they become restless and dissatisfied.[10] Women in America are not, as some people claim to think, the dominant sex, but having escaped from traditional bondages they are beginning to face the problems of freedom.

More generally, what I am trying to say is that permissiveness, liberating in its earlier installments, creates unanticipated

---

[9] I suppose some social scientists would argue that the division of labor here is both a good and a necessary thing. One could draw such an implication from the work of Parsons and Bales, linking the division of labor in small laboratory groups to the division of labor in the family. See Talcott Parsons and R. F. Bales, *Family, Socialization and Interaction Process,* Glencoe, Ill.: The Free Press, 1955.

[10] Compare Daniel Lerner, with the collaboration of Lucille W. Pevsner, *The Passing of Traditional Society: Modernizing the Middle East,* Glencoe, Ill.: The Free Press, 1958.

problems as it spreads. I am inclined to think that the more privileged young people need today some permission to resist permissiveness, that is, some form of adult protection for those who at the moment do not want to pursue each other or to feel that, if they are not doing so, they are missing what not only matters most in life, but what would define them in an ultimate way as men or women. Let me recall in this connection Bruno Bettelheim's book, *Symbolic Wounds*. He argues there that the initiation rites are a way of reducing the identity crisis for the initiates, a way of telling them with severity enough to make it stick, literally so, that they are a young man or a young woman now, as the case may be: they are that, and no other—how shall I say it?—no other selves can come in. Our society, because it is more permissive, does not countenance such impositions, but the problem remains of providing young people with what Erik Erikson calls a moratorium in which their identity can be at large and open and various, without worry that for all of life what happens in high school or college will freeze the pattern.

16

ON SOCIAL REGRESSION

PHILIP E. SLATER

Freud's later instinct theory has tended on the whole to
arouse puzzlement rather than stimulate theory, and with few
exceptions has been treated with contempt by his detractors
and embarrassment by his supporters. To some extent this is
due to the limitations of his own presentation, but much confusion has also arisen from the tendency to translate the "life"
and "death" instincts into psychological rather than biological
constructs, into human "motives" instead of panspecific impulses.[1] This problem of "level" is confronted directly by Parsons, when he suggests that "the pleasure principle is itself a

[1] American psychologists as a group have never become entirely reconciled
to the psyche's residence in the body, and most works mention "biological
drives" with the same dutiful haste generally accorded to the War of 1812
in elementary American History texts. It is no accident that psychoanalytic
ideas did not really become popular in the United States until they had
been Americanized by the neo-Freudians, who eliminated the instinctual
and biological elements. This transformation undoubtedly sprang from
the same discomfort with the body that has inundated the land with
deodorants.

SOURCE: Philip E. Slater, "On Social Regression," *American Sociological
Review*, XXVIII (1963), 339–64. Reprinted by permission of the author
and publisher.

mechanism of control, a way of imposing order on *still lower level processes* and 'needs' of the living system which is the human individual. These needs, it has been suggested, are those concerned with the physical aspects of the organism, which again is far from being a simple matter of a single level, but is itself a complex hierarchically organized system."[2]

With this in mind, let us consider Freud's own statements on the matter:

> As a result of theoretical considerations, supported by biology, we assumed the existence of a death-instinct, the task of which is to lead organic matter *back into the inorganic state;* on the other hand, we supposed that Eros aims at *complicating life* by bringing about a *more and more far-reaching coalescence of the particles* into which living matter has been dispersed, thus, of course, aiming at the maintenance of life. . . . both instincts would be active *in every particle of living substance,* although in unequal proportions.[3]

> The aim of [Eros] is to *establish ever greater unities and to preserve them thus*—in short, to bind together; the aim of the [death instinct], on the contrary, is to *undo connections* and so to destroy things.[4]

Although the phrase "every particle of living substance" make it quite clear that Freud is talking about a biological rather than a psychological process, the generality of these statements as a whole suggests that these "instincts" operate in some fashion in all aggregations of living matter, and hence have as much relevance for sociology as for psychology.

SOCIOLOGICAL IMPLICATIONS. Although Freud clearly intended the two instincts to be viewed as opposites, he did not describe

---

2 Talcott Parsons, "Some Reflections on the Problem of Psychosomatic Relationships in Health and Illness" (unpublished), pp. 18–19. Italics mine. In practice, of course, it is difficult to avoid psychologizing these impersonal biological concepts, so clumsy is our language. It must simply be borne in mind that when we talk about a "longing for death" it has the same meaning as would a reference to a "longing to breathe" or the blood "longing to circulate."

3 *The Ego and the Id,* London: Hogarth, 1949, pp. 55–56. Italics mine.

4 *An Outline of Psychoanalysis,* New York: Norton, 1949, p. 20. Italics mine.

them in precisely complementary terms.[5] The death instinct is most often defined in terms of an ultimate goal, with very little being said about the process through which it pushes toward that goal. In the case of "Eros" quite the reverse is true: it is always defined in terms of an endless process, with no ultimate goal being apparent.

This latter approach seems more fruitful, from a scientific viewpoint, since it is less teleological. If we operate consistently within this framework, the two instincts can be defined simply as the associative and dissociative propensities of living matter, from the molecular to the societal level, from cell colonies to the social groups of animals and humans. If "Eros" is an expanding, complicating tendency, and the "death instinct" a contracting simplifying one, then it would be most appropriate to view the two instincts merely as opposing forces acting upon the same inert material, i.e., sexual energy or libido. We would then apply the term "Eros" to the expanding tendencies of the libido, i.e., to those forces driving it toward more and more remote objects, along more and more circuitous paths to gratification, toward involvement in larger and larger collectivities. The term "death instinct" would refer to the contracting tendencies of the libido, i.e., to those forces driving it toward more and more proximate and intimate objects, along more simple and direct paths to more immediate and complete gratification, toward involvement in smaller and smaller collectivities. Since the terms "libidinal diffusion" and "libidinal

---

[5] This may be due in part to some desire to represent his later instinct theory as more dualistic than it actually is. For if the two instincts merely express expanding and contracting tendencies of the libido we are operating with a one-dimensional system, one which has moved only a very little way from the interim monistic period that Marcuse discusses (*Eros and Civilization*, Boston: Beacon Press, 1955, p. 22). This is a very different matter from the two-dimensional approach of the early period, in which sexual and egoistic instincts were not opposite sides of the same coin but truly independent forces. Marcuse, to whom my discussion of Freud's instinct theory owes much, also questions the dualism of the later theory, but from a somewhat different viewpoint (*Ibid.*, pp. 27–29). The intensity of Freud's need to characterize his theory as dualistic may be seen in *Beyond the Pleasure Principle*, New York: Liveright, 1950, p. 72.

contraction" are somewhat more immediately descriptive of the processes to be discussed than are "Eros" and "death instinct," and since their conceptual identity is problematic, I shall use the former pair in the ensuing discussion.[6]

The notion which establishes the clearest connection between Freud's exposition of the two constructs and the substance of this paper is that of directness and immediacy of gratification. For Freud, death was the ultimate cessation of tension, and "circuitous paths to gratification" implies the prolongation of tension and with it the maintenance of life. Death is thus viewed as analogous to orgasm, and life as analogous to the perpetuation of sexual tension. The conflict between the two instincts is thus the struggle between the continuance and the cessation of tension, the seeking and the avoiding of stimuli, the persistence and the suspension of movement.

Causes of Libidinal Diffusion

But if libidinal diffusion involves not only an increase in the number of objects cathected by the individual, but also an increase in the extent to which gratification is "sublimated," circuitous, delayed, and incomplete, one might well ask, why does it occur at all? What prompts the organism to make these "ever more complicated detours"?

6 Some readers may not feel that the fit between Freud's instinct theory and the observations which follow is as close as I have maintained, and in fairness to them it must be admitted that (a) many of the ideas set forth here were developed prior to my acquaintance with that theory, and (b) that Franz Alexander, who interprets Freud's two instincts in a manner identical with mine, nevertheless regards his interpretation as a new departure: "*instead of assuming* two kinds of instincts, one towards life and one towards death, it is more promising to speak of a trend towards organization, which counteracts the entropy principle, the most universal law of all natural process: the trend from more organized towards less organized states." Alexander, "Unexplored Areas in Psychoanalytic Theory and Treatment," *Behavioral Science*, 3 (October, 1958), p. 298. Italics mine.

Without getting too deeply into this rather abstruse issue[7] we might simply point out the competitive advantage in natural selection enjoyed by those organisms which participate in collectivities, and the still further advantage held by collectivities which are highly organized and integrated. Libidinal diffusion is the social cement which binds living entities together. The more objects an individual can cathect at once, the larger the number of individuals who can co-operate in a joint endeavor. Furthermore, as libido becomes further diffused, and gratification becomes less complete, the individual experiences a constant tension and restless energy which can be harnessed to serve socially useful ends.

This characteristic of libidinal diffusion is implicit in psychoanalytic writings. Thus Flugel, for example, describes normal sexual development as a series of successive displacements of libidinal cathexis, from the mother, to the father, to siblings, to parental surrogates, to peers with resemblances to the original incestuous objects, to peers who neither resemble nor contrast with these objects but are simply independent of them.[8]

Yet it should be abundantly clear from clinical analysis of dreams and projective materials collected from normal individuals, not to mention the universality of incestuous longings in mythology and folklore, that these earlier libidinal cathexes are never entirely uprooted. Indeed, so long as there is sufficient libido left over for completely free choice of objects, it is not important that they should be. But let us consider the consequences of this fact: "healthy" human growth in all existing societies *requires* that libidinal gratification must always be partial and incomplete. For no matter how perfectly gratifying the individual's mature erotic relationships may be, they cannot discharge those fragments of libidinal tension which have been "left behind," attached to their original incestuous objects.

---

[7] *Beyond the Pleasure Principle*, pp. 49–51; Sandor Ferenczi, *Thalassa: A Theory of Genitality*, New York: The Psychoanalytic Quarterly, 1938, p. 44 ff.

[8] J. C. Flugel, *The Psychoanalytic Study of the Family*, London: Hogarth, 1957.

This is, of course, of little practical psychological significance. Such residual libidinal tensions can be discharged in dreams or humor, or sublimated into filial devotion or artistic creativity. But it is important for social theory, since it means that *so long as an individual cathects more than one object he will be unable to achieve a complete absence of libidinal tension,* and hence remains always available for collectivization.

One of the best examples of the way in which libidinal diffusion provides competitive advantages in natural selection may be found in Parsons' analysis of the functions of the incest taboo. Parsons points out that the actual prevention of incest is less important than the fact that it enforces "marrying out." That is, it bars the nuclear family from becoming a completely autonomous collectivity, and blocks the withdrawal of libidinal cathexis from those larger coordinated aggregates the maintenance of which has long been essential in most parts of the world to tolerable human existence. "It is only on the impossible assumption that families should constitute independent societies and not be segmental units of higher-level organizations, that incest as a regular practice would be socially possible." Involvement in incestuous relationships, in which emotional needs could be more fully and immediately gratified, would weaken the individual's bonds to the larger collectivity. Parsons seems to be referring to this issue when he talks about the necessity of "propelling the child from the family."[9]

LIMITATIONS OF LIBIDINAL DIFFUSION. At this point, however, we find ourselves in another dilemma. Whereas at first we were puzzled to discern the basis for the prevalence of an inferior mode of gratification, we now seem to be in the antipodal difficulty of wondering why there should be any limit to libidinal diffusion. For while one can assume that the superior gratificatory attraction inhering in libidinal contraction would always exert a kind of gravitational drag on this trend, the advantages in terms of natural selection would seem to push inevitably toward endless increases in the diffusional direction.

[9] Talcott Parsons, "The Incest Taboo in Relation to Social Structure and the Socialization of the Child," *British Journal of Sociology*, 5 (June, 1954), pp. 101–117. See pp. 106, 107–8.

Even from a societal viewpoint, however, unlimited libidinal diffusion would be a doubtful blessing.[10] The most obvious limitation is the necessity for motivation of procreation. Those few attempts, by totalitarian religious communities of a utopian nature, to sublimate and diffuse all sexual tendencies, illustrate this point rather dramatically. Ultimate diffusion led to ultimate extinction. We must thus qualify our statement that natural selection favors libidinal diffusion, and say rather that it favors individuals and groups in whom diffusion is ascendant but nonetheless strongly opposed by tendencies toward libidinal contraction—in other words, those who are strongly conflicted on this dimension.

Such a modification helps to explain the intensity of the incest taboo, which may be attributed to the fact that it is indeed the conflicted who have survived. Ultimately, it derives from the specificity of the prohibition; libidinal contraction must be permitted to go far enough to ensure sexual union and procreation but not far enough to threaten the existence of suprafamilial collectivities. Since the incest prohibition marks the point at which prescription is suddenly transformed into proscription, and since the forces propelling the individual across this line are very powerful, the barrier required to interrupt this momentum must be correspondingly powerful.

Three Threats to Aggregate Maintenance

Although violation of the incest prohibition constitutes the nearest danger to suprafamilial collectivities, there are other and more extreme forms of libidinal contraction than that against which the taboo most specifically militates. If libidinal cathexis can be withdrawn from larger collectivities and centered in the nuclear family, it can also be withdrawn from the

[10] In raising this issue I do not mean to imply a disbelief in the possibility of further vast increases in the collectivization of human life.

family and centered in any single dyadic relationship, and
finally, it can be withdrawn from all object relationships and
centered in the ego, as in the classical psychoanalytic discussions of narcissism. All three are simply positions on a continuous dimension of social regression. Incest itself has long
been viewed in this manner, with Parsons twice referring to it
as a socially regressive withdrawal, from the "obligation to
contribute to the formation and maintenance of suprafamilial
bonds on which the major economic, political, and religious
functions of the society are dependent," and citing Fortune
and Levi-Strauss in support of this position.[11]

The normal response of others to signs of libidinal contraction in an individual with whom these others participate in
some collectivity, is what we shall call "social anxiety." They
may also display anger, moral indignation, ridicule, or scorn,
but the anxiety is clearly the primary response from which the
others are derived. Since it is a rather common and familiar
sensation to all of us, experienced whenever someone deserts,
either physically or psychically, a group in which we are emotionally involved, little need be said about it. The latent danger with which it is concerned is the collapse of the group.
It does not spring, however, from any rational consideration
of the advantages of societal existence, but is emotional and
automatic, and appears concurrently with awareness of group
membership, whether in the family of orientation or elsewhere.
Presumably its universality is a result of natural selection.

Social anxiety generally elicits, in those who experience it,
behavior designed to reform this deviant member who has
"regressed," i.e., transferred his libido from a more inclusive
to a less inclusive object. But social control is never entirely
post hoc, and in all surviving societies we find an elaboration
of anticipatory institutions which serve to hinder such cathectic
withdrawal. It is primarily with these institutions that the
remainder of this paper will deal, although *post hoc* sanctions
will also be discussed.

We have said that there exist three principal forms of libidi-
11 *Ibid.,* pp. 106, 107, 114.

nal contraction or cathectic withdrawal. Each of these forms has a primary anticipatory institution which tends to preclude its emergence:

1. The most immediate form—withdrawal of cathexis from larger aggregates to within the confines of the nuclear family —we will call "familial withdrawal." Its principal anticipatory institution is the incest taboo.
2. Withdrawal of cathexis from larger aggregates to a single intimate dyad we will call "dyadic withdrawal." Its principal anticipatory institution is marriage.
3. The most extreme form—withdrawal of cathexis from all objects to the self—we will call "narcissistic withdrawal." Its principal anticipatory institution is socialization.

These institutions are for the most part so successful in counteracting libidinal contraction that we are usually unaware of the conflict taking place; it is only at certain rough spots in the social fabric that it becomes visible. Since space limitations forbid detailed discussion of all three forms of withdrawal, I shall concentrate most heavily on the second or dyadic type, which yields some of the most dramatic examples. Little can in any case be added to Parsons' discussion of the function of the incest taboo in preventing familial withdrawal, while narcissistic withdrawal receives extensive treatment in the psychoanalytic literature. Analysis of these forms will therefore be cursory in this presentation.[12]

[12] The examples which follow are presented, for the sake of clarity and simplicity, in an interpersonal form, pitting individuals experiencing cathectic withdrawal against others who are not. This should not mislead the reader into assuming that there is no inner struggle in all this, or that we are talking of different types of people. There is no one who does not at some time in his life experience and defend cathectic withdrawal, and no one who never fights against it.

In the same way I have ignored the issue of guilt. Guilt is not aroused by libidinal contraction itself, but only by violation of the norms associated with the anticipatory institutions. For to the extent that cathectic withdrawal has occurred the individual is by definition emotionally unavailable to the collectivity in question. He feels no commitment to it and cannot therefore perceive himself as having violated that commitment.

I. Narcissistic Withdrawal

Narcissistic withdrawal takes many forms, the most familiar of which are psychosis and somatic illness.[13] In these instances, the internal emotional process is given some kind of concrete physical or behavioral manifestation, but this need not always occur. Furthermore, there are types of behavioral social withdrawal, such as reclusiveness or anchoritism, which may not involve a corresponding degree of withdrawal of libidinal cathexis.

The social control mechanisms which come into operation in the case of either type of illness have been discussed at length by Parsons.[14] For our present purposes we need only underline the fact that the principal control mechanism in this re-socialization is the same one upon which the initial socialization process is based: the kindling and fanning of dependency needs. By placing him in the sick role and catering to his needs, the deviant is seduced into once again directing his libido onto social objects. For the more severe "crimes," the sick person is incarcerated, partly to facilitate the induction of dependency, but partly also to offset the possible contagious effect of such libidinal contraction.

The logical extreme of both of these types of narcissistic withdrawal—in fact of all libidinal contraction for the human organism—is death.[15] Death naturally arouses more social an-

---

13 Freud's paper "On Narcissism: an Introduction," *Collected Papers*, Vol. IV, London: Hogarth, 1953, is still the best single discussion of this process.
14 *The Social System*, Glencoe, Ill.: The Free Press, 1951.
15 Freud never discusses the fate of the libido when the ego is destroyed. For although he says that "throughout life the ego remains the great reservoir from which libidinal cathexes are sent out on to objects and into which they are also once more withdrawn, like the pseudopodia of a body of protoplasm," he also says that "there can be no question that the libido has somatic sources, that it streams into the ego from various organs and parts of the body." (*Outline of Psychoanalysis*, pp. 23–4). From this it would seem to follow that libido is "psychic" energy only after it is drawn into the "reservoir" of the ego and assimilated to that structure, just as, to use Parsons' analogy, money becomes public only when it is collected

xiety than illness, however, because it is total, permanent, and irreparable. Furthermore, the dead man does not even decently take himself off, but leaves a putrefying corpse as a material reminder that he has "laid his burden down" and that others may do the same if they wish. For this corpse is impervious to social pressures and sanctions—no matter how others plead, nurture, threaten, and cajole, it is obstinately, defiantly asocial. Death is thus a desertion without the saving grace of absence. Nor is there any threat of punishment involved, for the corpse is clearly immune, insensible, and beyond retribution.

All of this serves to make funeral rituals an urgent necessity. First of all, the social fabric must be repaired, the ranks closed, and the virtue and unity of the collectivity dramatized[16] in such a way as to bolster the waverers who might be seduced into following in the footsteps of the departed. This aspect is tediously familiar to us from the writings of anthropologists.[17]

in a governmental treasury. But it is drawn, as Freud points out, from more primitive, lower-level sources, and if it can "stream into" the ego there is no logical reason why it cannot "stream back" whence it came. This presumably occurs in a very limited and partial way in very disturbed individuals, but it occurs altogether when any individual dies. For while it is quite proper to say that the ego "dies" when the organism dies, it is not proper so to speak of the libido. The ego is a structure, and it is quite obvious that death involves the dissolution of all higher level structures. But the libido is by definition energy, and energy does not "die." The libido as we are used to thinking about it—in its psychic mold, that is—dissolves, and reverts to its somatic components, ultimately to cellular and chemical components. The loss seems total, so impressive are the accomplishments of organic structures: we are similarly impressed with the way in which a money economy collapses when the political entity which supports it is dissolved. Yet wealth does not vanish, but only becomes latent and fragmented, and the same is true of libidinal energy.

16 An extreme example of this in our society is the practice of permitting stragglers in a funeral procession to cross an intersection against the lights. The danger involved underlines the importance attached to social cohesion at such times.

17 Cf., e.g., Bronislaw Malinowski, *Magic, Science and Religion*, Glencoe, Ill.: The Free Press, 1948, pp. 29–35; and A. R. Radcliffe-Brown, *The Andaman Islanders*, Glencoe, Ill.: The Free Press, 1948, p. 242, on which the following is largely based. It might be noted here that anthropologists and sociologists make altogether too little use of the concept of over-determination, which would eliminate many of the foolish controversies which encumber the literature.

Second, the corpse must be incarcerated in the ground or in some other way isolated so as to remove the "bad influence" from sight and awareness. Third, the "independence" of the corpse must be symbolically denied in some way through ritual interaction between mourners and mourned. The corpse is thus almost always bathed, cosmetically treated in some way, and decorated or dressed—in some societies even held in the arms, rocked and kissed—as if, by treating it like an infant, to make one last effort to re-socialization through gratification of the now extinguished dependency needs. Furthermore, by performing these various operations on the corpse, and particularly by disposing of it, the group recaptures the initiative from the prodigal. Instead of being abandoned by him, they have now expelled him, and often do not consider him officially dead before doing so. This desire to deny the independent initiative of the deceased is also revealed by the almost universal denial of the possibility that death could be a voluntary act of cathectic withdrawal, which, as every general practitioner knows, it often is.[18] In primitive societies this denial takes the form of a belief that all death is caused by sorcery. In our own society it takes the form of an insistence on a specific somatic "cause of death" on death certificates, even in those cases where no lesion can be found to serve as the scapegoat. Finally, the social immunity of the deceased may be denied by the myth that societal existence does not cease with death but continues in another world, so that he has not in fact "escaped," and, in the more fully elaborated of these myths, may even be punished.

In some instances the initiative of the individual in causing his own death cannot be denied. Although suicides are sometimes attributed to sorcery in primitive societies, the more usual response is to accept such blatant evidence and condemn the deceased. For disapproval always varies in accordance with the degree of personal responsibility for the crime, and as malingering is the most disapproved form of illness, so suicide

[18] Avery D. Weisman and Thomas P. Hackett, "Predilection to Death," *Psychosomatic Medicine,* 23 (1961), pp. 232–256.

is the most disapproved mode of dying. This disapproval, it must be emphasized, is a response to the suicide's shocking individualistic conclusion that his life is his own affair. In the absence of a theory of libidinal contraction or its equivalent the societal attitude toward suicide becomes incomprehensible. Durkheim seems to have had this in mind when he stated that both egoistic and anomic suicide "result from the fact that society is not sufficiently in the individual's consciousness," and when he refers to individuals "evading their duties through death." Durkheim's law that suicide rates vary inversely with the totalitarianism of the collectivity (in the sense of the depth, breadth, and intensity of its impingement upon individual activities) is also worthy of note here. We shall see that this law holds for all forms of libidinal contraction.[19]

THE WITHDRAWAL IN STRENGTH. The forms of narcissistic withdrawal thus far considered have been those associated with a weak and beleaguered ego. This corresponds to the implicit psychoanalytic assumption that in "healthy" states the libido flows out onto objects, while only a weak ego draws it back upon itself in the manner of a wound. But although as a recognition of the statistical correlation between "narcissism" and "ego-weakness" such an assumption is quite useful, it should not mislead us into ignoring the fact that more robust forms of narcissistic withdrawal do exist in reality, and play an even more important role in fantasy.

Of greatest interest in the present context is the combination of strong cathectic withdrawal with a complete absence of behavioral withdrawal—in other words, an individual actively engaged in collectivities with no emotional commitment to them. Insofar as others are aware of his total self-interestedness, he will be viewed as an ambitious and unscrupulous manipulator, and the term "psychopath" may even (rather loosely) be applied. In his paper on "Libidinal Types" Freud appropriately designated this personality constellation as "narcissistic," and saw it as ego-oriented, in contrast to the id-oriented

[19] *Suicide*, Glencoe, Ill.: The Free Press, 1951, pp. 208–210, 258.

"erotic" type and the superego-oriented "obsessional" type.[20] Both of the latter he considered dependent, the erotic through fear of loss of love, the obsessional through guilt,[21] while the narcissitic type he called "independent and not easily over-awed." He is active, aggressive, concerned primarily with self-preservation: "indeed, starting from this type one would hardly have arrived at the notion of a super-ego."[22]

There is no lever by which such an individual can be persuaded to serve social ends. He is the complete "economic man," motivated solely by rational self-interest. He will conform when it is dangerous not to, but will never scruple to violate any social norm or betray any individual or group if it will further his ends. He thus operates exclusively on the reality principle, which, as Freud notes, "indeed pursues the same ends [as the pleasure principle] but *takes into account* the conditions imposed by the outer world."[23] Such conscious weighing of alternatives is not the kind of conformity which will bring peace of mind to those who are emotionally identified with their society, for social order now exists only when conformity is automatic, unconscious and nonrational.

All of this may seem rather obvious, but it bears some emphasizing in view of the rather widespread tendency to regard the role of society in the internecine struggles of id, ego, and superego merely as one of helping the ego control instinctual demands and pressures. In some respects, however, this alle-

---

[20] *Collected Papers*, Vol. V, London: Hogarth, 1953, pp. 247–251.

[21] He makes this distinction in terms which correspond precisely to Riesman's distinction between other-directed and inner-directed modes of conformity. Cf. *The Lonely Crowd*, Garden City, N.Y.: Doubleday, 1955, pp. 29–42, 55 ff.

[22] Freud, *op. cit.*, p. 249.

[23] Freud, S. *The Problem of Lay Analyses*, New York: Brentano's, 1927, p. 70. Italics mine. It is absurd to argue, as is sometimes done, that the rational man will conform because he is aware of the manifold benefits conferred upon him by societal existence, and reckons that if others follow his deviant path some kind of annulment of the social contract will take place. The existence of his society is in fact non-problematic, his acts are not necessarily contagious, and there is absolutely no *rational* reason for not violating social norms and laws whenever the gain is great and the risks and losses small.

giance is reversed. Freud notes, for example, that the primary
opposition of religion is to the "egoistic instincts" rather than
the sexual ones.[24] What is insufficiently recognized is that the
socialization process almost invariably guarantees that impulse
control is *not* based entirely on the reality principle, but is
firmly grounded in a socially manipulable, nonrational basis.
Some of the ego's controlling functions must atrophy in order
to permit the essentially competitive social institutions—
whether in the ancient version of external authorities or the
more sophisticated form of an internalized superego—to operate. For social control is more homogeneous, more consistent
from person to person than individual, rational control. It
permits a smooth predictability in the affairs of men.

This relationship becomes quite clear when we consider the
nature of those figures considered to be the great villains of
literature and mythology. It is only here that we find that lack
of enmity between ego and id which Freud considered to be
healthy and natural.[25] These characters are not in the least
impulse-ridden,[26] nor do they suffer from superego anxiety. As
a result they are courageous, ambitious and proud, but also
heartless, calculating, and unscrupulous. They achieve their
goals without "going through channels." The epitome of this
type is Milton's Satan, who is egregiously individualistic and
hostile to any social organization he cannot dominate. His self-
sufficiency and sturdy ego defenses enable him to withstand
extreme tortures:

[24] "Obsessive Acts and Religious Practices," *Collected Papers*, Vol. II, London: Hogarth, 1956, p. 33.
[25] *Problem of Lay Analyses*, p. 71; *Outline of Psychoanalysis*, p. 19; *New
Introductory Lectures*, London: Hogarth, 1949, p. 102.
[26] Occasionally there is an attempt to link the villain's ultimate downfall
to an uncontrolled impulse, usually sexual ("a woman was his undoing"),
which causes him to drop his guard against his many enemies.
  One of the most interesting of these villain types is the shrewd pirate
captain, who usually appears almost ascetic relative to his impulsive crew.
Although utterly unscrupulous, he attracts identification as the wily and
heroic ego, satisfying but maintaining control over the fierce and lustful id.
The cinematic portrayal of Blackbeard by Robert Newton epitomizes this
type.

The mind is its own place, and in itself Can make a Heaven of Hell, a Hell of Heaven, What matter where, if I be still the same?[27]

The fact that "pride" is the cardinal sin in most religious systems should suffice to make it clear that the strong ego is seen as a greater menace to societal existence than the rampant id. The grossly impulsive individual is too ineffectual to menace anyone for very long and quickly destroys himself by stupid blunders. In our own legal system his inability to control his impulses is regarded as an extenuating circumstance. It is not the crime of passion but the premeditated crime that is most severely punished, which is equivalent to saying that the stronger the ego the greater the crime.

We must of course make clear here what viewpoint we are taking. As a member of a collectivity, social anxiety is aroused in the individual by narcissistic withdrawal—by "Satanic pride." But as a boundary-maintaining organism, instinctual anxiety is aroused in him when he observes a crime of passion or other manifestation of uncontrolled impulses. For the personality system, evil resides in the id, while for the social system, it resides in the ego.

This is the reason why great villains are so ambivalently regarded. Freud says that narcissistic types impress people as "personalities," and it cannot be denied that they invariably steal the show from the "good" characters. They are villains to society, but as representations of the ego they are heroes to the individual. Their deaths are doubly satisfying, for while social control is thus reestablished and evil punished, the villain achieves a secret victory, having established his narcissistic withdrawal on a permanent and invulnerable basis.

In sum, the "strong-ego" narcissist arouses most social anxiety because he appears to have overcome the dependency and guilt which are used as levers to resocialize the less healthy narcissist, and because his is an organization which can more effectively compete with the collectivity in which he is em-

27 *The Poetical Works of John Milton,* New York: Crowell, 1892, p. 49. Cf. Radcliffe-Brown's description of the "asocial" man in *Structure and Function in Primitive Society,* Glencoe, Ill.: Free Press, 1952, p. 176.

bedded. The most important anticipatory institutions which have arisen to meet this threat are the subversion of the reality principle in the socialization process, and the tendency of the family and peer group to punish narcissistic behavior with deprivation of love before the ego is hardy enough to tolerate such deprivation. These mechanisms are on the whole so effective that we have been forced to cull our major examples from fiction, wherein their existence serves further to ensure their absence from real life.

Before leaving the subject of narcissistic withdrawal we should take cognizance of one fact which seems at first to contradict much of what has been said. In his discussion of the narcissistic type, Freud says that "it is on them that their fellow-men are specially likely to lean: they readily assume the role of leader, give a fresh stimulus to cultural development or break down existing conditions."[28] While we would expect narcissistic individuals to be radicals and innovators, it is rather strange to think of them as leaders, even of a charismatic sort. How can they be feared as evil villains and followed as saviors at the same time?

The answer to this question is twofold. First, it seems to be true that strongly narcissistic individuals have a certain seductive fascination for most people, particularly for those with intense dependency needs. This fascination is non-normative and in no way incompatible with a considered appraisal (at a distance) of the narcissistic leader as totally villainous. Its prototype may be seen in the experiment of von Holst, who removed the forebrain (and hence the schooling response) of a fish, which thereupon became the leader of the swarm.[29] At the human level great leaders are similarly sought among those who are deficient in the need to depend on others—i.e., people who are willing to sacrifice security to vanity.[30]

[28] *Loc. cit.*, pp. 248–9. This is contrasted with the "conservative" obsessional type who is an "upholder of civilization."

[29] Bertram Schaffner (ed.), *Group Processes* (1957), New York: Macy Foundation, 1959, pp. 244–245.

[30] It should be emphasized that it is only when narcissism is combined with a strong ego that we expect to find weak dependency needs. In most forms of illness both narcissim and dependency are exaggerated.

But there are conditions under which this tendency becomes normative. Narcissistic withdrawal is usually tolerated in individuals who are expected to confer some great benefit upon society: leaders, prophets, shamans, inventors, artists, scientists, innovators of all kinds. This expectation allays social anxiety and social control mechanisms are waived—there is no harm if the prophet temporarily leaves the group and goes into the desert because he will return in time, replete with marvelous visions.[31] Similarly, if the leader is selfish, unfeeling, unscrupulous, and vain, this is acceptable because he will take upon himself the group's burdens and lead them to the promised land.[32]

The basis of this tolerance is perhaps some vague awareness that great enterprises require an abundance of libidinal energy, which must hence be withdrawn from the usual social objects. The more robust varieties of narcissist have this libido available for creative innovation, and to the extent that the social value of such innovation is perceived, the price will be paid with commensurate willingness.

31 Arnold Toynbee stresses this theme of withdrawal and return in his *A Study of History* (Somervell abridgement), New York: Oxford University Press, 1946, pp. 217–230. I do not wish to convey the impression of a smoothly-working system here, however. The expectation is probably more often than not misplaced, with the tolerance extended to the unworthy and denied to those who merit it, or bestowed after the fact. It is not that the collectivity is ever other than conservative, or that it is in any way "responsible" for the benefits it derives from a creative narcissistic withdrawal. It is merely that there is a general social recognition of the need for such withdrawal when great enterprises are to be undertaken.

32 This is the basis for the intensive use of narcissistic rewards, (in the form of deference, flattery and exhibitionistic display) to motivate leaders in all cultures and all ages. Shakespeare shows a brilliant if somewhat prejudiced understanding of the nature of this exchange in *Henry V*, Act IV, Scene 1, when the king reflects dolefully on the heavy burden of responsibility laid upon him by his subjects:

"what infinite heart's-ease
Must kings neglect, that private men enjoy!
And what have kings, that privates have not too,
Save ceremony?"

Yet the next day (Scene 3) Henry reveals that he is not an unwilling victim to the contract by wishing he had fewer soldiers with whom to share his glory.

In the case, however, of the charismatic leader, the relationship is simpler and more primitive. The individual who has stored up narcissistic libido will attract the libido of others to him, after the physical principle that the greater the mass the greater the attraction. Libido thus has a social significance akin to that of *mana*, and an individual of this kind can be a focus for group loyalty. This is usually achieved by seducing the potential centripetal agent with narcissistic rewards and power.[33]

We might then summarize these observations by saying that a group will not apply negative sanctions to narcissistic withdrawal if such withdrawal seems to increase the libidinal diffusion of other group members. We shall see that the same principle applies to other forms of cathectic withdrawal.

It is interesting that Freud saw this principle as operating on the biological level. Starting with the familiar observation that the association of cells is a means of prolonging life (one cell helping to preserve the life of another and the community surviving all individuals), and that the temporary coalescence of two unicellular organisms "has a life-preserving and rejuvenating effect on both," he interprets this process in terms of libido theory, seeing the cells as cathecting one another and "sacrificing themselves" for the object. Then he notes that the germ-cells constitute an exception to this rule, behaving "in a completely 'narcissistic' fashion. . . . The germ-cells require their libido . . . for themselves, *as a reserve against their later momentous constructive activity.*"[34]

---

[33] As the collectivity increases in size, the personal narcissism of the individual becomes less important, since it is "built into" the role. In their official capacities, heads of state behave narcissistically and are treated like narcissists whether they fit the part or not. This is not to say, of course, that narcissism is a sine qua non of leadership. It is of importance primarily when social integration is problematic and social change imminent. In stable and peaceful collectivities it is usually of very little or even negative significance.

[34] *Beyond the Pleasure Principle*, pp. 67–68. Italics mine. Cf. also Bertram Lewin's remark that regression to a simpler structural state always releases surplus energy. *The Psychoanalysis of Elation*, New York: Norton, 1950, p. 29.

II. Dyadic Withdrawal

Our discussion of narcissistic withdrawal would suggest that the social danger it raises is almost entirely hypothetical. Where it is combined with a weak ego it is impotent as a social force, while where it appears in conjunction with ego-strength, mechanisms have evolved which tend to channel it into what are often socially constructive paths. What diminishes the threat of both forms, then, is the fact that all human beings have needs which can best be satisfied through other human beings. Where the ego is weak the individual is compelled to depend upon others. Where it is strong he will seek out others because they will maximize his gratification. He will expend very little love on them, will in fact try to use and exploit them, ruthlessly, but in order to do so successfully he will in most cases be forced to bargain and compromise (which his inherent pragmatism finds quite natural and easy).

But what if most of the physiological and psychological needs of the individual could be satisfied without immediate[35] recourse to the larger collectivity? Suppose that the libido of the individual were concentrated upon only one other person, who served to gratify all of these needs, and that a reciprocal concentration were made by that other person. A lower level of ego-strength would then be required to make an effective cathectic withdrawal from larger collectivities, and the anticipatory institutions described in the previous section would no longer be adequate.

This is the situation which obtains with dyadic withdrawal. An intimate dyadic relationship always threatens to short-circuit the libidinal network of the community and drain off its source of sustenance. The needs binding the individual to collectivities and reinforcing his allegiance thereto are now satisfied in the dyadic relationship, and the libido attached to

[35] I.e., over and above that societal dependence which is automatic, unconscious, and universal.

these collectivities and diffused through their component members is drawn back and invested in the dyad.

There are several reasons why the dyad lends itself so well to this kind of short-circuiting. One is that, as Simmel pointed out, "the secession of either would destroy the whole. The dyad, therefore, does not attain that superpersonal life which the individual feels to be independent of himself."[36] Another is that all other groups consist of multiple relationships which influence one another, while the dyad consists of only one relationship, influenced by none. In triads and larger groups the libidinal cathexis of the individual is divided and distributed, and there are many points of "leverage" at which he may be influenced or controlled. Furthermore, if part of the attachment of two persons is based upon a common attachment to a third party it may also be based upon attachment to a superindividual concept, to collective ideals.[37]

One may, of course, exaggerate the special qualities of the dyad. In part it is merely the extreme case of a general law which says that intimate involvement of an individual with a group is an inverse function of its size. It is possible, however, to make a sharp separation of the dyad from other forms by virtue of its low combinatorial potential. The intimate dyadic relationship thus forms a nodal point for libidinal contraction. Libidinal cathexis which is withdrawn from larger collectivities can "stick" to the dyad, in a manner analogous to the stopping-places in Freud's parable of fixation.[38]

THE DYAD AND THE COMMUNITY. If we assume a finite quantity of libido in every individual, then it follows that the greater the emotional involvement in the dyad, the greater will be the cathectic withdrawal from other objects. This accords well with the popular concept of the oblivious lovers, who are "all

[36] Kurt H. Wolff (trans.) *The Sociology of Georg Simmel,* Glencoe, Ill.: The Free Press, 1950, pp. 123–4.

[37] Theodore M. Mills, "A Sociological Interpretation of Freud's *Group Psychology and the Analysis of the Ego*" (unpublished).

[38] Sigmund Freud, *A General Introduction to Psychoanalysis,* Garden City Books, 1952, pp. 297–299.

wrapped up in each other," and somewhat careless of their social obligations. All of the great lovers of history and literature were guilty of striking disloyalties of one kind or another —disregard for the norms governing family and peer group ties, in the story of Romeo and Juliet, becomes, in the affair of Antony and Cleopatra, a disregard for societal responsibilities which embrace most of the civilized world. In Shakespeare's drama, a war of global significance is treated by the lovers as a courtly tournament, and their armies are manipulated as if the outcome were related only to the complexities of the internal dyadic relationship. This is epitomized in a remark by Cleopatra, who expresses her satisfaction with a day of military victory by saying to Anthony, "Comest thou smiling from the world's great snare uncaught?"

Given this inverse relationship between dyadic cathexis and societal cathexis, another correlation suggests itself. We may hypothesize that the more totalitarian the collectivity, in terms of making demands upon the individual to involve every area of his life in collective activity, the stronger will be the prohibition against dyadic intimacy. We have already seen that a similar relation holds for suicide, and it may equally be applied to other forms of narcissistic withdrawal.

Strong opposition to dyadic intimacy is often found in youth groups which are formed on the basis of common interests, such as music, camping, travel, or mountain-climbing. Solidarity in such groups often runs high, and avoidance of even momentary pairing is usually a firmly upheld norm. Extreme prohibitions are also characteristic of utopian communistic communities, religious and otherwise, such as the Oneida experiment. In some instances the dyadic intimacy prohibition is enforced at the same time that sexual promiscuity is encouraged, thus clearly revealing that the basis of the proscription is not fear of sexuality but fear of libidinal contraction —fear lest the functions which the state performs for the individual could be performed for each other by the members of the dyad. Soviet Russia and Nazi Germany also made abortive experiments in this direction, before realizing that as a device for providing societal control over dyadic intimacy, the institution of marriage could scarcely be improved upon.[39]

In some nonliterate societies, the prevention of privacy is managed through such devices as barracks-type living arrangements. I stress this fact because of the widespread notion that "romantic love" is simply an idiosyncrasy of Western civilization, and has no relevance for primitive societies. This view has been challenged by Goode, who argues that it is less rare than supposed, and seems to associate its infrequency, as we have done here, with the notion that "love must be controlled." He sees the need for such control, however, as based on the more limited necessity of preventing the disruption of lineages and class strata. Of particular interest to our purpose is the passage from Margaret Mead which he cites as illustrating the presumed irrelevance of romantic love to primitive living. This passage states that the Samoans "laughed with incredulous contempt at Romeo and Juliet."[40] Similar laughter is often evoked by this drama among pre-adolescents and adolescents in our own society, but I wonder if we would infer from this that it had no meaning to them. Primitive peoples often laugh at hypothetical and "unheard-of" violations of major taboos, and it would perhaps be more appropriate to interpret the laughter as an expression of social anxiety rather than of the "irrelevance" of romantic love.

Goode cites many types of control of dyadic intimacy, similar to those we will discuss in relation to Western society. Child marriages, restriction of the pool of eligible spouses, isolation of adolescents from prospective mates, and peer group control. Of isolation he says, "It should be emphasized that [its] primary function . . . is to minimize informal or intimate social interaction." He also notes that relatively free mate choice (in *formal* terms) is always associated with the "strong develop-

---

[39] An insightful literary portrayal of this antagonism may be found in Orwell's *1984* (New York: Harcourt, Brace, 1949), in which a highly centralized collectivity evinces overwhelming hostility to dyadic intimacy, as a potential refuge from the all-pervasive state.

[40] William J. Goode, "The Theoretical Importance of Love," *American Sociological Review*, 24 (February, 1959), pp. 38–47. See esp. p. 42.

ment of an adolescent peer group system," for reasons "that
are not yet clear." From our perspective, the reasons are simply
that societal control has shifted to the peer group, and thus
does not need to be exercised parentally.[41]

One principal issue, then, in this conflict between dyadic
intimacy and collective life, is whether the relationship shall
be an end in itself (as in "romantic love") or a means to a
socially desired end. In this connection let us consider Alexander's remark that *"the erotic value of an action is inversely
related to the degree to which it loses the freedom of choice
and becomes coordinated* and subordinated to other functions
and becomes a part of an organized system, of a goal structure." On the individual level he points to the fact that the
growing child "first practices most of his biological functions
playfully for the mere pleasure he derives from them," but
that later they are directed toward utilitarian goals, integrated
into a larger system of action, and lose their erotic value. Similarly he sees society as "losing its playful hedonistic qualities
as it becomes more and more organized and thus restricts the
freedom of the activities of its members. . . . Play requires
utmost freedom of choice, which is lost when the activities of
man become closely knit into a social fabric." He contrasts the
individualistic and playful cat to the collectivistic, organized
and unplayful ant, and goes on to note that in the insect states
"organization progressed so far that the majority of the members became asexual and what erotic expression remains for
them consists in an occasional communal ritualistic performance consisting in to and fro rhythmic movements collectively
performed."[42]

This discussion pinpoints the source of the antagonism of
"totalitarian" collectivities toward dyadic intimacy. The intimate, exclusive dyadic relationship is essentially "playful" and

[41] *Ibid.*, pp. 44–5. This perhaps explains the one important departure of
the musical "West Side Story" from its Shakespearean original, which is
otherwise as timely as it was then. But Romeo and Juliet portrayed
decathexis of *both* family and peer group, and is thus the best single portrayal of dyadic withdrawal in adolescence. Even "Marty" adds little to
the street corner scenes Shakespeare depicted.
[42] *Op. cit.*, pp. 302–303.

non-utilitarian. Some kind of organized societal intrusion, as in the institution of marriage, is required to convert it into a socially useful relationship, and insofar as this intrusion is successful the playful aspect of the relationship will tend to disappear. As Alexander points out, "the process toward increased organization or less freedom of choice takes place at the cost of erotic gratification of the individual members of a system, be these organic functions of the body or members of a social organization."[43] Parsons is stressing precisely the same point in his paper on the incest taboo, when he says: "marriage has direct functional significance as a mechanism which establishes important direct ties of interpenetration of membership between different elements in the structural network. Under such circumstances marriage cannot be merely a 'personal affair' of the parties to it."[44] We may thus directly equate libidinal diffusion with the de-eroticizing of the sexual life of the individual—the transformation of hedonistic activity into utilitarian activity as Alexander describes it.

Freud and Bion lay similar emphasis on the opposition between hetero-sexual dyadic attachments and group solidarity. Both view the latter as dependent upon sublimation of sexuality, and see the dyadic bond as a subversion of this sublimation. Freud says flatly that "directly sexual tendencies are unfavorable to the formation of groups," remarking that the sexual act is the one condition "in which a third person is at the best superfluous."[45]

> Two people coming together for the purpose of sexual satisfaction, in so far as they seek for solitude, are making a demonstration against. . . . the group feeling. The more they are in love, the more completely they suffice for each other . . .
> Even in a person who has in other respects become absorbed in a group the *directly sexual tendencies preserve a little of*

[43] *Ibid.* The process is thus analogous to the "routinization of charisma" at the level of narcissistic withdrawal. Cf. Weber, *The Theory of Social and Economic Organization*, New York: Oxford University Press, 1947, pp. 363–368. Cf. also footnote 1.
[44] Parsons, *op. cit.*, p. 106.
[45] Sigmund Freud, *Group Psychology and the Analysis of the Ego*, New York: Liveright, 1951, pp. 92, 120 ff.; W. R. Bion, "Experiences in Groups: III," *Human Relations*, 2 (No. 1, 1949), pp. 13–22.

his individual activity. . . . Love for women breaks through the group ties of race, of national separation, and of the social class system. . . .[46]

THE PREMARITAL DYAD. Let us now look at examples of dyadic withdrawal in our own society. Although it first appears much earlier, as we shall see, its most familiar manifestations are those occurring in adolescence, when experiments in enduring heterosexual intimacy are first essayed, and soon encounter various kinds of resistance and control from parents, other authorities, and the peer group. The arena of the struggle is often the issue of "going steady," which is generally opposed by adults whether it involves a cathectic withdrawal or not, but which is handled by the peer group with the ardent inconsistency characteristic of fledgling social enterprises. In some groups zealous opposition is the rule, while in others there is an equally enthusiastic group endorsement of the practice, transformed in such a way, however, by group regulation, as no longer to constitute dyadic withdrawal. Criteria of sexual desirability are established with fanatical specificity by group norms, so as virtually to eliminate the importance of personal psychological characteristics. The partners are expected to spend the bulk of their time in group activities and to have a relationship of short duration (often measured in weeks). Such institutionalization of the "going steady" relationship is clearly a far more effective instrument against libidinal contraction than adult opposition.

A special example of this type of peer group control is found in the "rating-and-dating complex" described by Waller.[47] Here the most desirable dyadic partner becomes the one who best lives up to group norms, which tend to replace sexual strivings with status and prestige needs. Under these conditions personal intimacy is rarely achieved. If by some accident compatible partners should come together, the rules regulating behavior in the situation would tend to prevent the existence of this compatibility from becoming known to either person.

[46] Freud, *op. cit.*, pp. 121–123. Italics mine.
[47] Willard Waller, "The Rating and Dating Complex," *American Sociological Review*, 2 (1937), pp. 727–734.

Norms in many such groups also emphasize sexual antagonism and exploitation. The male often achieves prestige within the male group by maximizing physical contact and minimizing expenditure of money on a date. The female achieves prestige within her group by maximizing expenditure and minimizing sexual contact. The date becomes, in the ideal case, a contest between adversaries. Each has much to win or lose in the way of prestige, depending upon how effectively control of tender and sexual feelings can be maintained. It is not difficult to see how dyadic intimacy is minimized in this situation. If each partner, even in the midst of sexual caresses, is "keeping score" in terms of the peer group norms, little emotional involvement can take place. The boy, for example, knows that his friends will later ask him if he "made out," and his sexual behavior may be determined more by this than by any qualities inherent in his partner.[48] It is of no little significance that the beginning of dyadic intimacy and withdrawal is always signalled by the boy's sudden reluctance to talk about the relationship, a reluctance which invariably arouses social anxiety and ridicule.

The control mechanisms of the adult community during this early period are less subtle. Like the peer group, adults depend heavily on ridicule, and lay similar stress upon promiscuity and an exploitive attitude toward the opposite sex. In the adult's exhortation to the adolescent, however, to "play the field," or "keep 'em guessing," or "don't get tied down at your age," it is not difficult to detect the expression of suppressed promiscuous urges—so that the advice serves a psychological function as well as a societal one.[49]

Adult opposition is not limited to these casual admonitions,

[48] David Riesman sees this as a peculiarly "other-directed" phenomenon, but it undoubtedly occurs whenever the peer group is strong. *The Lonely Crowd*, pp. 96–97.

[49] Cf. Talcott Parsons, "Age and Sex in the Social Structure of the United States," *American Sociological Review*, 7 (1942), pp. 604–616. The requirement that the adolescent unlearn this injunction upon marrying constitutes a discontinuity of the type discussed by Ruth Benedict, "Continuities and Discontinuities in Cultural Conditioning," *Psychiatry*, 1 (1938), pp. 161–167. But as in so many other instances, the adult's response to his own stress perpetuates the conflict in the next generation.

however, but often takes more organized forms, and were it not for some such concept as social anxiety it would be difficult to explain why a practice which seems admirably suited to prepare the adolescent for a monogamous adult life should be decried by church and school authorities. "Going steady" is in practice a form of serial monogamy, through which the individual learns not only how to select those qualities most important to him in a mate, but also the obligations and interpersonal expectations appropriate to a monogamous system.

Prohibitions by these authorities are an expression of the breakdown, under changing social conditions, of older and more subtle methods of control. Institutions such as marriage or peer group regulation of dyadic relationships block dyadic withdrawal through social intrusion upon the dyad—ritualizing and regulating it, and drawing its members back into their other relationships. For the most part these forms of control are so effective that it is only in large, "loose," pluralistic societies such as our own that dyadic withdrawal occurs with sufficient frequency and intensity to permit easy observation of the forces opposing it. In many primitive societies dyadic relationships are so highly institutionalized and diluted by group bonds that withdrawal has little opportunity to emerge.

In more mutable societies, however, sudden outbreaks of dyadic intimacy in unexpected areas are always occurring, due to the obsolescence of old mechanisms (e.g., chaperonage) or the emergence of new and unregulated areas of contact (e.g. earlier dating). Sporadic accelerations in the process of collectivization (such as occur in utopian religious communities) may also generate a demand for more extreme action. In such circumstances prohibition becomes more common.

The "going steady" controversy in our society is a good example of this phenomenon, in that it revolves around an extension of heterosexual dyadic intimacy into a younger and younger age group in an era in which teen-age marriage is felt to be socially undesirable. In the colonial period, when an unmarried girl of twenty was considered an old maid, the threat of dyadic withdrawal in adolescence was dissipated by marriage, but this is less feasible today, when the educational process is so prolonged and so valued.[50] Furthermore, we have entered an age in which, through geographical mobility and mass communication, libidinal diffusion has achieved new heights of virtuosity.

Our hypothesis would lead us to expect that the strongest opposition to "going steady" would come from the more "totalitarian"[51] collectivities, and this seems to be the case. A few years ago a Roman Catholic organ expressed unqualified disapproval of the practice, and a parochial school "banned" it. Arguments stressed, as usual, the dangers of sexual transgression, but since sexual intercourse may also occur within the context of a promiscuous dating pattern, something more than sexuality is clearly involved. Other remarks concerning the parochial school ban revealed the intense social anxiety over possible dyadic withdrawal and consequent loss of interest in (i.e., decathexis of) church, state, school, community and God. Thus the priests argued that going steady "creates distractions to *make concentrated study impossible*," and "often leads to marriages between couples too immature emotionally to assume the *obligations of the married state*," while a school superintendent claimed that it "interferes with good school work, and robs the youngster of one of the finer experiences of growing up: the friendship and companionship of *as wide a circle of acquaintances of both sexes as possible*."[52] It is, of course, not the "youngster" but the community and the peer group which are "robbed" in these ways, and the absolute and unqualified nature of the italicized phrase reveals the chronic anxiety of the social man when he is reminded that the entire societal structure, upon which he is so utterly dependent, rests upon borrowed libidinal cathexis, the creditors for which are never still.[53]

[50] It may again become the solution, however, as in-school marriages are on the increase. It is interesting how seldom, in these two popular controversies, going steady and early marriage are seen as alternatives.

[51] Once again it should be stressed that this term refers to the diminutiveness of that sphere which is considered private and personal by the collectivity, rather than to the degree of autocracy which it evinces.

[52] *The Boston Globe*, October 19, 1956. Italics mine.

[53] Parsons, in his paper on the incest taboo, makes this same point in relation to socialization. *Op. cit.*, p. 115.

THE MARRIAGE CEREMONY AS AN INTRUSION RITUAL. The real
focal point of the conflict between dyadic intimacy and societal
allegiances is, of course, the marital relationship. It would be
tedious to review here the many functions of marriage, but it
may be profitable to examine the mechanisms which serve to
maintain its social nature and prevent dyadic withdrawal. For
every marriage poses the threat of this type of social regression,
inasmuch as it creates the possibility of a self-sufficient and
exclusive sub-unit, emotionally unaffiliated with the larger collectivity.

This danger is not a particularly serious one in many primitive societies, where the proverb "blood is thicker than water"
is not merely a psychodynamic reality but also a sociological
one. Even in monogamous societies such as that of the Dobu,
the marital bond is often a very weak one due to the divisive
effects of exogamy.[54]

In a society such as ours, however, with small nuclear family
units, monogamy, neo-local residence, and relatively weak kinship ties, the threat is a very real one. The marriage ritual then
becomes a series of mechanisms for pulling the dyad apart
somewhat, so that its integration complements rather than
replaces the various group ties of its members. The discussion
which follows is primarily concerned with the social rituals
surrounding the typical Protestant middle-class marriage in
our society, but the pattern differs only in detail from those
found elsewhere.

As the marriage approaches there is a rapid acceleration of
the involvement of the families of the couple in their relationship. Increasing stress is placed upon an awareness of the
ritual, legal, and economic significance of the relationship, and
the responsibilities which must be assumed. In addition to the
traditional evaluations made at this juncture of the bread-

54 Reo F. Fortune, *The Sorcerers of Dobu*, London: Routledge, 1932. The
kinship systems of many primitive societies, particularly those involving
complex exogamous clans and unilineal descent, often seem themselves to
be, in part, elaborate defenses against dyadic and familial withdrawal—
defenses that are reminiscent, in their rigid, hypertrophied quality, of the
neurotic mechanisms of individuals.

winning and home-making capabilities of the two individuals, there may even be, as Whyte has suggested, a concern about the social appropriateness of the wife for the organizational setting in which the husband must move.[55]

But societal invasion of the free and exclusive intimacy of the couple (assuming this to have been the nature of the relationship prior to this time) is not limited to such overt influence. The entire ceremony constitutes a rehearsal for the kind of societal relationship which is expected of them later.

First of all, the ceremony is usually a sufficiently involved affair to require a number of practical social decisions from the couple in preparation for the occasion. Much of their interaction during this period will thus concern issues external to their own relationship, and there will be a great deal of preoccupation with loyalties and obligations outside of the dyad itself. Guests must be invited, attendants chosen, and gifts for the attendants selected. The ceremony has the effect of concentrating the attention of both individuals on every *other* affectional tie either one has ever contracted.

Similarly, the ceremony serves to emphasize the *dependence* of the dyadic partners on other collectivities. In addition to the gifts given to the couple, it is made clear to them that much of the responsibility for their wedding rests with their families, who bear a far greater burden in this regard than they themselves. They are, in essence, "given" a wedding.

Their feelings of harassment and anxiety over the coming event, coupled with the realization that their role is at the moment a relatively minor one, and will throughout be a passive one, inculcates a feeling that the dyadic relationship is not their "personal affair." They become more aware that after marriage, too, life will involve instrumental responsibilities, extra-dyadic personal obligations, and societal dependence. It is usually during this period that the impulse toward dyadic withdrawal reasserts itself, and one or the other will half-

[55] William H. Whyte, Jr., "The Wife Problem," in Robert E. Winch and Robert McGinnis, *Selected Studies in Marriage and the Family*, New York: Holt, 1953, pp. 278–295.

seriously suggest elopement. By now there is a feeling that
they have set in motion a vast machine over which they no
longer have any control. But it is usually felt that things have
"gone too far"—parents and friends would be disappointed
and hurt, eyebrows would be raised—there is no turning back.
The impulse is overwhelmed by the feelings of loyalty and
obligation which the impending ceremony has aggravated, and
the crucial moment passes.

The role of the clergyman who is to unite the pair is of
the utmost importance during this period. It is he who usually
verbalizes the societal intrusion most explicitly, and he speaks
from a position of considerable prestige, regardless of the
religiosity of the betrothed couple. In the first place he is
the central person in the proceedings, and represents, emotionally, the paternal figure who can fulfill or deny their
wishes. It is he who will speak the magic words which will join
them, and the accumulated experience of hundreds of movies,
novels, serials, and comic strips tells them that until the last
word is spoken the marriage is in danger of being thwarted.

Second, he is the only person on the scene with expert
knowledge regarding the ceremony itself. As such he is also
typically the least anxious person involved, and thereby provides an important source of support. Sometime prior to the
wedding he generally has a "talk" with the couple, partly to
reassure, but more important, to stress their societal and
religious obligations.

The form of this statement is of particular relevance to the
concept of societal intrusion. In many denominations it is
explicitly stated that marriage is a contract involving three
parties—husband, wife, and God, and that He is always
"present" so long as the marriage lasts. It would be difficult to
find a more vivid symbol of the institutionalization of the
dyad than this, nor a more clear illustration of the Durk-
heimian equation of God with society. The dyadic relationship
not only is no longer a "personal affair," it is no longer even
a dyad. The privacy of the relationship is seen as permanently
invaded. It is interesting to note how this supernatural symbol

of societal intrusion is given more concrete form in Orwell's *1984*, in which the dyad cannot escape from Big Brother, who is "always watching."[56]

The actual process of intrusion, however, is more mundane. As the time for the wedding draws near, the forces drawing the couple apart become more intense. It is often believed to be "bad luck" for the groom to see the bride in her wedding dress before the ceremony, and, in general, contact between the couple on the day of the wedding is considered bad form. When they enter the church it is from opposite ends, as leaders of separate hosts of followers. Prior to the wedding day there are showers or a bridal supper for the bride and a "bachelor's dinner" for the groom, in which peer group ties are very strongly underlined. This tends to create the impression that in some way the couple *owe* their relationship to these groups, who are preparing them ceremonially for their marriage. Often this is made explicit, with family and friends vying with one another in claiming responsibility for having "brought them together" in the first place. This impression of societal initiative is augmented by the fact that the bride's father "gives the bride away." The retention of this ancient custom in modern times serves explicitly to deny the possibility that the couple might unite quite on their own. In other words, the marriage ritual is designed to make it appear as if somehow the idea of the dyadic union sprang from the community, and not from the dyad itself. In this respect, marriage in our society resembles the ritual of the parent who discovers a child eating candy, and says, "I didn't hear you ask for that," whereupon the child says, "May I?" and the parent says, "Yes, you may." The families and friends may actually have had nothing to do with the match, or even have opposed it. The members of the wedding party often come from far

---

[56] One wonders what effect this fantasy of an omnipresent parental figure has on the sexual relationship of couples who take it seriously. Ultimately, of course, societal intrusion is incarnated in a child, and the notion of a scoptophilic deity dwindles into the reality of the curious child before the primal scene.

away, and some of them may be strangers to one another. The
ceremony itself, however, its corollary rituals, and the roles
which pertain to it, all tend to create an image of two individuals, propelled toward each other by a united phalanx of
partisans.

THE HONEYMOON. To everything that has been said thus far
the honeymoon would seem to be an exception. The wedding
ritual seems designed to emphasize the fact that, indeed, marriage is *not* a honeymoon. Yet this wedding is actually followed immediately by a socially sanctioned dyadic withdrawal,
involving the very kind of exclusive, private intimacy—undis-
turbed by any external ties or obligations—which is at all
other times in the life of an individual forbidden. The couple
is permitted, even expected, to "get away from it all," and remove themselves entirely from collective life. To facilitate this
withdrawal they typically absent themselves from the community, travelling to a place where they are unknown. Some
secrecy is usually preserved about their destination, with only
a few chosen persons "in on" the secret. Seldom in the life of
the average individual are the threads binding him to society
so few and so slackened.

At the honeymoon resort they are entirely without obligations or responsibilities. No one knows them or expects anything from them. They are more or less taboo, and others have
them to themselves. The emotional privacy so difficult to obtain at all other times, before and after, is for the moment
almost universally granted. But the period of license is characteristically brief, save for the very wealthy; the couple return
to the community, establish a household, resume old ties,
assume new responsibilities, "put away childish things," and
"the honeymoon is over."

But how are we to account for this exception? Should we
write it off as simply another example of the universal social
tendency to permit norms to be violated on certain festive
occasions? The most reasonable interpretation would seem to
be the same as was applied to the narcissistic leader: the mar-

ried couple are allowed to hoard their libido between themselves, "as a reserve against their later momentous constructive activity." By this I refer not merely to the begetting and raising of children, but rather to the more general process of creating a home and becoming a family—the basic unit upon which the societal structure is built. For marriage is after all a compromise institution—one which attempts to generate a substructure which will be solidary enough to perform its social functions without becoming so solidary that it ceases to be a substructure and begins to seek autonomy. The wedding ceremony tends to guard against the latter, while the honeymoon helps to ensure the former. Some marriages, after all, do not begin with a withdrawn dyad, but with one which has scarcely experienced any privacy, intimacy or freedom. Either extreme is socially inutile, as we have noted.

At the same time we should not be carried away by this functional interpretation to the point of assuming that some sort of folk wisdom is operating here. It is not the community, nor the individual's allegiance to it which inspired this custom, but rather his hatred and fear of society and its pressures toward rationalization and de-eroticization of his instinctual life. In other words, the honeymoon is a manifestation of dyadic withdrawal which is tolerated because it has never in fact (for the reasons given above) showed the slightest sign of being socially disruptive.

Nor do I mean by this to attribute any undue rationality or reality-sense to individuals in their group identities. It would be perfectly reasonable to expect that, although the practice never called attention to itself as a social danger, the very threat of dyadic withdrawal in so concrete a form would arouse social anxiety, and that despite the experience of centuries the participants would stupidly reiterate this anxious reaction and the types of behavior to which it gives rise.

This is indeed the case, the reaction expressing itself primarily in going-away pranks of various kinds, whereby the most serious honeymoon taboos may be broken in a joking context. A great deal of hostility is expressed directly toward the departing couple in the form of diffuse anal-expulsive gestures such as throwing rice and confetti. Some of the customary jokes unveil the basis of this hostility, in that they have the covert purpose of hindering the couple's departure. These include tampering with the couple's automobile, hiding their luggage, etc. Furthermore, a number of devices, such as signs, streamers, or tin cans fastened to the automobile, stones placed in the hub caps, and, again, the confetti, serve to make the couple conspicuous, and thus have the effect of minimizing or negating the sense of privacy which has been granted to them. The importance of this maneuver appears when we recall that lack of self-awareness is commonly seen as an essential attribute of intimate lovers. Finally, attempts are often made to invade the privacy of the couple directly, and to forestall, by symbolic means the breaking of peer group bonds. Thus objects may be placed in the couple's suitcases, or the couple's clothes may be tied in knots—a rather pathetic blending of hostile and wistful sentiments. In the more extreme case every effort is made to find out the couple's destination, and to communicate with them in some way.

In these practical jokes the intensity of the social anxiety aroused by this institutionalized dyadic withdrawal is graphically displayed. It should be noted, however, that physical withdrawal is not a prerequisite to this type of reaction. In more totalitarian communities in which the honeymoon does not exist, the mere possibility of an emotional withdrawal on the part of the newly-weds may call forth more extreme anticipatory anti-withdrawal mechanisms such as the shivaree, which serve as a reminder that the couple has not and cannot evade the community in which it is rooted.

POST-MARITAL INTRUSION. The advent of the first child in itself tends to weaken the exclusive intimacy of the dyad, first by providing an important alternative (and narcissistic) object of cathexis for each member, and second, by creating responsibilities and obligations which are partly societal in nature, and through which bonds between the dyad and the community are thereby generated.[57]

In addition, the marital partners are to a considerable extent drawn apart by their participation in same-sex groups in the community, particularly in the occupational sphere. But the phenomenon is also striking in recreational activities, which fall largely into two categories: those which separate the sexes, and those which involve a reshuffling of partners. Occasionally we find both, as in the case of the traditional Victorian dinner party, during which husband and wife are always seated apart and after which the sexes retire to separate rooms. In our society separation by sexes is perhaps the more dominant form in the lower class, while the reshuffling of partners prevails in the middle class. It would not, in fact, be too much an exaggeration to say that all types of mixed-group recreational activities in the middle class are rooted in more or less larval forms of adulterous flirtation. Married couples who stay too much together in such situations are disapproved.

The extent of such flirtation varies a good deal. The more traditional groups limit themselves to mixing bridge and dancing partners, etc., and frown on spontaneous expressions of sexual interest. Today one more frequently finds groups in

[57] Simmel makes the following comment on the impact of the child on the marital partners: "It is precisely the very passionate and intimate husband and wife who do not wish a child: it would separate them: the metaphysical oneness into which they want to fuse alone with one another would be taken out of their hands and would confront them as a distinct, third element, a physical unit, that mediates between them. But to those who seek immediate unity, mediation must appear as separation." *Op. cit.,* pp. 128–9.

This "immediate unity" is the same desire for fusion that de Rougement discusses at such length in contrasting "passion-love" with "Christian love," and in his analysis of the Catharist heresy, *Love in the Western World*, Garden City, N.Y.: Doubleday, 1957. It involves loss of identity and essential rejection of role relationship—i.e., relationships that are collectively defined. In *Civilization and Its Discontents,* Freud also emphasizes this point. "When a love-relationship is at its height no room is left for any interest in the surrounding world: the pair of lovers are sufficient unto themselves, do not even need the child they have in common to make them happy." London: Hogarth, 1953, pp. 79–80.

which open flirtation in a joking context is expected, but must be carried on in the presence of the group. A third type, found in many sophisticated upper middle-class communities, involves less rigid control. Couples may indulge in sexual caresses away from the group, but it is felt that these should not culminate in intercourse nor lead to any expectation of future interpersonal involvement on the part of either individual (a norm which is perhaps more honored in the breach than in the observance). Finally, there are those communities which are organized on a completely adulterous basis, wherein "wife-trading" is widely practiced. Here the group norms merely proscribe permanent attachments.

While this latter form is something of a special case, it may in general be said that adulterous flirtation in social groups is a cohesive force which prevents the marital bond from atomizing the community. We have noted at many points, particularly with regard to the adolescent dyad, how dyadic intimacy may be blocked by converting sexual drives into strivings for status and prestige. In the married community, however, these strivings tend to unite rather than divide the couple, inasmuch as their status position is shared. This is important in neighborhood gatherings, in which there is typically a fair amount of competitive conversation centering around children and material possessions (such as houses, furnishings, cars, lawns and gardens). Extramarital flirtation tends to vitiate the divisive effect of such invidious comparisons (and vice versa).

SOCIETAL INTRUSION IN EXTRAMARITAL DYADS. If the marital dyad is institutionalized, the extramarital dyad usually is not. In our society extramarital sexuality is generally prohibited, although often sanctioned by subgroups within it. Since it is forbidden, one would expect the extramarital dyad to be the most free from societal intrusion and control. It would thus provide, theoretically, the most favorable context for dyadic withdrawal.

To a certain extent this seems to be the case. It is not accidental that most of the great love affairs of history and fiction are extramarital, nor is it due entirely to the Oedipal cast provided by triangularity. In most societies, past and present, there has been very little free choice in marriage, and dyadic intimacy has often been restricted to the more voluntary extramarital relationship. But it is easy to exaggerate the freedom of such relationships. In general it may be said that the higher the incidence of extramarital affairs in a given collectivity, the greater will be the societal intrusion upon such affairs, especially with regard to sexual choice. In many societies in which extramarital sexuality is universal, choice is restricted to a few relatives.[58] This means, in effect, that the degree of freedom of choice is relatively constant. The stronger the prohibition, the more individual choice will be thereby limited by situational factors; while the weaker the prohibition the more choice will be limited by group norms.

To begin with, there are the general norms which legislate the criteria for sexual attractiveness, and which of course apply to all relationships, not only the extramarital. Thus sexual appeal has been based upon painting the face and body, wearing bizarre clothing, putting rings in the nose, in the ears, around the neck, on the wrists, fingers, ankles, or arms; disfiguring (by scarring, stretching or pitting) parts of the body— to mention only the cosmetic conventions. To foreigners these embellishments often seem strikingly ugly and sexless, and in a complex society such as our own, it is not unusual to hear complaints to this effect even from natives.

Left to themselves, human beings would mate entirely in response to instinctual demands and psychological affinity. The establishment of socially defined aesthetic norms brings sexual choice under social control—one can maximize one's sexual attractiveness by conforming to social canons of taste. The fact that such canons may create an effect which is asexual or even repulsive (by some absolute standard) is merely an indicator of the need and ability of collectivities to control eroticism—to socialize sexuality.

An excellent example of this process may be found in our

[58] George P. Murdock, *Social Structure*, New York: Macmillan, 1949, pp. 4 ff.

own society. Comments have often been made upon the enormous emphasis placed upon deodorants, perfumes, and colognes in the United States. Body odors are of paramount importance in the sexual life of animals, and have always played a large, but apparently decreasing role in human sexuality. Sexual appeal was once determined primarily by the intensity of odors emanating from sexual secretions. But these have now become taboo. Erotic value is instead attached to *absence* of natural odors, the interest in which has been displaced onto odors which are advertised and packaged and may be purchased in a store. This means that sexual appeal can be restricted to certain people, and made conditional upon certain acts. It also means that the criteria of attractiveness may be integrated with the other values of the society (e.g., if beauty can be bought it becomes a part of the monetary reward system).

But societal conditioning extends beyond visual and olfactory canons of sexual taste. We have seen how in adolescent peer groups the appeal of personality affinities is transformed into a group-defined appeal, wherein the sexually attractive individual is one who behaves appropriately.

What applies to choice also applies to the conduct of the affair. When extramarital relationships are tolerated or encouraged by a community, they are usually governed by a variety of restrictive conventions which tend to forestall the kind of dyadic intimacy which leads to cathectic withdrawal. These conventions may be grouped roughly into three categories:

1. IMPERMANENCY. It is usually considered poor form in such groups to retain the same mistress or lover for long periods. The individual who changes partners rapidly gains the most prestige, while the one who is slow in shifting cathexes suffers ridicule from the group. In such a situation the termination of the relationship becomes almost a more important issue than its inauguration. Each partner is constantly on the alert for signs of flagging interest in the other, lest he or she be caught in the embarrassing predica-

ment of not being the first to find a new partner. (This anxiety is a prominent theme, e.g., in Restoration Comedy, which is a fairly accurate reflection of aristocratic life during that era.) The effect of this pattern is to keep the dyadic ties weak and shallow, and prevent the kind of emotional commitment which is a pre-condition for dyadic withdrawal.

2. ROMANTIC STYLIZATION. Collectivities which sanction extramarital sexuality often develop elaborate and detailed customs for initiating, maintaining, and terminating love affairs. This has generally been the rule in aristocratic groups. When it occurs, intimacy (except in the purely physical sense) becomes difficult, due to the formal, gamelike manner in which the affair is conducted.

Romantic stylization is simply one further example of the socialization of sexuality through appeal to vanity. It is the behavioral counterpart of societal influence over sexual choice. Just as there are fashions in sexual desirability, so also are there fashions in sexual etiquette, and these rules, while they last, will be just as indispensable and just as asexual as a ring in the nose or paint on the face. The important issue is that behavior, like perception, be socially conditioned, and not left to the instinctual tendencies of the dyadic partners. In any given collectivity, behavior which is defined as seductive will often seem as bizarre to the outsider as those cosmetic factors which are socially defined as beautiful.

3. TEMPORAL-SPATIAL CONSTRICTION. Whether an extramarital relationship is ephemeral or lasting, stylized or free, it is often the rule that it must be conducted only at specified times and places. Such constriction of the relationship may, of course, arise purely from situational factors, i.e., factors associated with the fact that these relationships are forbidden. But often it is a socially prescribed limitation. The affair is approved so long as it is "kept in its place."

One example of the operation of this factor is the frequent existence of a demand that affairs be conducted on a clandestine basis even when everyone knows of their existence. The explanation usually offered for this phenomenon is the alleged attractiveness of "forbidden fruit,"[59] but this does not account for the motivation of the community to collaborate in this pretence. I would suggest that the demand for clandestine behavior is a mechanism for limiting the scope and depth of the relationship. Temporal-spatial constriction ensures that each of the partners is drawn away from the dyad and into the community during the greater part of his or her everyday life. The intimacy of the relationship is decreased by the fact that each partner knows the other only in a very limited and narrow context. Each is unfamiliar with those personality traits in the other which are irrelevant to the secret rendezvous, and would be unlikely to manifest themselves even in an infinite number of them. Should a degree of intimacy nevertheless arise in such a relationship, its first expression is a demand for more freedom and "sunlight," but should the couple come into the open the reaction among other group members is typically one of shock and contempt. Extension of the dyadic relationship into other areas of everyday life is considered "out of place."

DYADIC WITHDRAWAL AND DEATH. In the preceding discussion it might seem as if we had pursued dyadic withdrawal into its last remaining stronghold only to watch this stronghold collapse. Insofar as such intimacy is frequent, it appears to be ephemeral, and insofar as it is lasting, it seems to be rare. Societal intrusion and absorption seems effectively to forestall tendencies toward dyadic withdrawal whenever and wherever they appear.

It is perhaps for this reason that dyadic withdrawal is such a popular theme in the myths, legends, and dramas of Western Civilization. Yet even in fantasy such withdrawals are always short-lived, ending usually in dissolution or death. Apparently

59 Cf. Freud, "Contributions to the Psychology of Love. The Most Prevalent Form of Degradation in Erotic Life," *Collected Papers,* Vol. IV, pp. 211–212.

a permanent lifelong dyadic withdrawal is unimaginable, for to my knowledge there is no instance of such a phenomenon in the fantasy productions of any culture.[60]

This statement, however, is somewhat misleading. In death a kind of permanent dyadic withdrawal *is* achieved, and this is the appeal that stories of tragic lovers hold. In real life, and in comedies, dyadic withdrawal usually ends in societal absorption, unless the couple separates. This does not mean, of course, that the relationship is any less satisfying—the couple may indeed "live happily ever after" as in the fairy tale. It means only that the dyad loses some of its exclusiveness and self-sufficiency and ceases to be a social threat. Some of the cathexis previously withdrawn into the dyad flows back onto larger collectivities, and some of the needs funneled into the dyad for satisfaction there now begin to seek fulfillment in a wider setting.

The great tragic lovers of fiction, however, are always set in opposition to societal forces and are always destroyed by them. But their relationship is not. They always die or are buried together, with the dyadic bond untainted by societal intrusion. The immortality of this bond and of their withdrawal is often symbolized by plants or trees growing out of their graves and entwining.

It may be recalled that we have encountered this theme before, in our discussion of the death of the narcissistic villain-hero: the crime of narcissistic withdrawal receives public punishment, i.e., death, and private reward, i.e., escape from socialization. So also with the crime of dyadic withdrawal in fiction. It is initially achieved, satisfying the desire of the spectator for libidinal contraction, and subsequently punished, relieving his social anxiety and assuaging his moral outrage. But in spite of the punishment, society is really cheated, since the withdrawal is never reversed, and both the dyad and the withdrawal remain immortally intact. A moral victory is won

[60] George du Maurier's *Peter Ibbetson* comes rather close, but the dyad is subject to a rather severe form of temporal-spatial constriction.

for the forces of regression—one in which the spectators can
privately participate with secret applause, like Irishmen ap-
plauding an Irish villain in an English play.

Thus, as de Rougemont has stressed, the great tragic lovers
of fiction, most notably in the Tristan and Isolde legend, actively desire and seek death. But this longing for death is a
longing for an end to life in a societal context. It is a turning-
away from what is felt as an over-extension, over-diffusion,
over-sublimation, and over-rationalization of libido, and a
desire to return to a more primitive, more simple, and more
fully satisfying form of libidinal involvement. It is the association of this regressive, anti-societal impulse with the yearning
for death which justifies Freud's use of the term "death-
instinct."

THE POST PARTUM DYAD. Let us now complete the circle and
return to the living, for while in fantasy life may end in a
dyadic withdrawal, in reality it begins in one (a correspondence that is, of course, far from coincidental). The dyad in
question is that of the mother and newborn infant.

We cannot correctly speak of cathectic withdrawal on the
part of the child, since its libidinal investment does not yet
extend beyond its own body and some fragmentary percept of
the mother. But it is extremely rare for a woman to undergo
pregnancy without a certain amount of narcissistic withdrawal,
or to tend an infant without entering into a dyadic relationship with it which involves considerable decathexis of other
social objects. The nonmutuality of the process—the fact that
one member is experiencing libidinal contraction while the
other merely has not yet undergone libidinal diffusion—differ-
entiates it from all other forms of dyadic withdrawal, but
should not prevent its inclusion in the category.

Both the earlier narcissistic and the later dyadic withdrawal
are tolerated by the community for reasons which the reader
will by this time have anticipated. Temporary contraction is
permitted because it is perceived as creative, and as leading
to greater long-run diffusion on the part of all concerned.

Narcissistic withdrawal during pregnancy is described by

Gerald Caplan in terms quite reminiscent of Freud's germ-cells, although he calls it "introversion" and lays somewhat greater emphasis on increased dependency needs: "The woman who previously may have been quite an outgoing person and . . . a giver, an active person, now . . . becomes someone who wishes to receive instead of to give. She becomes preoccupied with herself." Caplan employs the metaphor of a battery, which must be charged with nurturance in order later to nurture. We would add that she must be allowed to hoard libido in order later to extend it to include another major object. Such inclusion is in fact facilitated, as Caplan notes, by a narcissistic definition of the child as an extension of herself.[61]

In many primitive societies, this libidinal cathexis of the child is ensured by post partum sex taboos.[62] Since intercourse with the husband is forbidden, all of the mother's libido is concentrated on the neonate, often until it is weaned. In our society, the post partum sex taboo is of relatively short duration, the mother-child involvement being encouraged by less drastic means.

We may think of this libidinal contraction on the part of the mother as analogous to the techniques of many psychotherapists who work with schizophrenics—entering into the psychotic framework of the patient in order to seduce him out of it.[63] So the mother re-traverses the lowest levels of libidinal contraction in order to seduce the child—through emotional involvement, narcissistic rewards, and nurturant gratification —into normal libidinal diffusion.

But whenever libidinal contraction takes place there is a

[61] Gerald Caplan, *Mental Health Aspects of Social Work in Public Health,* Berkeley: University of California School of Social Welfare, 1955, p. 63, pp. 105–7.

[62] William N. Stephens, *The Oedipus Complex,* Glencoe, Ill.: The Free Press, 1962. Like so many crude social mechanisms which are based upon prohibitions and taboos, it overshoots the mark and generates a whole series of noxious institutions in its turn.

[63] John N. Rosen, *Direct Analysis,* New York: Grune and Stratton, 1953; A. Burton (ed.), *Psychotherapy of the Psychoses,* New York: Basic Books, 1961.

social danger. Here the danger is that the mother will be unable to reverse her regressive journey. She may remain fixed in her narcissistic withdrawal, as in the case of post partum psychoses, or, having crossed this threshold, be unable to relinquish her early symbiotic relationship with the child.[64]

There are a number of social mechanisms which help to facilitate her *anodos,* although they are only moderately effective. Rituals taking place when the child is born, for example, resemble the marriage ceremony in their tendency to stake a social claim in the new relationship. In our society it is the hospitalization rite which serves to create the illusion that the mother would be unable to bear a child without community assistance—the physicians merely replacing the old women who gather round in so many primitive societies. Instead of producing a child herself, it is given to her, first by the obstetrician, later by nurses; and her own role in the situation is obliterated by anaesthesia. It is typically several days before she can call it her own, and by this time she will be highly conscious of the extent to which the birth of her child has been a group effort.

At a more informal level, there are of course showers and other gift-giving arrangements to provide reminders of group ties, to let everyone participate in the event in some way, and to create group obligations which must be repaid.

Normally this flurry of social activity around childbirth serves to inhibit dyadic withdrawal to a considerable extent, and if the marital dyad is at all strong the likelihood of a marked withdrawal is infinitesimal. Where this latter condition does not hold, however, dyadic withdrawal in the form of a continued mother-child symbiosis is rather frequent, and if it becomes well established it is extremely hardy, resisting unanimous social disapproval and successfully circumventing the impotent endeavors of social and therapeutic agencies when they are applied.

64 Caplan, *op. cit.,* pp. 108–109.

III. Familial Withdrawal

A major social limitation of the withdrawn dyad is that, however self-sufficient it may appear to be, it cannot reproduce itself. This limitation is remedied when we move to the third potential product of libidinal contraction, the autonomous nuclear family. Here for the first time we encounter a true collectivity, a miniature society which is potentially immortal. In this sense it is the least regressive of the three forms we have discussed. As we move from narcissistic withdrawal through dyadic withdrawal to familial withdrawal we are tracing the waxing of the erotic instincts as defined by Freud, "which are always trying to collect living substance together into ever larger unities."[65] At the same time, it falls considerably short of the expanded libidinal cathexis necessary for full societal existence: "[The] rift [between love and culture] expresses itself first in a conflict between the family and the larger community to which the individual belongs. We have seen already that one of culture's principal endeavors is to cement men and women together into larger units. But the family will not give up the individual. The closer the attachment between the members of it, the more they often tend to remain aloof from others, and the harder it is for them to enter into the wider circle of the world at large . . . Detachment from the family has become a task that awaits every adolescent, and often society helps him through it with pubertal and initiatory rites."[66]

Familial withdrawal occurs whenever a nuclear family becomes emotionally or libidinally sufficient unto itself, and partial expressions of this state are often seen. But it is quite

[65] *New Introductory Lectures*, p. 139.
[66] *Civilization and Its Discontents*, p. 72. Note the similarity of these remarks both to Parsons' discussion of the functions of the incest taboo, and to the argument of the school superintendent quoted above against "going steady."

obvious that such a condition can neither go very far nor persist very long without the occurrence of incest—not on the fragmentary and disruptive basis which we find in reality, but in a stable and organized manner which provides at least one sexual partner for most family members.[67]

The success of the incest taboo in avoiding this outcome is due in part to its self-maintaining momentum. Once an individual has divided his libido between a family of orientation and a family of procreation he is less likely to foster a new family situation in which familial withdrawal reaches a level of intensity at which incest becomes a logical extension.

It is therefore reasonable to ask, however, since the danger of total familial withdrawal is as hypothetical as in the case of the other forms, and since it is in fact the least regressive of the three, why the incest taboo is stronger and less often violated than the taboos surrounding more severe forms of libidinal contraction? It is not enough to stress the manifold benefits arising from the prevention of familial withdrawal, for although it is quite true, as Parsons says, that "there is an intimate connection between the overcoming of the excessive autonomy of the nuclear family and the possibility of a cultural level of social development," the same may be said *a fortiori* of the other two forms. And if the incestuous nuclear family is too "ingrown" culturally, how much more so is a withdrawn dyad or an isolated narcissist.[68]

---

[67] See S. Kirson Weinberg, *Incest Behavior*, New York: Citadel Press, 1955. Some readers will object to this whole line of thought on the basis of theories which see the primary function of the incest taboo as one of maintaining the internal solidarity of the nuclear family. Space limitations forbid examination of these arguments (most of which, if taken seriously, would force us also to deny the viability of the polygamous family), except to point out that they rest on three questionable assumptions: (1) that jealousy does not exist in the nonincestuous family, (2) that authority is dependent upon a pompous and waspish demeanor, and (3) that the latter are incompatible with a sexual relationship. Freud would seem adequately to have refuted the first, our entire society is a refutation of the second, and the marital relationship in any strongly patriarchal culture, e.g., Germany, refutes the third.

[68] Parsons, *op. cit.*, p. 117.

The answer is that the incest taboo does not militate specifically against familial withdrawal, but against any degree of libidinal contraction. It is a general "out-pushing" force, and can be seen as having its most direct influence against incestuous dyadic withdrawal. The three points on our continuum necessarily partake of each other, and we must not become too enamoured of their unique particularities. Dyadic withdrawal is far more likely to occur if the attachment is narcissistic (i.e. based on resemblances between the partners)[69] and incestuous relationships are in part tabooed for the reason that they are closer to absolute narcissism than any other relationship can be.

An incestuous dyadic relationship need not lead to familial withdrawal. If it did so we would regard it as showing an increase in social consciousness—a de-eroticizing of the relationship. Conversely, a dyadic withdrawal could occur *within* an autonomous incestuous family, and be as disruptive to the security of that collectivity as to a larger one.

Let us also bear in mind that while there are only three types of incest, (excluding homosexual combinations), there are almost as many possible types of family organization which could be based on permission of some form of incest as there are presently combinations which exclude all forms. This is usually ignored in discussions of the functions of the incest taboo—it being assumed that unbridled promiscuity and chaos would follow from a lifting of the great ban, like the indiscriminately incestuous mating habits of most animals. Yet when we look at the variety of family patterns in primitive and civilized societies it seems inconceivable that no limiting and structuring would take place. This is true, for example, of the only two instances of a full-fledged and enduring incestuous family pattern that we have: the Ptolemaic and Hawaiian royal families both based on brother-sister incest alone.[70]

---

[69] I shall discuss this point in greater detail in a subsequent paper, along with the complex question of homosexual attachments.

[70] Murdock, *op. cit.*, Chapter 10.

Even if we assumed some kind of primeval normlessness, with the family structure based on power alone, we would not expect random mating, but rather a pattern reflecting the power structure. The prevailing form of incest would thus be father-daughter incest, with the other forms strongly inhibited by force. This would be the primal horde pattern described by Freud—a collectivity of normless narcissists held together and subjugated by the power of an absolutely narcissistic leader. It would cease to exist, as Mills points out, with the advent of any normative or collective action.[71]

It would be more difficult to envision a stable family structure built upon mother-son incest, simply because the potential for dyadic withdrawal would be so high. Intimate communication is enormously facilitated between incestuous partners, due to the biological and cultural similarities between them, not to mention the great range of shared experiences. But this essentially narcissistic component is particularly strong in the relationship between mother and son, since each has at one time viewed the other as a part of or extension of the self. It is in part for this reason that mother-son incest is of all forms the most severely prohibited.[72]

We should not leave the topic of familial withdrawal without considering the tolerated "exceptions" which we have found in the other forms of libidinal contraction. Murdock points out that institutionalized violations of the incest taboo (excluding momentary violations on special tribal occasions) are restricted to royal or aristocratic families, with the conscious purpose being to keep such families separate and impermeable.[73] The position of these families is identical to that of the narcissistic leader, in whom libidinal contraction is

[71] Cf. Mills, *op. cit.*, pp. 6–7, 11–12.

[72] Freud, *Collected papers*, Vol. IV, pp. 44–49; Caplan, *op. cit.*, 81 ff; Weinberg, *op. cit.*, pp. 222.

[73] Murdock, *op. cit.*, Chapter 10. Although this view has been convincingly challenged by Russell Middleton, "Brother-Sister and Father-Daughter Marriage in Ancient Egypt," *American Sociological Review*, 27 (October, 1962), pp. 603–611, as yet too little is known about the social context of these marriages to tell whether they constitute evidence for or against the theory presented here.

encouraged so that he may bear the burdens of responsibility more easily.

But if this phenomenon appears but rarely in terrestrial royal families, it is very much the rule in mythological ones. Not only are all major deities the world over inveterate narcissists,[74] but in all polytheistic systems the divine families are incorrigibly incestuous. In order to create a powerful and attractive nucleus which will focus libidinal diffusion for the earthly collectivity, the libido of the gods must be concentrated and intense, according to the principle that libido attracts libido. For upon these deities rests the solidarity of the community.

But it is not only as leaders and libidinal foci that the gods must hoard their libido, it is also as creators. The demiurges and progenitors of the gods are most particularly likely to be incestuous—theirs, after all, is the most "momentous constructive activity" imaginable.

A LITERARY ILLUSTRATION. Freud maintained that condensation, rather than brevity, was the soul of wit, and it may also be responsible for the fact that the best examples of social and psychological processes always come from literature. Although inadmissible as evidence, they provide superior illustrations, by forcefully condensing many processes into a compact and dramatic instance.

Thus the best example of libidinal contraction is a story by Thomas Mann entitled "The Blood of the Walsungs," which deals with an incestuous relationship between a twin brother and sister, identical in feature, personality and attitude.[75] Familial withdrawal is expressed in the contrast drawn between the family and outsiders; dyadic withdrawal in the twins' gaze "melting together in an understanding from which everybody else was shut out"; narcissistic withdrawal by Mann's comparing them to "self-centred invalids," in the brother's con-

[74] One of the few traits held in common by Greek and Judaic gods is that they are motivated almost exclusively by vanity, and are aroused to anger only by narcissistic injuries.

[75] *Stories of Three Decades*, New York: Knopf, 1936, pp. 279–319.

stant contemplation of his own image in the mirror, and in the final outburst of identification which immediately precedes their climactic copulation, an outburst in which the brother mutters (with rather careless oversight), "everything about you is just like me."[76]

The "erotic" (in Alexander's sense), non-utilitarian quality of the relationship is emphasized repeatedly by Mann. He speaks of their absorbing themselves in "trifles," of days passing "vacantly," of their having "doffed aside the evil-smelling world and loved each other alone, for the priceless sake of their own rare uselessness." The lower senses, particularly the olfactory, are insistently stressed: "they loved each other with all the sweetness of the senses, each for the other's spoilt and costly well-being and delicious fragrance."[77]

Finally, the absence of other social ties is conveyed both explicitly and symbolically. The most telling expression, however, is their journey to the theatre in a carriage, in which their social isolation is dramatized by the nearness of the city: "round them roared and shrieked and thundered the machinery of urban life. Quite safe and shut away they sat among the wadded brown silk cushions, hand in hand."[78]

This relationship epitomizes libidinal contraction in its introversiveness, its rejection of partial and scattered libidinal cathexes, its conservatism. One can argue about its satisfactoriness at a psychological level, but it is clear that it does not leave a sufficient residue of tension upon which to build a group structure. Only when an individual falls in love with a stranger while some of his libido is still harnessed to an incestuous object will he be inclined to attach himself to a larger agglomeration which embraces them both. In so doing he sacrifices total gratification and gains whatever benefits accrue from societal existence. One might also maintain that he gains life, for it is only in death that utter quiescence is found.

76 *Ibid.*, pp. 301, 305, 307, 317–319.
77 *Ibid.*, pp. 305, 307–8, 309, 316, 317, 319.
78 *Ibid.*, pp. 307, 309, 312, 314, 316.